D1368150

Lies,
damned lies
and **Iraq**

Lies, damned lies and **Iraq**

Peter Kilfoyle MP

Harriman House Ltd
3A Penns Road
Petersfield
Hampshire
GU32 2EW

Tel. +44 (0)1730 233870
Fax +44(0)1730 233880
Email: enquiries@harriman-house.com
Website: www.harriman-house.com

First published in Great Britain in 2007 by Harriman House Ltd.
Copyright © Harriman House Ltd

ISBN 1905641397
ISBN13 9781905641390

British Library Cataloguing in Publication Data A CIP catalogue record for this book can be obtained from the British Library

Printed and bound by Biddles.

To my daughter Lucy, without whose diligent research and
support this book would not have been possible.

Contents

Foreword

A charismatic, public school educated Prime Minister from County Durham takes the country to war in the Middle East. With a valued western ally, and Israel, in tow, a pre-emptive strike is launched on the basis of a false prospectus. The whole adventure falls apart when the truth becomes apparent. After a short interval, the Prime Minister resigns, and his Chancellor steps up to take his place.

This is not a reference to Tony Blair, but to the calamity which Sir Anthony Eden brought upon himself at Suez. Substitute America for France, and there is certainly a sense of *déjà vu* about the Iraq debacle.

There were, of course, voices in government – particularly amongst the Foreign Office Arabists – who could see the dangers facing both the Blair and Eden governments as they rushed into the military and political mire that is the Middle East. But headstrong leaders are able to force their way through the advice offered them, and through the constitutional checks and balances which offer restraint against the temptations of impetuosity. Sometimes, when obduracy meets reality, moderation is the outcome. On other occasions, self-delusion is the order of the day.

It is a short step from deluding oneself to trying to delude others. This book is an attempt to find a way through that delusion, through the smoke and mirrors of spin and propaganda. The objective is to show – using the words of the principal participants – just how the case for war was misrepresented. Let those who embarked on this illegal and immoral war be condemned from their own mouths.

Peter Kilfoyle MP
March 2007

Prologue

Our lives begin to end the day we become silent about things that matter.

Martin Luther King Jnr (1929-1968)

Iraq's history is a very long and – throughout many periods – very distinguished one. The first cities, such as Sumer, arose here, as did the earliest form of writing. It was here, in Mesopotamia – the land between the Two Rivers – that the fabled cities of Babylon and Nineveh flourished. Baghdad became a byword for the exotic east, as empires came and went across this ancient land. Iraq was formerly part of the Ottoman Empire. But by the end of 1918 when the empire broke up, it was occupied by British forces. By 1921, Faisal had been chosen as king in a constitutional monarchy and British occupation was formalised as a protectorate by the League of Nations.

By 1958, the Hashemite monarchy had been overthrown, and a republic put in its place. Brigadier Qasim became dictator and enjoyed a great deal of popular support. But over time, he made enemies with Iran, the US, and homegrown nationalists. Finally, in 1963, he, too, was deposed.

The quasi socialist, pan-Arabist Baath Party emerged triumphant from the regime change but was overthrown by the military after less than a year. A period of turmoil ensued, in which power rested with an inner core of military officers vying for supremacy. By the mid/late 1970s, Iraq seemed to be stabilising itself and retained many of its ancient characteristics – cultured, educated, enlightened. The first real cloud over this approach to life was Saddam.

Saddam rose through the Baath Party through the sixties and seventies. He ruthlessly suppressed opposition and appointed relatives and fellow Tikritis to key party and government posts. Out of his depth in foreign affairs, Saddam was a consummate insider politician, and absolutely ruthless in running his country.

He became President in 1979. The following year, he triggered the Iran-Iraq War which was to last for eight years, crippling both countries. Two years later, Saddam went to war again – this time against Kuwait. Saddam was now indelibly marked as a dictator and an aggressor, and became synonymous in the global mind with Iraq.

Neocons and other cons

The reasons behind the second Gulf War have been the subject of many books, and will continue to be a rich seam for historians to come. Our period is not an illustrious one in the history of this cradle of civilisation; and the most recent of the many wars fought there was not an illustrious war. Some now say it was a mistake; others say it was a criminal enterprise. History will judge the case even if contemporary realpolitik decides that the perpetrators of this attack on a sovereign state and the ensuing death toll of perhaps 650,000 men, women and children, should not be charged before a court of law.

After the first Gulf War there was a sense of unfinished business among Reaganites in George Bush Senior's administration. There were also covetous glances towards Iraqi oil. Nevertheless, the reasons ultimately given for the 2003 attack on Iraq were neither of these:

Saddam was connected to 9/11 (wrong); regime change was necessary for him to comply with UN resolutions (wrong); he possessed weapons of mass destruction (wrong); he was a danger to his neighbours (wrong). Only one thing could be correctly said about Saddam – he was a danger to his own people.

Equally dangerous in most people's eyes was the neoconservative faction in American politics. In alliance with fundamentalist Christians and Zionist groups, the neocons had a testosterone-charged view of geopolitics. In their opinion, all bets were off. The United States was at liberty to pursue its own interests in its own way regardless of treaties, agreements, and the rights of others.

Everything was up for grabs – Star Wars; nuclear weapons development; muscular trade negotiation; subversion of the United Nations – as long as the United States had 'full spectrum dominance'. Their goal was total American domination of the planet. Former Trotskyites allied with Christians expecting rapture, and Jews awaiting their secular Messiah, in order to kick the butt of the other ninety-five per cent of the world's population.

In this monochrome view of the world, slogans replace rational discussion For David Frum, Bush's speechwriter the, enemy became the 'axis of evil' – Iraq, Iran and North Korea. They also became by-words for terrorism, whatever that means, in the minds of western citizens.

In the United Kingdom – where most were highly sceptical about the United States, anyway, and extremely hostile to George Bush – the run up to war had another ingredient – the 'special relationship'. This is a peculiar, one-sided relationship whereby British leaders convince themselves that they hold a unique place in American hearts and minds, a sort of Athens to the modern American Imperium.

To validate this relationship, Prime Ministers defer to Presidents, and often prostitute the British national interest in order to maintain the fictitious communion of the two countries. It is a madness and a betrayal, it undermines our national sovereignty, and is an insult to intelligence on both sides of the pond. Yet it serves the purpose of bolstering the egos of Prime Ministers stuck in their own Imperial past. Hobnobbing it at a Commonwealth conference is one thing, a reminder of our glory years; but real power is in Washington. Prime Ministers delude themselves that the reflected 'glory' is real; but not so politically useful that Tony Blair will risk going to Washington for his congressional medal just yet.

Nevertheless, as the great tragedy of Iraq was to unfold, Tony Blair stood ready to play his part as the good ally, 'shoulder to shoulder' with President Bush. The neocons were in their intellectual and administrative bunkers, spinning away at an Iraqi fantasy, and what they saw as the new role of the United States. All that was required was to get the ducks lined up in a row – the pretext was in place (a real and imminent threat); they expected United Nations endorsement (wrong); the logistics had been computed (erroneously), and the political will was there in Bush and Blair.

All that was missing was truth and honesty. A large body of people in both the United States and the United Kingdom were awake to the lies and the spin. Unexpectedly, they opposed this 'righteous' war on Iraq, and they were to be proven correct.

However, we do need an overview of what arguments were being put forward in the build up to this diabolical war. That is the historical context necessary to look at what was said in support and what were the countervailing comments of those whom one would expect to make the case against war in a modern democracy. This is a small attempt to convey the principal arguments to the general reader, confused not only by the fog of war, but by the mist of misinformation put out by ever more pernicious spin doctors on behalf of their political masters.

On 23 November 1945, Ernest Bevin had told the House of Commons:

> There never has been a war yet which, if the facts had been put
> calmly before the ordinary folk, could not have been prevented . .
> . The common man, I think, is the great protection against war.

This proposition was to be tested to destruction over the Iraq War. Tony Blair said in Paris on 27 May 1997, just weeks into his premiership:

> Mine is the first generation to contemplate the possibility that
> we may live our entire lives without going to war or sending our
> children to war.

The road to war

There was a history to the Iraq War – an inconclusive war in 1991 which left Saddam Hussein in power, followed by years of sanctions, and what Ewen MacAskill and Richard Norton-Taylor described in the *Guardian* on 8 January 2001:

> The bombing (over the no-fly zones in Iraq) . . . is sometimes
> called 'the forgotten war'.

The sanctions were both crude and cruel, and Western governments tended to blame their devastating effects solely on Saddam. The much-reviled George Galloway had a different take in an early day motion of 5 February 2001:

> That this House welcomes the report of the Caritas Europa
> delegation including Julian Filochowski Director of the British
> Catholic Aid Agency CAFOD and Father Frank Turner SJ
> Assistant Secretary General of the Catholic Bishops Conference

on the 'humanly catastrophic, morally indefensible and politically ineffective' sanctions on Iraq; notes the report's description of Iraqi sanctions as a failed policy which must be changed; calls upon HM's Government to contemplate the churchmen's conclusion that the suffering of the Iraqi people cannot be regarded as unfortunate but collateral damage in what is otherwise an honourable course of action; and considers that the fact that sanctions are patently ineffective only adds insult to injury.

Our own government's hypocrisy towards Iraq was underlined in another early day motion, that of Andrew Stunnell, dated 20 February, 2001:

That this House notes the fifth anniversary of the publication of the Scott Report into the arms to Iraq scandal: shares the dismay recorded by the Quadripartite Committee last year that the Government has not afforded greater priority to bringing forward a Bill to implement the recommendations made in the Scott Report; further notes that the draft bill to improve the transparency of export controls promised in the Queen's Speech has yet to be published; and urges HM's Government to publish without delay a new bill on strategic exports which will control arms brokering and shipping agents through registration and licensing of all deals, promote democratic accountability through the prior Parliamentary scrutiny of arms export licences to sensitive destinations, establish a strict controls on licensed production and technology transfer, and establish a system for monitoring the end-use of arms after export.

In a Parliamentary debate held on the 4 October 2001, the late Tony Banks was one who sought to illustrate the West's double standards:

I was an MP when we were busy arming Saddam Hussein in the war against Iran. We said he was a despot who killed his own people, but we still supplied him with arms.

Alice Mahon had a different slant in the same debate:

> Why do we not listen to the friendly voices in the Gulf who tell us that we are alienating millions of Muslims by constantly bombing the people of Iraq and starving them through sanctions.

Nor were the Tories immune to voices of conscience. Thus, on 8 October 2001, Sir Teddy Taylor could declare:

> I remember the time when Iraq and Saddam Hussein were our secret cousins in the Middle East. They did our work for us and got help, finance and aid from the United States and the United Kingdom.

I took a wider swipe at the direction of United States policy, in a Guardian article published on 6 December 2001 entitled 'Taking Liberties over US Foreign Policy'.

> A simplistic notion that 'the United States is most certainly a force for good' has little resonance with disinherited Palestinians, starving Afghans and chemically bombed Colombians . . . Nor are those many millions living under the shadow of globalisation and environmental peril any better disposed to the United States than those who are witness to the realities of unleashed United States firepower . . . (Charles) Clarke refers to lots of 'indicators' of changes in the United States towards international relations, but no hard evidence. I suggest that he judges nations by their deeds, not by the exigencies of a deteriorating international image.

I was to return to this theme on 10 March 2002, in a Mail on Sunday article entitled 'Saddam: Could he be Blair's nemesis?'.

> Then there is the unresolved matter of Iraq, and, specifically, Saddam Hussein. It appears that the American administration

has simply to decide when to mount a wholesale attack on Iraq; it is no longer a traditional threat. More than a decade after the Gulf War ended, this should not be a surprise to any of us. After all, Richard Perle, formerly known as the 'Prince of Darkness' and a key Pentagon strategist as then chairman of the Pentagon's Defence Review Board, gave us on the night of September 11 a shopping list of alleged rogue states with which the United States would be dealing. Naturally, Iraq was high on that list. The American Administration considers its military action in Afghanistan a great triumph, despite its failure to date to account for Osama bin Laden and Mullah Omar. Their logic is to transfer their military approach from Afghanistan on to Iraq. This is where major problems occur for the British Government – political, economic, diplomatic and military . . . What the Government must ask itself is firstly, what is the justi-fication for a full-scale war on Iraq, and secondly, where do British interests lie in such a conflict?.... Does public opinion , so ready to support America after September 11, favour the involvement of British forces in a questionable venture aimed at Saddam? Perhaps most immediate in the minds of some Ministers will be the political turmoil eventuating at home from British participation. They will recognise that, detestable though Saddam is, there are other equally repugnant regimes at work in the world. They also know that there is nothing to link Iraq to the September 11 atrocities. It may be that Iraq is trying to develop so-called WMDs, but they know Israel has developed such weapons with impunity.

It was not as if these were particularly arcane issues. They were there for those who wished to see. The dangers were many – and not all on one side. The proposed development of a new generation of nuclear weapons and delivery systems prompted Jeremy Corbyn to post an early day motion on 13 March 2002:

That this House notes with grave concern reports of US plans to build new nuclear weapons that would be suitable first strikes against China, Iran, Iraq, Libya, North Korea, Russia and Syria; deplores further reports that the United States would be willing to use nuclear weapons in several scenarios, including an Arab-Israel conflict, a war between China and Taiwan, an attack by North Korea on South Korea and an attack on Iraq by Israel or another country in the event of a surprising military development; regrets that the United States is deliberately undermining international peace and security; and urges HM's Government to send a clear message to the US that they are opposed to these plans and demand that the US abandons them.

As opponents of another war in Iraq made their arguments, the Government machine was ever more strident in its attacks on opponents of the war. Thus I took the argument directly to Tony Blair at Prime Minister's Questions on 10 April 2002:

Given the Prime Minister's reported comments that those who take a different view from him on events in the Middle East are utterly naïve, may I ask him whether it is naïve to be dismayed at the succour that has been given to Sharon by the mixed messages that have come from the American and British Administrations? Is it naïve to be aware of the bellicosity of elements in the American Administration, based on ideology; or is it naïve to believe in the centrality of the United Nations in resolving the problems of the Middle East?

The Prime Minister's reply was sophistry at its finest:

I have not described anyone who takes a different view from mine on Iraq as utterly naïve. I said that it would be utterly naïve to say that WMD were not an issue and I am sure that my Honourable Friend would not say that either. The issue is how we deal with that – I said what I said on Iraq a moment or two ago – but in relation to the Middle East, it is not correct to say that there have been mixed messages. We are absolutely clear that we condemn entirely those things that are happening in the Middle East at the moment, which is why Israel should withdraw from the occupied territories and do so now, as the American President has said, but we also – I hope that my Honourable Friend would do so too – condemn without reservation the terrorist attacks on Israeli citizens, both must be condemned.

He had some unlikely allies in his defence of the indefensible. Nick Cohen – hitherto, a scourge of the Establishment – had developed a tremendous weakness for the Bush–Blair line on Iraq. On 11 August 2002, In his weekly column in the *Observer,* he opined that:

> There are honourable grounds for upholding the authority of the United Nations and opposing American global domination. What is dishonourable – indeed insufferable – is the pretence of everyone from Trots to archbishops that their animating concern is the suffering of the peoples of Iraq!

How right he was about the American-British axis (and their Israeli satraps) in their disregard for the suffering of millions in the Middle East. Of course, one would have hoped that the forces of light, defended by Cohen, would have looked to credible NGOs to support their case. Yet on 12 September 2002, Amnesty International could say:

> Once again, the human rights record of a country is used selectively to legitimise military actions. . . . The United States and other western governments turned a blind eye to Amnesty International reports of widespread human rights violations in Iraq during the Iran–Iraq war, and ignored Amnesty's campaign on behalf of the thousands of unarmed Kurdish civilians killed in the 1988 attacks on Malabar.

Of course, not just a Nelsonian blind eye was turned, as Glen Rangwala wrote on 16 September 2002 (*Labour Left Briefing,* 'Who Armed Saddam?')

The United States in particular supplied the material, logistical information, political backing and finance to Saddam Hussein's regime.

Historically, too, we had a defence doctrine based on deterrence – the lynchpin of British strategy for many years, and the basis for the justification for the retention of nuclear weapons. The policy shift being contemplated, aping the most rightwing United States administration in memory, was dramatic, as Mark Prisk noted in the House of Commons on 17 October 2002:

> The Secretary of State seems to be suggesting that moving from the historic basis of our defence in the past 40 years – namely the principle of deterrence – to a principle of pre-empting is a minor step that does not need full explanation.

On 25 November 2002, there was a House of Commons Debate on United Nations Security Council Resolution 1441. Once again, I raised the question of the elephant in the room:

> . . . All honourable members want WMD to be removed from Iraq, if they are found there, and elsewhere. However, he has spoken at length about confusion and precursors to United Nations resolutions. Does he know about Paragraph 14 of Resolution 687, which demands the removal of nuclear weapons throughout the Middle East? Israel is the only nation with proven supplies of nuclear weapons – it has perhaps more than 200 nuclear warheads. Does the Right Honourable Gentleman believe that here is a link between the confused and what is perceived – rightly or wrongly – in the Arab world as a partial attitude towards Iraq when Israel can harbour such weapons with impunity?

Jeremy Corbyn had a different take:

. . . we are told that this is not a war about resources or oil. I beg to differ. This is not a war about human rights, democracy or peace: it is a war about United States commercial control in the Middle East.

Alice Mahon was a consistent and long time critic of the use of cluster bombs. She had noted in an EDM on 7 December 2000, that:

. . . during the Gulf War 30,000 tonnes of ordnance was dropped on Iraq. This included cluster bombs which are still killing people.

In another EDM, on 4 December 2002, she was perceptive in her analysis of the 'forgotten war' on Iraq:

That this House condemns the 300 per cent increase in bombs dropped on Iraq since March 2002: believes this increase has little to do with protecting Iraqi people but more to do with destroying Iraq's air defences as a prelude to war; is deeply concerned the United States Administration is trying to bully the UN weapons inspectors into aggressive inspections; and calls upon HM's Government to distance this country from President Bush's war aims and join with the majority of peace-living nations in the world to seek a non-military solution in Iraq.

Approaches which were not consonant with a very muscular American policy approach were dismissed by the British Government. In the *Guardian* of 27 February 2003, my suggested approach was straightforward:

My answer to this question is containment. It is being done already with the weapons inspectors in Iraq and they should be allowed to get on with the job they were sent to do. At the moment Saddam is effectively contained and effectively there is disarmament. With weapons inspection there is always the implicit threat of force, but I don't accept that. It is a matter for the UN and its good offices to decide what should be done. For me to support war, a case would have to be made. I have seen no such convincing case.

By 19 March, the die was cast and I could say in the *Guardian*:

We are having a nineteenth century gunboat war in the Gulf, when the real dangers of terrorism should be isolated and dealt with as the first priority . . . I believe that this act would be illegal, it would be immoral and it would be illogical – the idiocy of fighting the wrong war, in the wrong place, at the wrong time, against the wrong enemy . . . I am satisfied that without that second resolution we are getting into extremely dangerous ground and setting extremely dangerous precedents . . . Think of what that name [Shock and Awe – the name of the allied operation] implies The United States is aiming to put ten times as many missiles and precision bombs in the first forty eight hours as they committed in the whole of the Gulf War. This is against a country that has been decimated . . . I would say earnestly and honestly to the Government that their impatience will reap a whirlwind, a whirlwind which will affect us and ours for generations to come . . . [The second resolution is] a litmus test, if you like, of the Government . . . Tony Blair made it that way . . . Many people fear that, quite apart from the issue of Iraq, we are faced here with the virtual denouement of the United Nations as the most effective forum in the world for resolving international disputes.'

I was not unaware of the nature of the Iraqi regime. Indeed, at the beginning of January 2003, my website carried my view of Saddam's real crimes:

It is . . . a horrendous regime, but this has not generally meant Western intervention before . . . He (Saddam) has caused loss of face to the Americans and sits on top of a sea of oil which they covet. That is enough, in the blinkered eyes of this Administration, to justify a Western attack.

Many Members of Parliament pointed out the contradictions of United Kingdom Government policy towards Iraq. Harry Cohen, in an early day motion on 23 January 2003, made a particularly telling point:

> That this House notes that UK policy towards Iraq, prior to its support for the war effort of the United States, has had dire humanitarian consequences for the Iraqi people and this is confirmed by Mr Benon Sevan, the UN Under Secretary General in charge of Iraq's oil for food programme; notes that he has said that the new retroactive pricing initiative, introduced at the behest of the United Kingdom, whereby the Sanctions Committee sets the price for Iraqi oil several weeks after it is sold, along with the paralysis at the committee, has caused a 35 per cent drop in the country's crude oil exports since November and that this has diminished the amount of money available for humanitarian aid; and further notes that the vast majority of Iraqi people hold to the view that western powers such as the UK, rather than Saddam Hussein, are responsible for their economic impoverishment and that vindictive policies toward them such as the one highlighted by Mr Sevan give evidence of this.

What hope was there for the future well being of the Iraqi masses? On 3 February 2003, Llew Smith pointed out another inconsistency in government policy, tabling an early day motion:

> That this House believes the threat made in his interview with David Frost on 2 February by the Defence Secretary to use nuclear weapons against Iraq is morally repugnant and diplomatically suicidal; recognises that the use of nuclear weapons would have the capacity to kill and main tens of thousands of

people, as well as to contaminate radioactively huge areas of land and water, and to render ecologically dead parts of the ecosphere: insists that the United Kingdom's status as guardian of the 1968 nuclear non-proliferation treaty which this country co-authored with other nuclear armed states, and for which it is one of three depositary states, means the United Kingdom has a special responsibility to uphold the Treaty; recalls that at the latest review conference of the NPT (Non-Proliferation Treaty) at the UN in New York, the United Kingdom reaffirmed that it would not use nuclear weapons against non-nuclear weapon states parties to the NPT, except in the case of an invasion or any other attack on them, their territories, their armed forces or other troops, their allies, or on a state to which they have security commitments, carried out or sustained by such a non-nuclear weapon state in 'association of alliance' with a nuclear-weapon state; notes that these circumstances do not prevail with Iraq; and calls upon the Prime Minister to withdraw this unacceptable and incredible threat to humanity by the threatened use of WMD.

Llew Smith had his own ideological drum to beat and he did it consistently, pointing out that American behaviour was as responsible under its international obligations as that with which it charged Iraq (early day motion dated 4 February 2003):

That this House notes the USA signed the Chemical Weapons Convention on the Prohibition of Chemical Weapons to several chemical industry sites in the US on the grounds of 'protecting business proprietary information of US companies' according to the United States Bureau of Industry and Security in a statement on 10th October 2002; notes with disapproval that US escorts have also refused to allow inspectors to use approved inspection equipment (eg: weighing equipment) during inspections of some military facilities used for chemical weapon manufacturing or storage in the past; believes that the US has

imposed limits on inspections of its facilities that are contrary
to the requirements of the treaty, including reserving the right
for the President to block inspections and limiting what facilities may be inspected; records with disapproval that this stance
has led to a less thorough inspection regime; observes the US
has acted in a similar disruptive way in respect of the Biological
Weapons Convention, putting the interests of the secrecy of
biotechnology and pharmaceutical companies before global
security and anti-terrorist measures; points out that if Iraq were
to be similarly uncooperative it would incur the deadly wrath of
the United States Administration; and thus calls upon HM's
Government to put all possible pressure on the United States
Administration to enforce American compliance with these
treaties.

This was not merely an academic debate about the relative behaviour of two
sovereign states. As I pointed out to the House of Commons on 26 February
2003:

I recommend that people read Senator Riegle's report,
published by his Senate Committee, on where the biological
weapons originated . . . . [73 separate consignments] were
exported to Saddam by the US . . . it ill behoves people to stand
up as purer than Caesar's wife on the issue.

Given the cavalier disregard by many in the British administration for international law, it was very disquieting to contend with the utterances of people
like United States Defense Secretary Donald Rumsfeld. It dragged the United
Kingdom into supporting what would, if effected, be illegal action, as John
Barrett pointed out in an early day motion of 13 March 2003:

That this Houses notes the 1997 Chemical Weapons convention
signed by the United Kingdom, United States and over 140 other
countries, which prohibits the use of chemical agents that 'can
cause death, temporary incapacitation or permanent harm to

humans' in international military conflict; further notes that it is United Kingdom policy not to allow troops to participate in operations involving the use of non lethal or riot control gases such as o-chlorobenzylidene malonontrite (C5) gas and pepper sprays; is deeply concerned that the United States Defence Secretary, Donald Rumsfeld, has shown a willingness to use in military action against Iraq, similar toxic agents to those that resulted in the deaths of 129 hostages in the Moscow theatre siege of October 2002; is particularly disturbed by Mr Rumsfeld's suggestion that such gases could be used in situations involving women and children; and calls on the United Kingdom Government to press the United States Administration to uphold the provisions of the 1997 Convention by making a clear statement of intention not to use such toxic gases in any military action against Iraq.

The pro-war party assumed from the outset that a war in Iraq would be short, sharp, and clean. Tony Worthington perceptively thought otherwise (during a House of Commons debate on 18 March):

> ... It is worth remembering that the Six Day War in the Middle East is still going strong after 35 years. This war has similar potential.

After all, in this part of the world, as Malcolm Savidge commented in the same debate, 'friends' and 'enemies' are interchangeable:

> It is okay if our friends develop nuclear weapons, but not if our enemies do, and they (ie: the Americans) choose who are the friends and who are the enemies. Let us remember that Iraq was regarded as a friend and was supplied during the 1980's but is now regarded as an enemy. I find that approach capricious and destabilising.

With the actuality of war came ever more pressure for information from the Government, to test its claims and arguments. I sought in March, via a

Parliamentary written question, to draw out who was undermining whom over weapons inspections in Iraq prior to the war:

> To ask the Secretary of State for Foreign and Commonwealth Affairs how many times during the inspections in Iraq carried out prior to 1998 the Iraqi Government was recorded by the UN as non-cooperative, broken down by (a) minor delays and (b) actual inspection refusals.

It was to be increasingly important to garner all factual material possible from official sources as the Government spin machine made it ever more difficult to extract the unvarnished truth. Without that information it would be difficult, if not impossible, to dispute statements like those made by the Prime Minister on 30 March 2003, in an article circulated to the Arabic press:

> There has been no rush to conflict. Indeed, the international community has waited for twelve years for Saddam to rid himself voluntarily of his weapons of mass destruction as he promised in 1991.

A matter of some dispute, to put it mildly!

> . . . President Bush, Prime Minister Aznar and I have pledged Iraq's oil will be placed in a United Nations trust fund to benefit the people of Iraq.

A pledge that would be broken – to no one's surprise.
By the end of 2003, the context of debate about the war had changed. It was by then apparent that there were no WMD in Iraq. Their presence as a *casus belli* was shown to be utterly false, and the Prime Minister was moving to a far more defensive position on British involvement in Iraq. In a speech to his Sedgefield constituents on 5 March 2004, he coupled 9/11 with the war on Iraq:

> . . . .[9/11] was a declaration of war by religious fanatics who were prepared to wage that war without limit.

You might have said the same about the ultimatum to Saddam Hussein – it would be as accurate.

Remarkably, Blair insisted:

> It didn't matter that the Islamic extremists often hated some of these regimes.

It most certainly did matter, if one wished to understand the enormity of the mistake which was being made. As the *Daily Telegraph* was to quote an anonymous British officer just a few weeks later, on 11 April:

> My view and the view of the British chain of command is that the Americans' use of violence is not proportionate and is over-responsive to the threat they are facing. They don't see the Iraqi people the way we see them. They view them as Untermenschen. They are not concerned about the Iraqi loss of life. The United States troops view things in very simplistic terms. It seems hard for them to reconcile subtleties between who supports what and who doesn't in Iraq. It's easier for their soldiers to group all Iraqis as the bad guys. As far as they are concerned Iraq is bandit country and everybody is out to kill them. It is trite, but American troops do shoot first and ask questions later.

Already, Mr Blair's misreading of the realities in Iraq was having dire consequences. In truth, the British Prime Minister had already sold his political soul to the American President, as evidenced by his complicity that April with George Bush, in supporting Sharon's unilateral withdrawal from Gaza and 'disengagement' from the Palestinians, effectively destroying the Middle East road map.

All along, the United States Administration agenda was quite different from the public case put forward by Tony Blair. The United States was always about regime change – an illegal act. As Scott Ritter wrote in his book *Iraq Confidential*, there was a long standing US determination to remove Saddam:

As they crafted Security Council resolution 687 (in 1991), American diplomats had destabilising and undermining Saddam Hussein at the front of their minds rather than the complex business of disarmament. Disarmament was merely a vehicle for achieving the larger United States objective of regime change.

The question is just how much of this agenda did Tony Blair share – what did he know, and when did he know it? The narrow historical perspective of this debate is that many people had profound doubts about American policy towards Iraq, and were alarmed by Tony Blair's drive to co-ordinate British policy with that of the Americans in this area.

Many supported him – whether through conviction or opportunism. Many Parliamentarians opposed him. Parliament and public were sold the Government's case on what is now generally held to have been a false prospectus. It is perhaps time to look at some of the contentious areas of policy debate in the words of pundits and politicians who shaped the debate – not yet fully resolved – which will in turn define Tony Blair's much sought after legacy.

Warriors

At least two thirds of our miseries spring from human stupidity, human malice and those great motivators and justifiers of malice and stupidity, idealism, dogmatism and proselytizing zeal on behalf of religious or political idols.
Aldous Huxley (1894-1963)

Ever since the expulsion of Saddam from Kuwait in 1991, many on both the left and the right of American politics had Iraq filed under the heading of 'unfinished business', along with Iran, North Korea, Cuba and others. More than anyone, the neoconservatives clung to a sense of America's mission to cleanse the planet of such undesirable regimes as those they deemed 'rogue states'.

The Neocons

Neoconservatives (or 'neocons') is the name given to a group of right wing American intellectuals and policy makers, who have been influential under the President George W Bush. They took their lead from academics like Leo Strauss and Albert Wohlsetter, but there were numerous other influences. Many of the individuals concerned are former Trotskyists, perhaps accounting for their rather bizarre world view.

Both Strauss and Wohlstetter are dead, although their protégées – like Richard Perle and Paul Wolfowitz – live on. Like Marcuse for a previous generation, one can only wonder at what the late professors would have made of their acolytes in action.

One does not need, for the purpose of this book, to worry unduly about the genesis of neoconservatism. Suffice to say that within its embrace were many of the most powerful people in the Bush Administration – and beyond. Just look at the signatories of this letter, sent to President Clinton, on behalf of the Project for a New American Century – one of the many front organisations for the neoconservatives (others include the Heritage Foundation; the American Enterprise Institute: the Jewish Institute for National Security Affairs; the Centre for Security Policy): Elliot Abrams, Richard L. Armitage, William J.Bennett, Jeffrey Bergner, John Bolton, Paula Dobriansky, Francis Fukuyama, Robert Kagan, Zalmacy Khalilzad, William Kristol, Richard Perle, Peter W. Rodman, Donald Rumsfeld, William Schneider Jr., Vin Weber, Paul Wolfowitz, R. James Woolsey, Robert B. Zoellick.

> We are writing you because we are convinced that current American policy toward Iraq is not succeeding, and that we may soon face a threat in the Middle East more serious than any we have known since the end of the Cold War. In your upcoming State of the Union Address, you have an opportunity to chart a clear and determined course for meeting this threat. We urge you to seize that opportunity, and to enunciate a new strategy that would secure the interests of the United States and our friends and allies around the world. That strategy should aim, above all, at the removal of Saddam Hussein's regime from power. We stand ready to offer our full support in this difficult but necessary endeavour.
>
> The policy of 'containment' of Saddam Hussein has been steadily eroding over the past several months. As recent events have demonstrated, we can no longer depend on our partners in the Gulf War coalition to continue to uphold the sanctions or top punish Saddam when he blocks or evades United Nations inspections. Our ability to ensure that Saddam Hussein is not producing weapons of mass destruction, therefore, has substantially diminished. Even if full inspections were eventually to resume, which now seems highly unlikely, experience has shown that it is difficult if not impossible to monitor Iraq's chemical and biological weapons production. The lengthy period during which the inspectors will have been unable to enter many Iraq facilities has made it even less likely that they will be able to uncover all of Saddam's secrets. As a result, in the not-too-

distant future we will be unable to determine with any reasonable level of confidence whether Iraq does or does not possess such weapons.

Such uncertainty will, by itself, have a seriously destabilizing effect on the entire Middle East. It hardly needs to be added that if Saddam does acquire the capability to deliver weapons of mass destruction as he is almost certain to do if we continue along the present course, the safety of American troops in the region, of our friends and allies like Israel and the moderate Arab states, and a significant portion of the world's supply of oil will all be put at hazard. As you have rightly declared, Mr President, the security of the world in the first part of the 21st century will be determined largely by how we handle this threat.

Given the magnitude of the threat, the current policy, which depends for its success upon the steadfastness of our coalition partners and upon the cooperation of Saddam Hussein, is dangerously inadequate. The only acceptable strategy is one that eliminates the possibility that Iraq will be able to use or threatens to use weapons of mass destruction. In the near term, this means a willingness to undertake military action as diplomacy is clearly failing. In the long term, it means removing Saddam Hussein and his regime from power. That now needs to become the aim of American foreign policy.

We urge you to articulate this aim, and to turn your administration's attention to implementing a strategy for removing Saddam's regime from power. This will require a full complement of diplomatic, political and military efforts. Although we are fully aware of the dangers and difficulties in implementing this policy, we believe the dangers of failing to do so are far greater. We believe the US has the authority under existing UN resolutions to take the necessary steps, including military steps, to protect our vital interests in the Gulf. In any case, American policy cannot continue to be crippled by a misguided insistence on unanimity in the UN Security Council.

> We urge you to act decisively. If you are now to end the threat
> of weapons of mass destruction against the US or its allies, you
> will be acting in the most fundamental national security
> interests of the country. If we accept a course of weakness and
> drift, we put our interests and our future at risk.'

The date of this letter was 27 January 1998. Their clear and stated objective
is the removal of Saddam by military force. It also sets the seeds for the cover
story of the British Government when the time arrived – weapons of mass
destruction; authority of existing UN resolutions; a defiance of the Security
Council.

Look at the names – Khalilzad, now ambassador to Iraq; Bolton – until
recently ambassador to the UN; Wolfowitz – recently President of the World
Bank; Rumsfeld was Defense Secretary. Key men in key positions, as they have
been throughout President Bush's two terms. Bolton had already put down a
marker in the neocon house journal, the *Weekly Standard*, on 19 January,
1998:

> During the holiday season, Iraq all but slipped from public view
> – doubtless to quiet prayers of thanks from the Clinton admin-
> istration. Since Saddam Hussein effectively barred United
> Nations weapons inspectors from carrying out their responsi-
> bilities in late October, the administration's strategy has been to
> strike a macho pose for domestic consumption but do next to
> nothing diplomatically, and as little as possible militarily, to end
> Iraq's evasion of the Security Council's post-Gulf War
> constraints.
>
> Surprisingly, the president has escaped damaging criticism,
> not only for five years of waning attention to the Iraq problem,
> but even for his sloppy handling of the last three months. By
> now, the administration's Middle East policy has dwindled to
> sheer political image-making; characteristically, the president
> has invited Israeli prime minister Benjamin Netanyahu and
> PLO leader Yasser Arafat to the White House for photo oppor-
> tunities next week. The 'peace process' is nearly in ruins,

> Saddam is daily gaining confidence and resources, and the
> administration remains passive and unconnected to reality.

He went on to say that Congress 'should spell out for the administration, in
both political and military terms what, in Bob Dole's phrase 'a real president'
would do with Saddam Hussein.

The heat was being turned up in the Clinton administration. As two of the
leading neocons wrote in the *New York Times* on 30 January 1998 ('Bombing
Iraq isn't Enough', William Kristol and Robert Kagan):

> Saddam Hussein must go. This imperative may seem too
> simple for some experts and too daunting for the Clinton
> Administration. But if the United States is committed, as the
> President said in his State of the Union Message, to insuring
> that the Iraqi leader never again uses weapons of mass
> destruction, the only way to achieve that goal is to remove Mr
> Hussein and his regime from power. Any policy short of that
> will fail.

They went on to say that nothing short of a full scale military campaign
would do, raising the same scare stories of dangers from biological and
chemical weapons.

Within days, in the *Weekly Standard*, Kagan was comparing Saddam to Hitler
marching into the Rhineland, and warning of anthrax-tipped rockets. He
conveniently did not mention, as Senator Dan Riegle's report concluded, that
the anthrax spores were exported to Saddam by American companies.

Presciently, Kagan hypothesised that Clinton 'decides to go in alone, or
perhaps with the British as his only ally'. His fear – and that of the neocons
– was that the military action would not be heavy enough. This, he opined,
would only lead to failure:

> Perhaps some would even echo Anthony Eden's sentiments of
> sixty years ago and propose that the world conclude as far-
> reaching and enduring a settlement as was possible whilst Herr
> Hussein was in the mood to do so. This would be an unmiti-

gated victory for Saddam. And for a dictator, nothing succeeds like success.

He concluded that:

The only solution to the problem in Iraq today is to use air power and ground power, and not to stop until we have finished what President Bush began in 1991 . . . Only ground forces can remove Saddam and his regime from power

He went on:

If we're going to have a breach in the Security Council over Iraq, let's at least have it over a promising military effort rather than a doomed one.

The campaign of the neocons was unrelenting as the indefatigable Kagan rejoined Kristol, writing in the *Washington Post* of 26 Feburary 1998. Complaining now of a new deal to get UN inspectors back into Iraq, they fused the twin targets of the hated Saddam and the despised UN;

The fact that UNSCOM will be allowed to continue its mission in some form, moreover, does not mean the inspectors will be any closer to finding Saddam's biological and chemical weapons than they were before. After all, as administration officials acknowledge just last week, after six-and-a-half years of inspections, the United States still has no idea where the weapons are hidden. Saddam has now had four months to conceal his weapons. How many months, or years, will it take the inspectors to get back on the scent?

Confrontation remained the way forward.

It is clearer now than ever that there are only two real choices ever more: Kofi Annan-style concessions leading eventually to the full emancipation of Saddam and his regime. And let's not kid ourselves. In any such political-military strategy, the military element is central. Unless we are willing to live in a world where everyone has to 'do business' with Saddam and his weapons of mass destruction, we need to be willing to use US air power and ground troops to get rid of him.

Kagan and Kristol were not alone. Across at the *Weekly Standard*, John Bolton was growing ever more impatient with Bill Clinton's diplomatic approach to the Middle East. He was critically aware of the role of the Security Council in denying warmongers their head, and remained disposed to believing in the mythical Iraqi weapons of mass destruction:

First, given the United Nation's visibility, we can count on efforts in the Security Council by the Russians, French and Chinese to circumscribe our ability to use force 'next time' without the Security Council's prior, express approval.

Second, the weapons inspectors will not, under this agreement, be any better able to achieve their objectives; Saddam's efforts to develop, produce and deliver weapons of mass destruction will continue apace. The Iraqis believe that, since October, they have thwarted the inspectors and rolled back substantial amounts of previously achieved progress. They have done this at no cost – military, political, or diplomatic – which of course only increases the likelihood of further Iraqi transgressions.

Finally, the Iraq-UN pact itself singles out 'the lifting of sanctions' as something 'to bring to the full attention' of the Security Council. This is diplo-speak for the secretary general's implied commitment to urge the council to eliminate the sanctions of the Iraqis do not egregiously subvert the UN weapons inspectors' work.

This array of problems is not happy news for those who saw the need for stronger, decisive action against Saddam Hussein. But we are exactly where the administration's policy has predictably put us.

By September of 1998, the neocons were in high dudgeon over what they saw as Clinton's failure to topple Saddam. The stakhanovite Kagan wrote in the *Weekly Standard* of 28 September:

> It has been clear that the only way to rid the world of Saddam's weapons of mass destruction is to rid Iraq of Saddam. Last week, Paul Wolfowitz, a defence official in the Bush administration, laid out in testimony before Congress a thoughtful and coherent strategy to accomplish that goal . . . Any serious effort to oust Saddam must also be backed by US military might.

As the message began to percolate through the political classes, Senator Richard Lugar commented that airstrikes alone 'will not get the job done'. He continued that a 'credible programme for the removal of Saddam Hussein [is] going to involve US ground troops in due course.'
President Clinton had been cowed in 1998 into signing the Congress's Iraq Liberation Act of 1998. There is no evidence that he ever considered implementing it. Indeed, to the anger of the neocons, his National Security Adviser – Sandy Berger – was to bring on board Kenneth Pollack. Pollack had been a co-author of an article 'The Rollback Fantasy', which had outraged Paul Wolfowitz when it appeared in *Foreign Affairs* magazine. The original article was highly critical of the aggressive neocon policy towards Iraq:

> . . . That policy of containment. If that collapses – or when it collapses – the United States will face a Saddam who has new nuclear, biological, and chemical weapons and a renewed capacity to conduct conventional warfare and terrorism, and who is bent on avenging his 1992 defeat. That would risk many more lives than trying to overthrow Saddam by force.
>
> Neither side of this debate has a monopoly on responsible judgement, neither course of action is free from significant dangers. On balance, however, containment entails much greater long-term risks that using force to help the Iraqi people rid themselves and us of this tyrannical menace.

As the *Weekly Standard* had said again on 16 November 1998:

> There is a way to deal with Saddam that can work, and we've outlined it in these pages over the past year. It is to complete the unfinished business of the 1991 Gulf War and get rid of Saddam.

At least that publication and its contributors had the quality of consistency; and their message was being taken more seriously by more and more elected politicians. Nevertheless, they had all but given up on the Clinton administration's capacity for sorting out Iraq. The 11 January 1999 edition found Kagan putting their view succinctly:

> The Clinton administration is, in short, bereft of a policy toward Iraq, indeed more so today than before the missile strikes. It refuses to consider serious action to remove Saddam by supporting the Iraqi opposition. It won't even contemplate the idea of sending in US ground forces to do the job. Clinton's national security team utters vague promises about containment, about keeping Saddam 'in his box', but they cannot begin to explain how they intend to accomplish this. Guess who's in the box now.

The attempts of the neocons to prise the scales from the eyes of their fellow Americans were focused and unremitting. Gary Schmitt – executive director of the Project of a New American Century – was another zealot in that cause. He wrote a review in – you've guessed it – the *Weekly Standard*, of a book published by the American Enterprise Institute (a virtuous circle) the central thesis of which is that terrorism is generally state-sponsored, and Iraq is in the thick of it. Ergo, Schmitt wrote:

> If terrorism is state sponsored, then governments are faced with a choice between waging war in return and ignoring an act of aggression, neither of which is without consequences.
>
> It is precisely this dilemma that Middle East scholar Laurie Mylroie examines in Study of Revenge: Saddam Hussein's

Unfinished War against America. Are we willing to face the fact that most terrorism consists of acts of war being waged by identifiable nations? No, says Mylroie, as she focuses on the 1999 World Trade Centre bombing and the Government's apparent willingness to ignore the evidence that pointed toward Iraq's hand in the effort'

Yet the Hitlerism comparisons of Saddam – one neocon even claimed his wars with Iran and Kuwait were a hunger for lebensraum – became intensified. Not only must Saddam be overthrown, but it must be done with a particular style, including shock and awe:

America's hayba – its ability to inspire awe, the critical factor in the Middle East's ruthless politics – had vanished. And once hayba is lost, only a demonstration of indomitable force restores it. A US election, followed by President George W. Bush's slightly bigger bombing run over Iraq on February 16th , doesn't cut it after years of pointless raids accompanied by American braggaddio.

If we are to protect ourselves and our friends in the Middle East, who are many, we have to rebuild the awe which we have lost through nearly a decade of retreat.

Curiously, Reuel Gerecht, the neocon quoted above, shows how shallow the thinking of the neocons was. Ahmad Chalabi was to be the neocons' chosen leader of Iraq, notwithstanding that his reputation was tarnished:

Anonymous US diplomats and intelligence officers have repeatedly labelled Chalabi via the press as corrupt suggesting that he cares more about personal profit than anything else. A banker in Jordan in the 1970s, Chalabi is rumoured to have stolen millions from his Petra bank. The rumours are probably unfounded, the product of Chalabi's being on the losing side of Hashemite-Jordanian-Palestinian squabbles. He made enemies amongst influential Jordanians closely tied to Palestinian banking circles, which have a near monopoly over Jordan's commerce.

But even if the rumours are true, so what? Chalabi hasn't been trying for the last eight years to become the CEO of KPMG. He hasn't watched friends die because money is the center of his life. If Chalabi weren't rich, he couldn't devote so much time and money to the fight against Saddam Hussein. One would think that George Tenet's CIA which has probably been at the root of most of the attacks on Chalabi, would know well that good, even noble, men can take money. In the Middle East, there are much deadlier sins than greed.

As George Bush Junior settled into the White House the outriders for the neocons were still unsure whether or not the new administration would be suborned by the Washington bureaucracy. One early fear was that a defence review being carried out by Donald Rumsfeld might take Iraq off the American agenda.

Tom Donnelly reminded people that Rumsfeld and Wolfowitz had signed up to direct intervention in Iraq. Pointedly, he wrote that: 'the Republican Party platform demanded' a comprehensive plan for the removal of Saddam Hussein from power.

That same month – July 2001 – Reuel Gerecht wrote:

> From the spring of 1996, the Clinton administration's Iraq policy was in meltdown, under the Bush administration. It has completely liquefied.

They felt almost cheated:

> . . . in any case, in Middle Eastern eyes, the Butcher of Baghdad has checked, if not checkmated the United States.

And then came 9/11.

In their favoured medium – a letter – the leading neocons wrote to President Bush on 3 April 2002 asking:

Furthermore, Mr President, we urge you to accelerate plans for removing Saddam Hussein from power in Iraq. As you have said, every day that Saddam Hussein remains in power brings closer the day when terrorists will have not just airplanes with which to attack us, but chemical biological or nuclear weapons, as well. It is now common knowledge that Saddam, along with Iran, is a founder and supporter of terrorism against Israel. Iraq has harbored terrorists such as Abu Nidal in the past, and it maintains links to the Al Qaeda network. If we do not move against Saddam Hussein and his regime, the damage our Israeli friends and we have suffered until now may someday appear but a prelude to much greater horrors. Moreover, we believe that the surest path to peace in the Middle East lies not through the appeasement of Saddam and other local tyrants, but through a renewed commitment on our part, as you suggested in your State of the Union address, to the birth of freedom and democratic government in the Islamic world.

Influential signatories included Ken Adelman, William Kristol, Thomas Donnelly, Frank Gaffney, Reuel Marc Gerecht, Donald Kegan, Richard Perle, Norman Podhoretz, Gary Schmitt, and R. James Woolsey.

There were others who signed, and those who would have done so, but who were then in the administration; individuals like Richard Armitage, John Bolton, Donald Rumsfeld and Paul Wolfowitz.

The same people had, by and large, signed another letter to President Bush, dated 20 September 2001, in the immediate aftermath of the tragedy of 9/11. They agreed with Colin Powell that:

US policy must aim not only at finding the people responsible for this incident, but must also target 'those other groups out there that mean us no good' and 'that have conducted attacks previously against US personnel, US interests and our allies'.

Going on to specify Iraq:

We agree with Secretary of State Powell's recent statement that Saddam Hussein 'is one of the leading terrorists on the Face of the Earth . . . ' It may be that the Iraqi Government provided assistance in some form to the recent attack on the United States. But even if evidence does not link Iraq directly to the attack, any strategy aiming at the eradication of terrorism and as sponsors must include a determined effort to remove Saddam Hussein from power in Iraq. Failure to undertake such an effort will constitute an early and perhaps decisive surrender in the war on international terrorism. The United States must therefore provide full military and financial support to the Iraqi opposition. American military force should be used to provide a 'safe zone' in Iraq from which the opposition can operate. And American forces must be prepared to back up our commitment to the Iraq opposition by all necessary means.

Within a relatively short time, all of their dreams about Iraq and regime change were to come true.

Then came the nightmare.

Blair

Prior to 9/11, Tony Blair had not placed any great emphasis on Iraq. Along with the rest of the British Government, he was aware of the problem, but tended to reflect President Clinton's arms-length approach to Saddam. Even in his much quoted Chicago speech of 24 April 1999, the Prime Minister was three-quarters of the way through his comments before he mentioned Saddam.

Admittedly, he spoke of 'two dangerous and ruthless men – Saddam Hussein and Slobodan Milosevic'. But one paragraph in a very long speech does not place Iraq at the epicentre of the world's problems. The speech is more interesting for other reasons. Presciently, he remarked:

First, are we sure of our case? War is an imperfect instrument for fighting humanitarian distress; but armed force is sometimes the only means of dealing with dictators. Second, have we exhausted all diplomatic options? We should always give peace every chance, as we have in the case of Kosovo. Third, on the basis of a practical assessment of the situation, are there military operations we can sensibly and prudently undertake? Fourth, are we prepared for the long term? In the past we talked too much of exit strategies. But having made a commitment, we cannot simply walk away once the fight is over; better to stay with moderate numbers of troops than return for repeat performances with large numbers. And finally, do we have national interests involved?

Reform of the United Nations was then on the agenda, but based on the principles establishing the international rule of law:

I am not suggesting that these are absolute tests. But they are the kind of issues we need to think about in deciding in the future when and whether we will intervene.

Any new rules however will only work if we have reformed international institutions with which to apply them.

If we want a world ruled by law and by international cooperation then we have to support the UN as its central pillar. But we need to find a new way to make the UN and its Security Council work if we are not to return to the deadlock that undermined the effectiveness of the Security Council during the Cold War. This should be a task for members of the Permanent Five to consider once the Kosovo conflict is complete.

But the real rub came in his clarion call to the United States:

Realize that in Britain you have a friend and an ally that will stand with you, work with you, fashion with you the design of a future built on peace and prosperity for all, which is the only dream that makes humanity worth preserving.

After all, he had spelt out earlier in the speech that:

The most pressing foreign policy problem we face is to identify the circumstances in which we should get actively involved in other people's conflicts. Non-interference has long been considered an important principle of international order. And it is not one we would want to jettison too readily. One state should not feel it has the right to change the political system of another or ferment subversion or seize places of territory to which it feels it should have some claim. But the principle of non-interference must be qualified in important respects.

He had set out the background to his position in November 1997 and December 1998, long before his Chicago speech:

The goal of our foreign policy – tonight's subject – is clear. We cannot in these post-Empire days be a super-power in a military sense. But we can make the British presence in the world felt. With our historic alliances, we can be pivotal. We can be powerful in our influence – a nation to whom others listen. Why? Because we run Britain well and are successful ourselves. Because we have the right strategic alliances the world over. And because we are engaged, open and intelligent in how we use them.

So he told the Corporation of London on 20 November 1997. How many would agree with his final line.

Second principle: Strong in Europe and strong with the US. There is no choice between the two. Stronger with one means stronger with the other.

Our aim should be to deepen our relationship with the US at all levels. We are the bridge between the US and Europe. Let us use it.

When Britain and America work together on the international scene, there is little we can't achieve.

We must never forget the historic and continuing US role in defending the political and economic freedoms we take for granted, leaving all sentiment aside, they are a force for good in the world. They can always be relied on when the chips are down. The same should always be true of Britain.

We face another critical test of international resolve today. Saddam Hussein is once more defying the clearly expressed will of the United Nations by refusing to allow UN inspectors to fulfil their task of ensuring Iraq has no remaining weapons of mass destruction. It is vital for all of us that they be allowed to complete their work with no suggestion of discrimination against our US allies. Only then can the question of relaxing sanctions arise.

This Government's determination to stand firm against a still dangerous dictator is unspeakable. We want to see a diplomatic solution and will work with others to achieve this in the next few days, but Saddam should not take as a sign of weakness the international community's desire to find a peaceful way forward if possible. He has made this fatal miscalculation before. For his sake, I hope he will not make it again.

This part of Blair's speech overwhelmed the sections on his other three principles of foreign policy. It is almost a cry for attention to the American big-brother, and it helped create an American impression of Blair as a 'pushover' in any areas of difference.

Similarly, his statement to the House of Commons on 17 December 1998, was so supportive of Bill Clinton, that Blair was moved to say.

There are suggestions that the timing of military action is somehow linked to the internal affairs of the United States. I refute this entirely. I have no doubt whatsoever that action is fully justified now. That is my strong personal view. I know that President Clinton reached the same conclusion for the same reasons. Had he acted differently, out of regard to internal matters of US politics, that would have been a dereliction of his duty as President.

This was the occasion when Clinton launched strikes against Iraq at the height of the Monica Lewinsky scandal. It was also the beginning of the great deception in the United Kingdom:

Let us be clear, Saddam still has capability in this area, not least to develop more weapons in the future. To give only one example, over 610 tonnes of precursor chemicals for the nerve gas VX have not been found or accounted for.

What was to be echoed in the chamber over four years later, was the 'no choice' argument:

We had a stark choice. Either we could let this process continue further, with UNSCOM more and more emasculated, including its monitoring capability, Saddam correspondingly free to pursue his weapon-making ambitions, and this one-sided and unjustified bargaining over sanctions continuing. Or, having tried every possible diplomatic avenue, and shown endless patience despite all Saddam's deception, we could decide that if UNSCOM could not do its work, we should tackle Saddam's remaining capability through direct action of our own. In these circumstances there is only one responsible choice to make.

We are acting now because Butler's report, delivered on time, was so clear. And because, if we were going to act, it was obviously better that we should do so without giving Saddam unnecessary time to prepare his defences, and disperse whatever he could to new locations.

Thus, the stage was set not only for the future war, but for the litany of lies that was to be deployed as the excuse for it.

Much of the press seemed bored with Iraq, and let it pass by. Specialists in foreign affairs or defence were aware of its significance as a challenge for the United States and United Kingdom governments; but it was generally thought to be of little consequence in the everyday run of things, and, in the British case, the media's love affair with New Labour.

The *Evening Standard* flagged up the war of words between the west and Saddam after a briefing prior to Blair's Guildhall speech of November 1997, but in a rather low-key way. Such trading of threats had been *de rigueur* between Saddam and the west for years, and the focus was on air-strikes. No one envisaged at that time a reprise of the Gulf War.

By early 1998, there was a ratcheting up of the rhetoric. As the *Independent* reported on 28 January:

> The attacks would be intended to force Iraq to comply with UN resolutions on inspection of its weapons of mass destruction. Only Britain, of the five permanent members of the Security Council, fully supports the United States position on the use of force against Iraq. Tony Blair, the Prime Minister, told the Arabic daily al-Hayat: 'We hope that diplomatic efforts to end the crisis will succeed. But we are not willing to rule out any options at this stage.'

Ian McWhirter was a little more cynical in the *Scotsman* on 3 February:

> Of course, there's nothing like a small war in a land far away to bring folks together. Clinton needs Blair's backing in confronting Iraq, and Blair is keen to give it. They both need something to distract the public mind from sleaze. But this latest British-American posturing over Iraq is no mere contrivance to divert attention from the President's sex life and Tony Blair's domestic political problems. These guys really believe it – and they believe in each other.
>
> Imagine if, during the first Gulf War, someone had predicted that seven years on, a Democratic President and a Labour Prime Minister would be standing shoulder to shoulder, alone against the world in their resolve to bomb Baghdad? It would have seemed absurd.

And McWhirter forecast:

> . . . It will be post-socialist foreign policy that is the main feature. New Labour; New Hawks. Tony and Bill want to show that the Centre Left can kick butt too. It is both symbol and substance of

the new special relationship that Tony Blair has already signalled unconditional support for Bill Clinton on Iraq.

Tony Blair is in love with the idea of himself as a firm leader, like Thatcher. He needs a good war to efface forever the image of Labour defeatism, pacifism and unilateralism.

But he warned:

Blair would do well to be cautious about becoming merely an arm of American foreign policy. He should ask himself how far he wants this relationship to go, on and off the battlefield. For the Americanisation of Britain is not something any of us have actually voted for.

Even the *Birmingham Post* got in on the act. It mischievously asked some rather pertinent questions on 12 February 1998:

As events hot up in Iraq and Tony Blair's embarrassing prostration before his 'trustworthy friend' Bill Clinton means we are involved again up to our necks, how anxious are you about the threat from Saddam Hussein's stores of killer biological substances which could wipe out the world twice over? (a) Not worried? (b) Moderately scared? Or (c) It's a cure for constipation?

It's hard to know whether the answer should be (c) or not. Is all this talk about Saddam's arsenal of death merely a smoke-screen to deflect attention away from Clinton's zipper and its gravity problem?

We all know about truth being the first casualty of war. Could the propaganda agents really be whipping up the anti-Iraq panic that only a week or two ago we were actually predicting they would as a means of saving the Presidents' soiled reputation?

Now we all know that bombs were dropped and lives extinguished because of Bill Clinton's sexual proclivities – or, rather, his need to divert the American public from his seediness.

As the *Daily Mail* put it less than a fortnight later:

> Whatever happens about Iraq, Tony Blair has suffered collateral damage by being seen as Bill Clinton's poodle. He's despised by many Labour supporters.
>
> Cartoonist Gerald Scarfe has repeated a famous, obscene drawing he did for *Private Eye* in the sixties of Labour premier Harold Wilson and the then US President Lyndon Johnson's bottom. This time its Messrs Blair and Clinton.

The *Evening Standard* was clear:

> Foreign affairs offer a diversion from tales of Oval Office 'entanglements' and the Paula Jones sexual harassment case. Clinton's opinion poll ratings leapt during his confrontation with Iraq. Tony Blair and the G-7 summit in Britain (are) set to raise them still higher.

Later that year, Iraq's profile was raised still further. Clinton spoke from an Asian tour about UNSCOM, and Sandy Berger warned:

> Iraq has an obligation to produce the documents and we will support UNSCOM in that effort. The issue here is whether Iraq will meet its obligations and whether UNSCOM is able to do its work. If we reach the conclusion that the answer to those questions is negative, we are obviously prepared to act. The first signal to any attack will be the withdrawal of the weapons inspection teams from Iraq.

The British Prime Minister dutifully did his supporting act - as was, by now, the norm. Where America went, he would follow. It was reported that:

> Tony Blair was at his country residence Chequers with his family yesterday, but a Downing Street spokesman said 'The refusal to give the documents to the weapons inspectors is clearly a pretty bad

sign . . . Iraq has quickly chalked up another black mark. We have already made contact with the Americans to discuss strategy. Judgements on what action to take will be made soon.

This could be read as: 'The Prime Minister hasn't a clue about this, but we know our place in the scheme of things.'

As time wore on, further and further damage was being done to Iraq. Its air defences were being degraded, and innocent lives were being lost. Defence Secretary George Robertson – later NATO Secretary-General – was reported to have set out the line in *Evening News Scotland* on 17 December:

> Mr Robertson said military action had been necessary to send a message not only to the Iraqi leader but to other dictators intent on developing weapons of mass destruction . . . 'If we are going to stop the proliferation of these weapons everywhere in the world it is right that we should use force at this time because, unfortunately, it seems to be the only language that Saddam Hussein seems to understand.'

Clearly, not a very successful argument, given proliferation to India, Pakistan, and North Korea, with Iran possibly about to challenge Israel's nuclear hegemony in the Middle East. Nor a very moral argument: bombing innocent women and children in Iraq, to pressurise dictators in other countries. Robertson was, in truth, merely reflecting his Prime Minister's view on bombing Iraq, that:

> It would be a dereliction of our duty if we had not taken the action we have done.

A strange duty that kills and maims. Speaking of Saddam, Mr. Blair was reported as saying:

> This is a man who, every time he is given the chance to use violence and to use terror, will do so. Now I think that is why there is a great deal of understanding as to why we have taken this action.

Old sayings about 'pots' and 'kettles' come to mind. Then came one of the first chinks in Blair's case. As the *Western Daily Press* reported for the first time on 17 December 1998:

> Mr Blair rejected claims by Iraq that the United States and Britain had lied about breaches of arms control in a bid to provoke military action.

And as George Monbiot commented in the *Guardian* on 9 January 1999:

> Iraq, Tony Blair told us, had to be bombed because Saddam Hussein is 'a serial breaker of promises'. If the fickleness of a country's leader is now regarded as sufficient justification for blowing up its installations, we in Britain had better start building some bomb shelters.

The bombing went on and on, with mounting loss of life, and no discernible advantage – the world was not looking at the elimination of Iraqi air defences, particularly once Bush replaced Clinton. By February 2001 – just months before 9/11 – the *Northern Echo* was urging Mr Blair to 'tread warily' as it questioned the reasoning behind the intensified bombing:

> The reaction may not have been so strong if the world had been given warning of the increased anxiety over Saddam's activities. If, as we are told, there has been heightened cause for concern over the past month, why wasn't it flagged up to the international community more vociferously weeks ago?

While questions were raised in the House of Commons by Tam Dalyell, Alice Mahon, George Galloway and Ann Clwyd (at least, where Kurds were concerned) the country as a whole was sleepwalking into a contrived showdown with Iraq. The trigger was the entirely unrelated terror attacks on the twin towers of New York.

The gathering storm

In a time of universal deceit, telling the truth becomes a revolutionary act.

George Orwell (1903–1950)

In September 2000, a blueprint for a new *Pax Americana* had been laid out. The neoconservative think tank Project for a New American Century published *Rebuilding America's Defenses*. It predicted: 'Some catastrophic and catalysing event – like a new Pearl Harbour' was needed to kickstart a resurgence of America's dominance in the world.

9/11 was to trigger the 'war on terror' which, in turn, gave the impetus for achieving even wider goals. As commentator John Pilger was to write on 20 February 2003:

> Two years ago [the document] recommended an increase in arms spending by 48bn dollars so that Washington could 'fight and win multiple, simultaneous major theatre wars'. This has happened. It said the United States should develop 'bunker buster' nuclear weapons and make 'Star Wars' a national priority. This is happening. It said that, in the event of Bush taking power, Iraq should be a target. And so it is . . . 'While the unresolved conflict with Iraq provides the immediate justification,' it says 'the need for a substantial American force presence in the Gulf transcends the issue of the regime of Saddam Hussein'.

James Naughtie was later to say, in his book *The Accidental American*, that in July 2001:

Bush foreign policy was a worrying phenomenon [as by this time] it was clear that whatever it turned out to be, Blair would support it.

Naturally, 9/11 set the tone for Bush's 'worrying' foreign policy. As former counter-terrorism chief Richard A. Clarke wrote in his book, *Against All Enemies*:

> [On the 12th September 2001] I expected to go back to a round of meetings examining what the next attacks could be, what our vulnerabilities were, what we could do about them in the short term. Instead, I walked into a series of discussions about Iraq. At first, I was incredulous that we were talking about something other than getting Al Qaeda. Then I realised . . . that Rumsfeld and Wolfowitz were going to try to take advantage of this natural tragedy to promote their agenda about Iraq. Since the beginning of the administration, indeed well before, they had been pressing for a war with Iraq.

On 12 September, Blair was declaring:

> . . . be under no doubt at all – we stand with the United States of America in this matter.

On 16 September, he could praise President Bush:

> I think that the way President Bush has handled this is absolutely right. He has been very calm and measured in the way that he has approached it.

Although Trent Lott, Senate Minority Leader, was to suggest on 8 October this was all a façade:

One advisor that we have met says to remember that revenge is
better eaten cold. In other words, you know, you take your time,
have a plan, go after your first target, second target . . .

It was certainly the case that the United States Defense Policy Board met in
camera for nineteen hours on 19 September, to make the case against Iraq.
The State Department was not invited; nor were its Iraq experts. No briefing
was given to them of what was discussed or decided.

In Britain, Parliamentarians wanted any British involvement in a military
response to 9/11 to have broad support. Parliament debated the situation on
4 October, when Tony Lloyd asserted:

When we seek possibly to make war, those . . . constraints on
the Government of the will of the people and accountability to
the public must apply.

Tam Dalyell had a more specific question:

Could we be clear exactly what the attitude is towards Iraq?

Michael Ancram, Tory spokesman on Foreign Affairs, urged the neocon
obsession with Iraq onto a British Government that should have been
focussed on Al Qaeda:

What is the Government's current position in relation to
Iraq? For years, the regime has been publicly condemned as a
major sponsor of terror and a constructor of WMD. Now,
suddenly, we hear little or nothing about it. Do the
Government support a course of action aimed at eradicating
the virus of international terrorism within Iraq, and could
that be part of a second phase in the fight against international terrorism?

Tam Dalyell qualified the Opposition's conflation of Iraq and the Al Qaeda
tolerating Taliban in Afghanistan:

... the leader of the Opposition asked about action against Iraq and . . . [the Prime Minister's] response was somewhat ambiguous. Is this not an opportunity at least to start talking to the Government of Iraq?. . . the Iraqi Government loathes the Taliban. That is the fact of the matter. Might this not be the opportunity at least to start a dialogue?

On 8 October, Menzies Campbell asked Defence Secretary Geoff Hoon:

Is he aware that there is now some loose talk that military action [in Afghanistan] should be extended to other countries, for example, Iraq? Is he aware of any evidence that would justify the extension of military action in that direction?

Members of Parliament had already divined the wider agenda. George Galloway told the Commons a week later:

... it is clear from a cursory reading of the newspapers on Sunday that Afghanistan is not the only target in this coalition against terrorism.

Vernon Coaker agonised:

... like other Honourable Members, I am worried by some of the signals coming from Washington about an escalation into Iraq and other places.

And I wrote the following day:

Richard Perle, [known by] the sobriquet the 'Prince of Darkness', urged that we ought to widen our aims beyond Afghanistan. He named those other countries that he felt should be the object of our military ire, including Iran, Iraq, Syria and Libya. Subsequently, that has been reinforced by Donald Rumsfeld, Paul Wolfowitz, John Negroponte, and

others who would be fairly described as fully paid-up members
of the hawkish tendency . . .

The concern was widespread, and not just limited to Parliamentarians.
Websites were full of paranoid conspiracy theories, as Joseph Key demonstrated on the World Socialist Website, on 20 October:

> . . . a section of the Bush administration is working hard – overtly
> and covertly – to create a pretext for an American invasion of Iraq
> . . . The events of September 11 and more recently the anthrax
> scare, are being exploited by high level operatives within the
> American Government to promote a program that has long been
> sought by the military and intelligence establishment: the ousting
> of the Ba'athist regime of Saddam Hussein and the transforma-
> tion of Iraq into a state subservient to American interests . . . It is
> clear that the Pentagon is already drawing up plans for a [military]
> invasion of Iraq.

Nine days later, Geoff Hoon was to claim otherwise:

> There is no hidden agenda; this [Afghanistan] is not a prelude
> to a wider war.

Did he know? Did he care?
In an article in the *Sunday Telegraph* on 4 November, Matthew D'Ancona had
a different perspective on Blair's direction at least:

> He is applying precisely the techniques he has honed on the
> domestic front to his mission overseas. He is approaching the war
> on terrorism as if it were an extension of the New Labour project,
> the latest and greatest challenge for the arch moderniser.

D'Ancona almost presents Blair as a dreamer, a cross between Alexander the
Great, looking for new worlds to conquer, and Don Quixote, tilting at
windmills.

Another journalist – Bob Woodward, of Watergate fame – wrote in his book *Plan of Attack*, that Bush asked Rumsfeld after 9/11:

> What kind of war plan do you have for Iraq?

It was very clear to the media what the plan was. As the *Observer* set out on 2 December 2001:

> America intends to depose Saddam Hussein . . . President George W Bush has ordered the CIA and his Senior military commanders to draw up detailed plans for a military operation . . . The trigger for any attack . . . would be the anticipated refusal of Iraq to resubmit to inspections for the WMD destruction under the UN sanctions imposed after the Gulf War. United States proponents of extending the war believe they can make the case for hitting Saddam's regime over its plan to produce WMD.

The problem was that Saddam did not flatly refuse to resubmit to inspections. That was not to be a major hurdle. As James Naughtie wrote in *The Accidental American*; the British Embassy knew in January 2001 that:

> . . . a timetable had been set for the invasion of Iraq.

Britain, however, was not at this stage irrevocably committed to the American agenda. As Naughtie pointed out:

> There were six or seven moments in the Iraq story when he [Blair] could have drawn back. The first was probably early in 2002. He could have and he didn't. It was clear then where we were heading.

Blair was fond, in general political terms, of urging colleagues 'to use the bigger picture'. Others did exactly that with regard to Iraq. Thus, I wrote in an article in *Tribune* on 8 January 2002, 'Eyeless in Gaza':

For George W Bush and his acolytes, Arafat's impossible situation is of no matter. He is but one piece in a political jigsaw which puts him, along with the leaders of Iraq, Iran, North Korea and others who fall foul of America's gameplan, on a one-way ticket to nowhere.

On 10 September 2002, Philip Zelkow, executive director of the 9/11 Commission, made a telling connection in American thinking:

Why would Iraq attack America or use nuclear weapons against us? I'll tell you what I think the real threat is and actually has been since 1990 – it's the threat against Israel.

The Jewish Institution for National Security Affairs (JINSA) was extremely influential in neoconservative thinking, and Israeli considerations were certainly given disproportionate value by the Bush administration.

In an article for the *New Statesman* of 20 February, John Pilger set out what was in train:

[According to the PNAC] what was needed . . . was 'some catastrophic and catalysing event – like a new Pearl Harbour'. The attacks of 11th September 2001 provided the 'new Pearl Harbour' described as the 'opportunity of ages'.

The British position was by no means either as transparent or decided. As Naughtie's book suggests, Blair had made his own personal decision by March 2002. However, his cabinet had its first discussion on Iraq on the first of that month. Blair's line was that there was no choice – Britain would support President Bush. There was no debate or argument. The Prime Minister simply handed down his decisions to a supine cabinet, bereft of either information or principle. So much for cabinet collective responsibility.

Many others had made a decision, as well as the Prime Minister. Alice Mahon put her views into an early day motion on 4 March:

> That this House is aware of the deep unease among honourable Members on all sides of the House at the prospect that HM's Government might support United States military action against Iraq; agrees with Kofi Annan that a further military attack on Iraq would be unwise at this time; believes that such a course of action would disrupt support for the anti terror coalition among the Arab states; and instead urges the Prime Minister to use Britain's influence with Iraq to gain agreement that UN weapons inspections will resume.

Feeling left out of this 'great game' and despite their party's even stronger pro-American bias than that of government, some Tories simply grumbled ineffectively from the sidelines, like George Osborne on 12 March:

> ... the Prime Minister ... conducts his own presidential foreign policy without telling anyone about it.

The real opposition came from a broad alliance of dissident Labour backbenchers, a handful of Tories, various nationalists and the Liberal Democrats. From the latter, David Heath asked the Foreign Secretary on 12 March:

> Does the Foreign Secretary agree . . . that massive military confrontation with Iraq is certainly not inevitable and would indeed be foolhardy?

The Foreign Secretary, Jack Straw, did not provide a direct response. Without a hint of irony, he could tell the House that day:

> . . . It [military action] is not directly in contemplation at the moment.

In fact, it was the only option on the table. He went on to patronise the House:

> Of course . . . whenever military action has been determined,
> the House has had a crucial role to play.

The only 'crucial role' it was to play was to rubberstamp decisions already taken, and preparations already made. It was downright wrong of Straw to say:

> It [military action] cannot be ruled out in this situation.

It could, but the truth was that the Americans would not budge from their determination to attack Iraq (not that there is any evidence of British attempts to dissuade them. Au contraire, pressure came the other way, as when Lord Goldsmith was leaned on by the Americans to change his legal advice on the legality of war against Iraq). Straw continued:

> . . . nothing in my discussions with members of the Bush Administration suggested that they have in mind anything other than proceeding that way [i.e. in a cautious, proportionate manner, with international support and in line with international law].

If the Foreign Secretary was unaware of American intentions, he ought not to have been in the job; and the whole institution of the Foreign Office ought to have been closed down as a total waste of time. We must presume that he did know exactly what the Americans were up to.

The pressure was on the Government to guarantee a debate on British military involvement against Iraq. It was hoped that, despite the Royal Prerogative, Parliament could check any precipitate rush to war. It was by no means clear that such a debate would come about; or, if it did, that the Government would feel bound by its outcome. Menzies Campbell put down a marker on the 20 March:

> That this House calls upon HM's Government to ensure that there is a debate and substantive motion in the House before any further British forces are deployed in any military action

beyond present commitments against Iraq by land, sea, or air, and if necessary to recall Parliament during any recess for that purpose.

Aware of two very different audiences the Prime Minister spoke at the George Bush Senior Presidential Library, on 7 April:

> If necessary the action [against confluence of terrorism and WMD] should be military and, if necessary and justified, it should involve regime change. As for Iraq, I know some fear precipitate action. They needn't. We will proceed . . . in a calm, measured, sensible but firm way. But leaving Iraq to develop WMD, in flagrant breach of no less than nine separate United Nations Security Council resolutions, refusing still to allow weapons inspectors back to do their work properly, is not an option. The regime of Saddam is detestable. As I say, the moment for decision on how to act is not yet with us. But to allow WMD to be developed by a state like Iraq without let or hindrance would be grossly to ignore the lessons of September 11 and we will not do it.

He was happy to perpetuate the mythical linkage of 9/11 terrorism, rogue states, WMD and Iraq. Yet he had an eye to his domestic audience – everything was conditional. Again, he linked military action and regime change, both extremely problematical under international law:

> . . . we must be prepared to act where terrorism or WMD threaten us . . . If necessary the action should be military , and again, if necessary and justified, it should involve regime change.

This pleased Bush and his hawks, but his insistence that 'as for Iraq . . . we will proceed, as we did after September 11, in a calm, measured, sensible but firm way', was not to be borne out by events. Indeed, news from a conference at Ditchley Park in England confirmed that the broad approach of the United

States/United Kingdom alliance was already set in stone. William Pfaff, of the *International Herald Tribune,* reported:

> Those Americans at Ditchley Park who are close to the Bush administration insisted that the next step in the war against terrorism must be an attack on Iraq. They argued that the United States must unseat Saddam Hussein because only then will the other states of the Middle East . . . understand that Washington means to destroy its enemies wherever they are and will do so whether the Europeans or the 'international community' like it or not.

Indeed, the aerial bombardment of the targets in Iraq was already being stepped up, as Iraqi air defences were degraded, nearly a year before the war on Iraq officially began.

By 7 May 2002 it was clear to Alex Salmond, and to millions of ordinary Britons, what was afoot:

> That this House notes with concern reports of Pentagon sources briefing that the United States is planning a massive air led military campaign against Iraq of up to 1,000 bombing strikes a day, followed by a ground invasion involving at least one United Kingdom army brigade, and that plants producing so called smart bombs are currently working overtime in preparation for a military campaign in the autumn or next spring as reported in the Herald on 29 April; further notes the remarks of the Prime Minister in the House on 10 April in relation to Iraq that 'no decisions on action have been taken'; believes that these positions are mutually inconsistent; calls on the Prime Minister to make a full statement to the House outlining preparations for an attack on Iraq; and reiterates that any offensive military action against Iraq can only be morally justified if it carries a new and specific mandate from the UNSC.

Incredibly, President Bush could tell a press conference in Berlin on 23 May (repeating his claim in Paris three days later):

I have no war plans on my desk.

This was despite General Tommy Franks having given him 'the refined Generated Start Plan for war with Iraq' on 7 February. The President is said to have a short attention span – perhaps that is the explanation for it allegedly never having been on his desk.

By mid-July, British mobilisation preparations were under way, and for three weeks, staff officers had been making joint plans with the Americans for an attack on Iraq. However, the Prime Minister could tell Panorama on 16 July:

> No, there are no decisions that have been taken about military action.

Five days later, a briefing paper – *Iraq: Conditions for Military Action* – was given a limited circulation by the Cabinet Office:

> The United States Government's military planning for action against Iraq is proceeding apace . . . Depending on United States intentions, a decision in principle may be needed soon on whether and in what form the United Kingdom takes part in military action . . . we consider the following conditions necessary for military action and United Kingdom participation; justification/legal base; an international coalition; a quiescent Israel/Palestine; a positive risk/benefit assessment; and the preparation of domestic opinion . . .

Belatedly, official minutes and memos (not favoured by the Blair inner circle, as Lord Butler highlighted) began to catch up with reality. Thus a Downing Street aide, Matthew Rycroft, penned a memo on 23 July:

> [The Head of the Secret Intelligence Service reported that] . . . Military action was now seen as inevitable [in Washington]. Bush wanted to remove Saddam, through military action, justified by the conjunction of terrorism and weapons of mass destruction. But the intelligence and facts were being fixed

around the policy. The National Security Council had no patience with the UN route. There was little discussion in Washington of the aftermath after military action. The Defence Secretary said that the United States had already begun 'spikes of activity' to put pressure on the regime . . . It seemed clear that Bush had made up his mind to take military action, even if the timing was not yet decided. But the case was thin. Saddam was not threatening his neighbours and his WMD capability was less than that of Libya, North Korea or Iran. The Attorney General said that the desire for regime change was not a legal base for military action. There were three possible legal bases; self-defence, humanitarian intervention, or UN Security Council authorisation. The first and second could not be the base in this case. Relying on UNSCR 1205 of three years ago would be difficult . . . We should work on the assumption that the UK would take part in any military action.

The following day at Prime Minister's questions, Blair blandly commented:

> . . . we have not yet reached the point of decision. How we deal with [Iraq's weapons] is an open question . . . we have not taken the decision to commit British forces.

It is hard to reconcile that statement, with either the thrust of the Cabinet Office note, or Rycroft's memo.

Desperation crept into backbenchers' thinking. I was afraid of a quick decision on war being taken during a recess:

> In the eventuality of the United States commencing military action in the Middle East during the recess, will the Prime Minister undertake to recall the House, before any British forces are committed?

The Prime Minister was accommodating, although not quite clear as to what he meant by 'consulted':

> I have to say that we have not got to the stage of military action.
> If we do get to that stage, at any point in time, we will, of
> course, make sure that Parliament is properly consulted.

I had increasingly come to the view that, despite the arguments that a war on
Iraq was all a dastardly plot to secure America's oil needs, there was a large
element of revenge, or payback, in the American agenda. True, there were
considerations of ensuring that 'rogue states' understood the USA was no soft
touch; there was oil; and there was the huge Zionist influence on American
politics. There was also a gut reaction of wanting to hold someone or
somewhere more accountable for 9/11 than an amorphous, semi-anonymous
movement like Al Qaeda.

Saddam was easy to identify and demonise. He had 'form' and was generally
seen as a thoroughly reprehensible thug (which he was). It was easy to label
him as 'the bad guy' who had tried to assassinate George Bush Senior. Was
this sufficient reason, however, to wreak havoc on the Middle East with
possible global repercussions, and many thousands of lives lost? I thought
not, and wrote about it on my website on 9 September:

> Whilst there is a negotiable way forward, I ask of our leaders
> and their haste to fight this war: What is the point?

Meanwhile, on the same day, Clare Short – Secretary of State for International
Development, with a volatile political history – was noting in her diary:

> Tony Blair gave me assurances when I asked for Iraq to be
> discussed at Cabinet that no decision made and not imminent.

The next day, the Prime Minister addressed the Trades Union Congress
Conference:

> . . . and before there is any question of taking military action,
> I can categorically assure you that Parliament will be consulted
> and will have the fullest opportunity to debate the matter and
> express its view.

What did this mean in terms of substance? Blair had already defended the Royal Prerogative before the Liaison Committee in January. Expressing a view, and being consulted, did not mean that Parliament would decide.

I wrote in the *Guardian* on 21 September, that there was a need to move away from the American agenda over Iraq:

> There are some people in the party worried about urging caution because they fear being described as unpatriotic, but I think it will be a strength if we debate this at party conference . . . My fear is that certain elements in the United States would like to shape the evidence against Bin Laden to suit their own agendas, and much of that is about settling old scores, rather than meeting the needs of a coalition against terrorism.

Anatole Lieven took a direct view of the American agenda – it was reckless. In an article published on the *London Review of Books* website on 3 October – 'The Push for War' – he said:

> The most surprising thing about the Bush Administration's plan to invade Iraq is not that it is destructive of international order; or wicked, when we consider the role the US (and Britain) have played, and continue to play in the Middle East; or opposed by the vast majority of the international community; or seemingly contrary to some of the basic needs of the war against terrorism . . . The most surprising thing about the push for war is that it is so profoundly reckless.

Such views did not seem to matter to most politicians. The United States Congress approved an attack on Iraq on 11 October, under the War Powers Act. For President Bush there was now no barrier to war, although support from Britain, Australia and others would give him the appearance of international support with the American public. A new impatience to let loose the dogs of war now overtook his Administration.

It was not so clear cut for the Blair Government. On 17 October, Geoff Hoon was defensive in the Commons:

I must make it clear that any reference to, or suggestion of, any specific offer of forces by the United Kingdom is simply wrong . . . I can assure the House that no specific decisions have been taken on any commitment of British forces.

The hapless shadow defence secretary, Bernard Jenkin, was even more supportive of the Prime Minister's position than the most gullible New Labour Blairites, telling a parliamentary doubting Thomas, Paul Keetch MP:

I am amazed that the Honourable Gentleman should have the arrogance to believe that the Prime Minister and the President of the US would use military force except as a last resort.

Despite appeals for honesty – as from Alice Mahon on 29 October:

Many of us are deeply concerned about the latest threats from Colin Powell and believe they are evidence of the further intention and determination of the United States to start that sort of war. We think that it is time for the fancy footwork from those on our Front Bench to stop and for us to have a firm statement about exactly what our policy is on Iraq – the Government still pursued their grotesque charade.

On 5 November, an unlikely combination of Llew Smith MP and the Archbishop of Canterbury, surfaced in an early day motion:

That this House commends the article by Dr Rowan Williams, the next Archbishop of Canterbury in the Daily Telegraph on 5 November, agrees with his analysis that military conflict initiated by the United States with United Kingdom support against Iraq could escalate into a nuclear conflict involving Israel; recognises with horror the huge numbers of innocent civilians and military conscripts who would die if nuclear weapons were exploded over or near densely populated cities in the Middle East; further recognises that radioactively contaminated clouds show no respect for national borders, as the Chernobyl accident showed; and calls for all efforts to be made to reach a diplomatic solution to the Iraq crisis.

Michael Ancram tried to be constructive on behalf of the opposition on 13 November 2002:

> That this House welcomes the unanimous decision taken by the UNSC and applauds it determination to deal with Saddam Hussein's WMD; expresses the hope that the regime in Baghdad will not obstruct the UN weapons inspectors in any form; notes that Res. 1441 clearly states that any such obstruction will result in serious consequences as a result of its continued violations of its obligations; further notes that in the event of military action the Government should set out what plans it has for a post Saddam Iraq; expresses concern that Iraq as a country should not be fragmented; highlights that the international community must accept its responsibility to assist the people of Iraq with economic aid and humanitarian assistance, and notes that this is vital if the Iraqi people are to successfully rebuild the international infrastructure and economy of the country.

However, he had forgotten that the first duty of the opposition is to oppose the executive. His weak motion simply reaffirmed the Government's belief that the official opposition was no problem to their game plan. The real opposition to war took more direct action; as on 26 November, with an amendment which would have blocked military action against Iraq without explicit United Nations authorisation. As I told the *Guardian*:

> This is the only time we can log a protest against what I fear is a fait accompli.

I feared right – military action had been agreed. It was the presentation of that agreed position which was yet to be completed to the Government's satisfaction. The amendment had been put down by the Liberal Democrats, and Labour Members had a three line whip to vote against the amendment. No Member wishes to vote against his or her own party; but sometimes has no option in conscience. Meanwhile, a former CIA operative, Robert Baer, was telling the BBC's *The Case Against War*:

> . . .what we're inviting is World War Three in the Middle East. It's too late to invade Iraq a second time . . . I think all power in Washington has sort of gravitated towards the Pentagon which has set up its own intelligence unit which is reinterpreting intelligence to ensure the outcome they want.

He was right. The State Department and the usual security agencies were frozen out of the Pentagon by Rumsfeld and Wolfowitz. They set up their own autonomous 'agency' within the Pentagon.

A harder war than the intelligence operation was already under way. Figures were provided by the Ministry of Defence to Menzies Campbell on 10 December:

> that showed that ordnance dropped on southern Iraq had increased by 300 per cent since March that year. The increased attacks on Iraqi installations, which senior US officers admitted were designed to 'degrade' Iraq air defences, began six months before the UN passed resolution 1441, which the allies claim authorised military action.

Belatedly, the opposition leader Iain Duncan Smith recognised the obvious, on 18 December:

> It is clear that the Government are making preparations for a major deployment in the gulf.

The Prime Minister swatted him away:

> It is a contingency deployment.

Hoon was more detailed that day:

> I emphasise once more that these are contingency preparations, aimed at increasing the readiness of a range of options. This process does not lead inevitably to military action. The use of force is not inevitable. However, as long as Saddam's compliance with UNSCR 1441 is in doubt, the threat of force must remain and must be real.

Blair had carefully 'groomed' arch-Labour rebel Dennis Skinner over the years, but Skinner suspected a nefarious plot:

> Are the Government aware that outside this place there is probably a majority of the British people who are against a war on Iraq? I say to my Right Honourable Friend [Hoon] that vanity is not sufficient reason to spill the blood of innocent men, women and children, either here or in Iraq.

Three days later, across the Atlantic, President Bush approved the deployment of troops to the Gulf region. This was while the inspectors were busily doing their job. Clearly, military planning – like the increased aerial bombardment – had been underway for many months. Readers of A. J. P. Taylor's *Origins of the Second World War* would have recognised the momentum towards war due to the mobilisation of troops, and that carried over into the New Year.

On 1 January, the Foreign Office convened a conference of British ambassadors. They left sure of one thing – that there would be a war. They, like politicians, journalists and military people, could see this; none seemed able to stop it.

Bush and Blair maintained their double act with a New Year's Day joint press conference. Meanwhile, I was writing on my website:

> A combination of nationalism, religion, greed and perverse pride is taking us down the road to a most uncertain future. A vast agitprop exercise is designed to persuade a majority of us . . . that a war on Iraq is just, necessary and relatively benign. The truth is

rather different. In the United States . . . an unholy alliance of oil and defence interests, Likudniks and fundamentalist Christians, is trying to steer the world down its own narrow, bigoted, self inter-ested path. Iraq is for them both a litmus test for their hegemonic agenda, and a virility test for a giant of a nation unable to remove the irritation of Lilliputian terrorists.

On 7 January, Geraint Davies asked Geoff Hoon:

Can my Right Honourable Friend confirm that the sole ground for involving ourselves in military conflict with Iraq will be the material breach of UNSCR 1441, and that no other pretext will be used to commit British armed servicemen and women to a war that is designed to bring about regime change in Iraq through a pre-emptive strike?

The irony was that the pretext was UNSCR 1441. The key was to be what it meant, who evaluated its 'breach' and with what authority?
Even some Tories were getting impatient – Crispin Blunt, for example:

May I say to the Secretary of State that the formula whereby a decision has yet to be taken is beginning to wear a little thin.

Alex Salmond reminded Hoon of the obvious:

. . . does he [Hoon] appreciate the concern shared by many of us that those deployments and the vastly greater deployments by the United States army have their own momentum, making conflict almost inevitable? Does he appreciate the danger of being on a conveyor belt towards war?'

The lawyer in Hoon took over:

. . . this is a step-by-step process and it is not possible to secure overwhelming public support for military action before the explanation for that military action has been given and, therefore, before the justification for that military action has been identified. We have not yet reached the point in the process, and unless and until we do I accept that we cannot explain the justification for military action.

The following day Charles Kennedy put the essential question to the Prime Minister:

> . . . if the United Nations weapons inspectorate does not produce concrete evidence of WMD but the United States nonetheless decides to go ahead with military conflict against Iraq, will Britain be involved?

Blair's response was predictably inadequate:

> I am not going to speculate on the circumstances that might arise.

Iain Duncan Smith once more resorted to the blindingly obvious:

> . . . the Government are sending different messages to different audiences.

The Tories had still not understood how the New Labour spin machine operated. It could not fool veterans like Tam Dalyell, who repeatedly sought a debate which the Government did not want, as on 8 January:

> I beg to ask leave to move the adjournment of the House, under Standing Order No. 24, to debate an important matter that requires specific and urgent consideration, namely the urgent need for a House of Commons debate with a substantive vote, before any more British servicemen and servicewomen are committed to the Gulf.

The following day, Lynne Jones tabled one of her omnibus motions. These irked members of the Government, but were a useful way of raising publicly, valuable points about government policy and its inconsistency:

> That this House congratulates the Poet Laureate, Andrew Motion, on his verse about the motives for war in Iraq, Causa Belli, which reads 'They read good books, and quote, but never learn a language other than the scream of rocket burn. Our straighter talk is drowned but ironclad; elections, money, empire, oil and Dad'; supports the view that maintaining a close relationship with the USA is not a sufficient justification for United Kingdom participation in a war against Iraq; notes that a large proportion of the public do not believe that the threat posed by Iraq is sufficiently imminent or grave to constitute a moral basis for war; calls on the Government to be candid about the casus belli, meaning the causes, motives or pretexts of war, in relation to Iraq; further notes the comment of the Secretary of State for Defence on 7 January 2002 that there would be a vote in the House when rather than if military decisions have been taken and military action decided on; and calls for a substantive motion on whether there is a moral basis for attacking Iraq to be put to the House before any decision is taken to go to war.

John le Carré noted in a letter to *The Times* of 15 January how he believed that 'The United States of America has gone mad':

> The imminent war was planned years before Bin Laden struck, but it was he who made it possible. How Bush and his junta succeeded in deflecting America's anger from Bin Laden to Saddam Hussein is one of the great public relations conjuring tricks of history . . . The American public . . . is being browbeaten and kept in a state of ignorance and fear. The carefully orchestrated neurosis should carry Bush and his fellow conspirators nicely into the next election.

Deflecting what the Government and its supporters disparagingly dismissed as the 'chattering classes' view, he went on:

> What Bush won't tell us is the truth about why we're going to war. What is at stake is not an Axis of Evil – but oil, money and people's lives . . . If Saddam didn't have the oil, he could torture his citizens to his heart's content . . . Baghdad represents no clear and present danger to its neighbours, and not to the United States or Britain. Saddam's WMD, if he's still got them, will be peanuts by comparison with the stuff Israel or America could hurl at him at five minutes notice. What is at stake is not an imminent military or terrorist threat but the economic imperative of United States growth. What is at stake is America's need to demonstrate its military power to all of us.

This was a powerful stream of opinion in the United Kingdom – and among many in the United States – as well as in Europe, and it was foolish of the Blairites to simply dismiss it as anti-American. It has matured into an almost visceral dislike not only for Bush, but also for Blair, viewed as the American President's British apologist.

Meanwhile, an ever-faithful Geoff Hoon continued to parrot Blair's misrepresentations in Parliament, repeating on 20 January:

> A decision to employ force has not been taken, nor is such a decision imminent or inevitable.

He could not answer Glenda Jackson:

> As no material breach of Resolution 1441 has been presented to the UN by the weapons inspectors, does not my Right Honourable Friend's statement today that the movement of British troops is a contingency and not a commitment ring very hollow indeed? Is not the movement of troops taking place because ground troops will not be able to engage in military

action after the end of February or the beginning of March because the weather will become too inclement?

Nor Elfyn Llwyd:

> . . . the Secretary of State has gone out of his way to say that war is not inevitable. Committing thirty thousand ground troops, however, smacks of inevitability. Has he taken into account the fact that the IAEA has said the inspection might take up to a year?

Blair knew a war was going to happen. He gave that away to the Liaison Committee on 21 January. He was asked:

> Have you been given assurances that our armed forces will be sufficiently equipped to undertake what clearly is going to be a very, very difficult task ahead?

And he replied:

> I would never dream of committing British forces unless I thought they were properly and adequately equipped. I think you get these stories every time a conflict is about to happen.

Even so, he effectively told that committee that he wanted to have his cake and eat it:

> I have got absolutely no doubt at all that in the event of us having military action there will be a vote in the House of Commons. What I am not promising is that you can necessarily do that in all sets of circumstances before the action is taken.

There was still no commitment on war being subject to a Parliamentary vote, so Tony Wright asked the Prime Minister:

We have this mysterious thing called the Royal Prerogative which enables Prime Ministers and governments to wage war without Parliament . . . you do not think it is constitutionally bizarre that the House of Commons can have endless votes on whether it wants to kill foxes, but has no right at all to have a vote on whether we kill people?

Blair's response was pure casuistry:

. . . you can get into a constitutional argument about this, but the reality is that government are in the end accountable to Parliament, and they are, and they are accountable for any war that they engage in, as they are for anything else.

The next day, Tony Banks wondered why our European friends were not hot-footing it to Iraq:

We have dispatched a quarter of our forces . . . as a contingency force for possible action in Iraq. Will he explain to us . . . why it is that our European partners do not appear to share that concern? They do not appear to have deployed any of their troops.

Colin Breed knew what was happening:

. . . the deployment of more than 30,000 troops to the gulf is unique in size and has proceeded without any debate or vote in this House. The Secretary of State will be only too well aware that many consider this to be yet another example of proceeding down a predetermined route in conjunction with the United States.

And so did Tory MP Jonathan Sayeed:

To date the Government have not made the case for war or done enough to dispel the impression of the inevitability of a possibly unnecessary war.

I predictably gave my backbencher view through an unlikely medium – the socialist Campaign Group News – on 27 January:

> American and British apologists have switched their excuses for their belligerence from the 'war' on terrorism, to the 'need' for regime change, to Saddam's alleged possession of 'WMD'. They have twisted and turned to accommodate the inconsistencies of their various positions. They have contorted the processes of the UN, the Security Council and their agencies . . . Most disappointing of all has been the sycophantic posturing of the British Government. Every cliché in the book has been employed to justify its slavish adherence to each madcap notion to emanate from this most ideologically perverse of American administrations.

At Prime Minister's Questions on the 29 January, Blair was to loftily pronounce on our military commitments:

> The decisions whether to commit troops on behalf of this country are taken by our government, our House of Commons and our country.

That was certainly not the unanimous view of his ministers, or the lesson to be drawn from precedent. Besides, it was a minor point in 'the bigger picture'. Paul Flynn had a cinemascope view of the Iraq crisis:

> That this House condemns the brutal repressive regime of Saddam Hussein but regrets the Government's failure to provide convincing evidence that he is planning to use weapons of mass destruction; believes that the only likely use of such weapons would be if Saddam Hussein is facing defeat in war when he may, in a final act of desperation, use them against British soldiers; recalls that the most effective way to defeat terrorism is to win over the hearts and minds of terrorist supporters; fears that an attack on Iraq before there is a just settlement in Palestine will be judged by many

Muslims as a punitive assault on Islam which will increase the likelihood of a terrorist attack on the UK; and believes that the present
crisis is the result of the election of President Bush whose
supporters in the 'Project for a New American Century' have long
planned to reorder the world in the interests of the US.

After all, President Bush was challenged on the undeclared agenda at a press
conference on 31 January:

Mr President, an account of the White House after 9/11 says
that you ordered invasion plans for Iraq six days after 11
September – Bob Woodward's account. Isn't it the case that you
have always intended war and that international diplomacy is a
charade in this case?

Bush made no attempt to deny the charge. That was the same day that 26,000
British troops were ordered into the Gulf. The countdown to war had begun.
The United Nations? UNSCR 1441? Finds of WMD? All of this was by-the-
by – war was now inevitable. Not, of course, according to Prime Minister
Blair who told Parliament on 3 February:

Even now, I hope that Saddam can come to his senses, cooperate
fully and disarm peacefully, as the UN has demanded. But if he
does not – if he rejects the peaceful route – he must be disarmed
by force – Saddam's weapons of mass destruction and the
threats they pose to the world must be confronted. In doing so,
this country and our armed forces will be helping the long term
peace and security of Britain and the world.

Despite the wish of many to challenge the Prime Minister on his many assertions, nothing was guaranteed by way of a debate. Hence, I tried to draw
attention to the frustration of opponents of a war by way of a Point of Order:

You may be aware [Mr Speaker] that the elected Australian
Senate has passed a vote of no confidence in the Australian

Government's line on Iraq. Can you advise humble backbench Members on how they may be able to effect a debate to the same end in this House?

Hilton Dawson went down a different avenue:

> That this House requires that the Government arrange for a thorough debate on Iraq and a vote on a substantive motion before the Adjournment on 13 February.

Hoon was all at sea on the question of a debate on the possibility of war, telling Liberal Democrat Paul Keetch on 6 February, in contradiction of what the Prime Minister had said:

> I caution him against the insistence on requiring a substantive vote of the House before any military operations are conducted . . . I said that I did not anticipate that a vote would be needed before deployment took place.

The Government's critics were unrelenting, like Tony Lloyd on 12 February:

> Does [the Prime Minister] accept that the British public remains largely sceptical about the case for military action against Iraq, but that they believe that the Americans will take military action almost come what may? Will he tell the House and the country why we should believe that a war now will make peace in the Middle East more likely and in the end make Britain less of a target for terrorists?

Tony Wright stayed with the constitutional line:

> That this House notes that it has not approved any military action against Iraq; believes that any such action should require prior approval by a vote in this House and not rely on prerogative power alone; does not accept in this case that such a vote

would in any way compromise our armed forces; and demands an unequivocal confirmation that such a vote will be held.

Members could fulminate, argue, write and complain. What they could not do was shake the Prime Minister's steely determination not to be swayed from his decision. As I pointed out in a Point of Order on 24 February:

> Since we last debated Iraq, we have been presented with a risible, plagiarised dossier on WMD. We have also seen huge demonstrations in London and Glasgow and elsewhere round the world. We have had the Archbishop of Canterbury, the Cardinal Archbishop and His Holiness the Pope repudiating the assertion of some kind of moral justification for war on Iraq.

None of this diverted Blair; not even the views of eminent churchmen dented the sensibilities of the 'religious' prime minister. After all, as I noted that day in the *Guardian*:

> Tony Blair is not involved in a push for peace, but a drive for war.

Gordon Prentice tabled a motion on 25 February which congratulated Senator Robert Byrd on his condemnation of the American Administration. Senator Byrd echoed the charge of recklessness made by Anatole Lieven the previous October:

> That this House congratulates Senator Robert Byrd, former Democratic Leader in the US Senate and now Dean of the congress, on his thoughtful and persuasive speech on the floor of the Senate on 12 February in which he describes the Bush Administration as reckless and arrogant having initiated policies which may reap disastrous consequences for years, notes his trenchant criticism of the doctrine of pre-emption in which the USA or any other nation can legitimately attack a nation that is not imminently threatening but may be threat-

ening in future; and concurs with his conclusion that pressure appears to be having a good result in Iraq and that war is not necessary at this time.

The Prime Minister still insisted that there was no hard and fast timetable, telling the House that same day:

As for our own timetable, it is obviously open, but we have already said that this has to be resolved within weeks, not months.

Backbenchers had a variety of concerns. Thus, on the 26 February I said to the Foreign Secretary:

When the Foreign Secretary opened the debate, he gave the impression that we would have the opportunity later to hold a substantive vote on whether this country commits troops to action in Iraq. At the very least, the Government could get their act together.

Even the docile official opposition spokesman – Bernard Jenkin – had become exasperated:

Many honourable Members have genuine fears and concerns and the Government must take them seriously. It is now time they clarified their objectives and made the case more clearly.

Chris Smith feared that the United Kingdom was simply following President Bush's timetable. He was right:

I beg to move we add 'but finds the case for military action against Iraq as yet unproven'. If the Government motion [draft second resolution] is passed unamended by this House, a signal will have been given that this House endorses the timetable that is now upon us – which will lead, I fear, inevitably to war within the next three to four weeks . . . at the moment, the timetable appears to be determined by the decision of the President of the United States and not by the logic of events.

Ken Clarke worried:

I cannot rid myself of doubts that the race to war upon which we are now embarked was decided on many months ago, primarily in Washington, and there has been a fairly remorseless unfolding of events since that time. I am not alone in having heard and met American politicians of great distinction who gave the impression that a change of regime in Iraq was determined long ago and that the use of military force in a pre-emptive strike was justified in order to achieve that.

While John Gummer was definitive:

There is no MP who does not know that this war is war by timetable and the timetable was laid down before the United States had any intention of going to the UN. The truth is that it must be seen by the world that when, or if, we invade Saddam Hussein's Iraq, we do so not because of some prearranged timetable connected with ulterior motives but because we and the world are convinced that there is no alternative. That is the message that should be given to those who argue the case from moral grounds.

Behind the Parliamentary language, traditionally steeped in circumlocution and understatement, lay the truth of the matter, widely understood by Members in all parties. There was a timetable for war against Iraq, set in America, and impervious to argument about the United Nations, WMD, or anything else.

It was all the more incredible that on 28 February, Colin Powell should tell Radio France International:

> If Iraq had disarmed itself, gotten rid of its weapons of mass destruction over the past 12 years, or over the last several months since (UNSCR) 1441 was enacted, we would not be facing the crisis that we now have before us . . . But the suggestion that we are doing this because we want to go to every country in the Middle East and rearrange all of its pieces is not correct.

Iraq had rid itself of WMD, so his first claim was wrong. As for rearranging the map, there were only some of the Middle East countries in the frame – Iraq, Iran, Syria and Libya. Saudi, Egypt, Jordan and the Gulf States were seen as friendly. We only need to look now at Palestine and Lebanon to see where American policy has taken the wider region.

By 3 March, the Defence Secretary was assuring the House:

> I emphasise to the House that no decision has been taken about the use of military force, and I repeat that there is no substantial change in the operation of the northern or southern no fly zones.

This was simply untrue. Two days later, Iain Duncan Smith got it right for once, at Prime Minister's Questions:

> The fact that Saddam Hussein remains in material breach means that military action is more likely. Will the Prime Minister therefore spell out exactly what is happening in the no fly zone? Is it not now the case that British and American planes are making pre-emptive strikes on targets that would threaten our ground forces rather than just our aircraft? Surely this represents a substantial change in existing policy. Would not the Prime Minister help his own case if he more frankly spelled out to the British people what is exactly and really going on?

The war had effectively begun. By 16 March, Vice-President Cheney could confidently tell NBC's Meet the Press that the ground war would take 'weeks rather than months'.

Nevertheless, Jack Straw still brazenly proposed to the House that:

> As a result of Saddam Hussein's persistent refusal to meet the UN's demands and the inability of the Security Council to adopt a further resolution, the Cabinet has decided to ask the House to support the United Kingdom's participation in military operations, should they be necessary, with the objective of ensuring the disarmament of Iraq's WMD and thereby the maintenance of the United Nations.

All of this was patently untrue, but it fitted the Government's distorted picture of the situation. Resigning as a Cabinet member, Robin Cook pointed out the inconsistency of the case being put:

> We do not express the same impatience with the persistent refusal of Israel to comply . . . Britain's positive role in the Middle East does not redress the strong sense of injustice throughout the Muslim world at what it sees as one rule for the allies of the United States and another rule for the rest. Nor is our credibility helped by the appearance that our partners in Washington are less interested in disarmament than they are in regime change in Iraq. That explains why any evidence that inspections may be showing progress is greeted in Washington not with satisfaction but with consternation; it reduces the case for war.

The question of patience was not an irrelevance. Some, as I had pointed out in the House on 26 February, had confused impatience with the calculated plans of the Bush Administration:

> People who think it is a matter of us running out of patience misunderstand the mechanics of what is going on. The decision was not made in Downing Street or the Foreign Office but in the White House. It has taken until now and it is still not finalised, to mobilise and deploy the troops and units needed to hold a

campaign that accords with an American military doctrine that is nearly coming to a conclusion . . . The hard reality is that it will be an American military campaign . . . The reasons for the campaign are complex . . . the ideological hawks in the United States Administration have set out their stall for many years . . . the objectives of the new Pax Americana have been set out clearly and unequivocally.

Blair himself was to remark in the debate on 18 March:

Our fault has not been impatience.

John Randall's simile was appropriate:

. . . the military build up is like water behind a dam. We cannot keep it there forever. That is why I think what is going to happen is inevitable.

David Heath had a different figure of speech to illustrate his point:

Throughout the process, there was a ticking clock, and I agree with Sir Crispin Tickell, who asked who started the clock ticking. The British Government was trying to find a consensus on a military timetable rather than a process of disarmament.

Meanwhile, there were shades of Marie Antoinette in the comments of the President's mother, Barbara Bush, that same day to the ABC's *Good Morning* programme:

Why should we hear about body bags and deaths? Why should I waste my beautiful mind on something like that?

The following day was an inglorious one. The inspectors had not finished their work in Iraq, but their work to date had shown that Iraq was complying with the United Nation's demands, and that there was no evidence of a threat from weapons of mass destruction. On this day, President Bush declared war on Iraq:

> American and coalition forces are in the early stages of military operations to disarm Iraq, to free its people and to defend the world from grave danger . . . We have no ambitions in Iraq except to remove a threat and restore control of that country to its own people.

How wrong he was. 'Operation Iraqi Freedom' has turned out to be a pyrrhic victory. Back then, Donald Rumsfeld's excitement at the prospect of this war was almost childlike:

> What will follow will not be a repeat of any other conflict. It will be of a force and a scope and a scale that has been beyond what we have seen before.

Yet when it came, things were very different.

In a BBC interview with John Kampfner on 9 April, Anmar Uday, an Iraqi doctor, gave an Iraqi perspective on this American war:

> We heard the helicopters. We were surprised. Why do this? There was no military. There were no soldiers in the hospital. It was like a Hollywood film. They cried, 'Go, go, go' with guns and flares and the sound of explosions. They made a show, an action movie like Sylvester Stallone or Jackie Chan, with jumping and shouting, breaking down doors . . . all the time, the cameras rolling.

Iraq: The Movie was to become *Iraq: The Basket Case*. In Britain, one insider – Clare Short – was to reveal her own disillusionment to the Foreign Affairs Select Committee Inquiry, on 17 June:

> I think it is a series of half truths, exaggerations and reassurances that were not the case to get us into conflict by the spring

and I think that commitment had been made by the previous summer . . . I thought for a long time in this crisis that the United Kingdom was playing the role of trying to restrain the United States and trying to examine all other means, and I now think that we were not and that we pre-committed . . . By 9 September they [Blair and Bush] were both committed to military action.

The question had become just when was the United Kingdom committed to war? Alex Salmond noted on 15 September:

That this House notes the contents of the book Blair's War by Mr John Kampfner, the political editor of the New Statesman, which states that the Foreign Secretary sent a memorandum to the Prime Minister before the start of the Iraq war urging him not to commit United Kingdom forces, and that the Prime Minister agreed to go to war with the United States as early as April 2002 during a summit with President [George] W. Bush in Texas; and believes that these well-sourced claims make it essential that there is an independent judicial inquiry into the full background and circumstances of the Government's decision to go to war in Iraq.

Blair's response to such charges was predictable:

It is absolutely right that throughout the whole of 2002 the Americans were looking at and we were looking at what happens if there is no other way to deal with this issue other than military action. What is not true is that the Americans had decided to take military action come what may. That is not true.

Greg Thielmann, a former State Department expert on weapons proliferation, spoke for many insiders on the BBC's *Today* programme on 13 January 2004:

. . . the American public was seriously misled. The Administration twisted, distorted and simplified intelligence in a way that led Americans to seriously misunderstand the nature of the Iraq threat. I'm not sure I can think of a worse act against the people in a democracy than a president distorting classified information.

However, he was to lay most blame with officials, when speaking at the Arms Control Association on 3 February:

The Bush administration did not provide an accurate picture to the American people of the military threat posed by Iraq . . . most of [the fault] lies with the way senior officials misused the information they were provided . . . the senior leadership of the CIA and the National Intelligence Council . . . slanted the Intel to make the case against Iraq, to beef up the justification for a war against Iraq.

The key was in the political expectations, as was also the case with British intelligence. Thielmann told *60 Minutes*:

The main problem was that the senior administration officials have what I call faith based intelligence. They know what they wanted the intelligence to show . . . They were really blind and deaf to any kind of countervailing information the intelligence community would produce. I would assign some blame to the intelligence community and most of the blame to the senior administration officials.

Under continuous pressure, Prime Minister Blair became very defensive, as in a Sedgefield speech on 5 March 2004:

President Bush told me that on 9 September 2001 he had a meeting about Iraq in the White House when he discussed 'smart' sanctions, changes to the sanctions regime. There was no talk of military action.

Many just do not accept the Prime Minister's assurances. In another prime ministerial flight of fancy, he insisted:

> This is not a time to err on the side of caution.

How very wrong he was – again.

In May 2004, an article appeared in *Vanity Fair* called 'The Path to War'. It quoted Francis Brooke, an advisor to the exiled Iraqi National Congress (INC):

> I told them [the INC exile group, based in London] 'Go get me a terrorist and some WMD, because that is what the Bush administration is interested in'.

The Administration had, in short, made up its mind, and wanted evidence – evidence that would resonate with the American people, post 9/11.

That tragic date had had its effect also on the British Prime Minister. He had told Parliament that:

> My thinking has changed after 11 September.

The question is: how? The temptation is that, like the neocons, he saw opportunities in 9/11 and its aftermath. For Blair, it was as if he saw his destiny as a global leader in the fallout from Al Qaeda's devastating attacks. So much so, that Iraq became his personal cause. As Dan Plesch and Glen Rangwala put it in August 2004, in *A Case to Answer* (a report on the possible impeachment of Blair):

> . . . this Prime Minister made Iraq a matter of individual, not collective, responsibility, through practice . . . of . . . Government by cabal.

However, when it suited the Prime Minister, he passed responsibility onto other shoulders. In the Hutton Inquiry, he stressed repeatedly that the September dossier was:

the work of the Joint Intelligence Committee.

And on the timetable of the war:

> Frankly, we were months away (in March 2002) from deciding
> our strategy on this issue.

What the prime Minister could not avoid was the widespread analysis that 'war, war, war' had quickly overtaken 'jaw, jaw, jaw' in the Bush/Blair strategy. As Britain's former ambassador to the United Nations, Carne Ross, told BBC's *Panorama*:

> I think it's pretty clear, looking back, that the military timetable
> drove the diplomatic timetable.

Or as Senator Barbara Boxer summed up an American view on 6 July 2005, in a speech to the Commonwealth Club:

> *Iraq was a war of choice, not necessity.*

In fact, it was not only a choice, but one which involved very few people. On the British side, it was certainly Tony Blair's personal crusade, although he was aided and abetted by those who ought to have been more critical friends. It was most indicative that those whom one would have expected to be inside the loop on such a major commitment, were excluded. Thus, the former British Ambassador to the United States, Sir Christopher Meyer, could write in his memoirs:

> I find myself repeatedly answering the question; did something
> said by Jack Straw or Geoff Hoon represent the Prime
> Minister's views? Sometimes it did not. Indeed, throughout this
> period, the Foreign Office impinged little on my life. Between
> 9/11 and the day I retired at the end of February 2003, on the eve
> of war, I had not a single substantive policy discussion on the
> secure phone with the Foreign and Commonwealth Office.

Al Qaeda and terrorism

But the greatest menace to our civilisation today is the conflict between giant organised systems of self-righteousness – each system only too delighted to find that the other is wicked – each only too glad that the sins of the other give it the pretext for still deeper hatred and animosity.

Herbert Butterfield (1900–1979)

Iraq was a secular state under Saddam; hence, he was a sworn enemy of Osama bin Laden and his confederates. He used Islam where it was necessary, but he was not a theocrat like his Shia neighbours in Iran. He was certainly not one to fund Islamic fundamentalist terror groups, reasoning – quite correctly – that he would be a likely target of their radical zeal.

Far more worrying to the American leadership were the ayatollahs of Iran. On the basis of the old Arab adage that 'my enemy's enemy is my friend', Saddam had actually been an ally of the United States in their attritional struggle with Iran. The United States and the United Kingdom, among others, had provided him with weapons, including the components of chemical and biological weapons.

All of this changed with the Iraqi invasion of Kuwait. Even then, President Bush and General Colin Powell had held back on attacking Baghdad after the successful liberation of Kuwait. Saddam was left to regroup and reassert his control, although with limitations on his ability to operate freely in the north and south of his country. The real change came with two events wholly unconnected with Saddam.

The first was the rise of the neoconservative ideologies parallel to, and feeding on, the accession of Bush to the Presidency. A unique cocktail of influences was brought to bear on that presidency – pro-Zionist bias on an unprecedented scale; Christian fundamentalism with its crude view of 'the Holy

Land' and antipathy towards Islam; neoconservative foreign policy – muscular and imperial; and the vested interests of the oil and armaments corporations.

The second event was 9/11. For Bush, everything changed – most believe that to be true, although some of his most cynical colleagues saw it more as an opportunity. For Blair, by his own account, 9/11 also fundamentally reordered his world view. This was as much a statement of his emotional reaction as anything else – he was becoming more American than an American, tending at times to forget that he was British, and Prime Minister of the United Kingdom. The United Kingdom, in turn, was no satrapy of an imperialist United States. He stated his case in the House of Commons:

> 9/11 was an attack . . . on the very notion of democracy . . . .
> We all agree that this attack is an attack on the world, which demands our complete and united condemnation, our determination to bring those responsible to justice and our support for the American people at this time of trial . . . the interests of our country are engaged . . . the world now knows the full evil and capability of international terrorism which menaces the whole of the democratic world. The terrorists responsible have no sense of humanity, of mercy or of justice . . . To commit acts of this nature requires a fanaticism and wickedness that is beyond our normal contemplation . . . there are issues connected with such terrorism that the international community as a whole must consider; where these groups are, how they operate, how they are financed, how they are supported, and how they are stopped.

No one could disagree, although he notably turned an attack on the United States into a global issue. As he said:

> This was not an attack on America alone. This was an attack on the free and democratic world everywhere and this is the responsibility that the free and democratic world has got to shoulder together with America.

This was in response to a journalist asking him:

> Are there no limits to which you would cooperate with the
> United States Government in pursuing the terrorists and, given
> the possibility, the real possibility that Britain could become a
> target if you either endorse or insist on reprisals, to what extent
> do you think the British public is prepared for that?

By 14 September, the seeds of Blair's latest cause, in a long list of noble aspirations, had been planted. He stressed 'evidence', 'judgement', 'care' – words
which were to ring hollow, given his subsequent actions. Indeed, it was one of
Tony Blair's 'inspirations' which afflict him from time to time, in the search
for his destiny:

> These attacks on the basic democratic values in which we all
> believe so passionately and on the civilised world . . . In the
> most direct sense – we have not just an interest but an obliga-
> tion to bring those responsible to account . . . First, we must
> bring to justice those responsible. Rightly, President Bush and
> the United States Government have proceeded with care. They
> did not lash out. They did not strike first and think afterwards.
> Their very deliberation is a measure of the seriousness of their
> intent. They, together with allies, will want to identify, with
> care, those responsible. This is a judgement that must and will
> be based on hard evidence. Once that judgement is made, the
> appropriate action can be taken. It will be determined, it will
> take time, it will continue over time until this menace is
> properly dealt with and its machinery of terror destroyed. But
> one thing should be very clear. By their acts, these terrorists and
> those behind them have made themselves the enemies of the
> civilised world. The objective will be to bring to account those
> who have organised, aided, abetted and incited this act of
> infamy; and those that harbour or help them have a choice;
> either to cease their protection of our enemies; or be treated as
> an enemy themselves . . . we need to rethink dramatically the

scale and nature of the action the world takes to combat terrorism . . . We know that these groups are fanatics, capable of killing without discrimination. We know that they would, if they could, go further and use chemical or biological or even nuclear weapons of mass destruction. We know, also, that there are groups of people, occasionally states, who trade the technology and capability for such weapons.

On 16 September, CNN quoted him in full mission mode:

This is a time for cool heads and calm nerves and an absolute and fixed determination to see this thing (the fight between the civilised world and fanaticism) through . . . Whatever the technical or legal issues of that declaration of war, the fact is we are at war with terrorism . . . this (possible military strikes) is something obviously we discussed with the American president . . . so it (action) is right for reasons of justice, but it is also right for reasons of self preservation.

Christopher Meyer was to report that on 20 September, just nine days after Al Qaeda's devastating attack, the agenda was already shifting. Meyer wrote of the Bush–Blair meeting, which he attended, that Bush had said:

'I agree with you Tony. We must deal with this [the Taliban and Al Qaeda]. But when we have dealt with Afghanistan, we must come back to Iraq.' Blair said nothing to demur.

Bush was already intent on attacking Iraq, and Blair was going along with him. The approach was reinforced by a letter to Bush on the same day from the leading neoconservative ideologues under the aegis of the Project for a New American Century:

We agree with Secretary of State Powell's recent statement that Saddam Hussein 'is one the leading terrorists on the face of the earth'. It may be that the Iraqi Government provided assistance in some form to the recent attack in the United States. But even if evidence does not link Iraq directly with the attack, any strategy aiming at the eradication of terrorism and its sponsors must include a determined effort to remove Saddam Hussein from power in Iraq.

Nothing had, in fact, changed. The leading lights of the Administration had long standing plans to take out Saddam. Blair did not dissent. He was to hint at darker things to the House of Commons on 8 October:

Even when Al Qaeda is dealt with, the job is not over.

This referred back to Bush's reminder nineteen days earlier. Blair's hint did not go unnoticed. John McDonnell told him:

We cannot broaden it to a battle against Iraq.

He had no chance of keeping Iraq out of the war plan. A link to justify Iraq's inclusion would be found or fabricated. As the *Financial Times* pointed out on 10 October:

Mr Bush's war against terrorism is therefore much broader than simply focusing on Mr bin Laden and the Taliban. It encompasses the Al Qaeda network outside Afghanistan, Hezbollah, Hamas and other groups of 'global reach' as well as the states that continue to sponsor them – including possibly Iran, Iraq, and Syria.

The press were well aware of the wider Bush Administration plan, as was Prime Minister Blair. Not that he or his Government would admit it. His Defence Secretary, Geoff Hoon, told a press conference on 29 October:

There is no hidden agenda: this [Afghanistan] is not a prelude to a wider war. Our objectives are linked to the events of 11

September ... there is no evidence linking Iraq to the events of 11 September ... It's important we emphasise those things.

Yet it was *de rigueur* for Prime Minister Blair to hedge his bets. His official spokesman declared on 4 December:

There is no evidence that implicates Iraq in the events of September 11. That said, we have always acknowledged that the fight against international terrorism will take two phases.

Our European friends had more sense. The *Morning Star* reported on 22 December 2001 that Hubert Verne, French foreign minister, had declared:

No European country believes it is in the logic of the anti-terrorist drive to undertake something against Iraq.

Stella Remington, former head of MI5, was reported in the *Observer* on 30 December as remarking:

A war on terrorism implies that you are going to exterminate terrorism and I don't see how anyone can do that. It's like exterminating evil. It can't be done.

Her scepticism on the evolving 'war on terror' was well founded and well informed. 'War on terror' was a glib phrase, resonating in the American heartlands, perhaps, but it meant nothing of itself, eluding definition and practical meaning. Yet in truth, some states had sponsored terrorist organisations – including the United States (one needs only look at the Nicaraguan Contras). I probed the Prime Minister on terrorist states on 22 May 2002:

Does the Prime Minister agree with the American Government's assertion that Cuba is a terrorist state?

Mr Blair was his usual evasive self:

I think that America is entitled to its position on Cuba, which it takes for obvious reasons. We, however, take our position.

On Iraq, Condoleezza Rice had no public doubts, telling the Associated Press on 22 September:

> There clearly are contacts between Al Qaeda and Saddam Hussein that can be documented.

Bush followed up this groundless assertion on 14 October:

> And I also mentioned the fact that there is a connection between Al Qaeda and Saddam Hussein.

Blair was more circumspect. He simply implied a connection between Iraq and terrorism at a press conference with Bush on 21 November 2002:

> The whole world wants to see us now take this very firm stand against terrorism, against issues of weapons of mass destruction.

I tried to pin him down at Prime Minister's Questions on 4 December:

> Does the Prime Minister accept the assessment of the intelligence service that whatever else Saddam Hussein is guilty of, he is almost certainly innocent of the charge of associating with Al Qaeda?'

Blair's response gave the clear impression that there was a linkage between Iraq and terrorism, while seeming to accept that it was not the case:

> What I have said is that we have no evidence directly linking the Iraqi regime to the attack on 11 September. That is true. I would also say, however, that I believe that the issues of WMD and international terrorism are linked directly. I believe, however,

that unless we tackle that issue they will at some point be directly linked.

Hoon stepped up the argument in a debate on 20 January 2003:

We are aware of some contact between the Iraqi regime and Al Qaeda over a number of years.

This was probably the most direct claim of a link between Iraq and Al Qaeda, and wholly untrue in the implication that Iraq was supportive of Al Qaeda. The following day, Tony Blair appeared before the House of Commons Liaison Committee. He phrased his line carefully:

Whenever I am asked about the linkage between Al Qaeda and Iraq, the truth is there is no information that I have that directly links Iraq to September 11 . . . there is some intelligence evidence about loose links between Al Qaeda and various people in Iraq . . . There is none that I know of (a direct linkage) that directly links Al Qaeda, Iraq, terrorist activity in the United Kingdom but . . . there is some intelligence evidence about linkages between members of Al Qaeda and people in Iraq . . . it would not be correct to say there is no evidence whatever of linkages between Al Qaeda and Iraq . . . I am not suggesting there is evidence directly linking members of the regime with Al Qaeda. I am simply saying that there is some intelligence evidence about linkages between people in Iraq and Al Qaeda and I do not think that is in quite the same sense, if you like, as links between Al Qaeda and, say, people in this country.

Written down, it looks a less lucid response than his oral presentation had been. Remember, too, that prior to this meeting with the committee, he had had a classified intelligence briefing (in mid-January) written by defence intelligence staff, stating that there were no links between Iraq and Al Qaeda; and that bin Laden's aims ' are in ideological conflict with present day Iraq'.

On the same day that Blair waltzed around the Liaison Committee, Jack Straw was to conflate terrorism, WMD and Iraq to the House of Commons:

> The two greatest threats facing Britain and its citizens in the next decade are terrorists and rogue states with WMD. The most dangerous terrorist organisation is Al Qaeda. The most aggressive rogue state is Iraq.

Alice Mahon was quick to spot the manoeuvre:

> The policy of merging the issue of WMD in Iraq with the aims of the war on terrorism is no substitute for any hard evidence of WMD or indeed, a link with Al Qaeda. Does the Foreign Secretary realise that many will view this attempt as disingenuous? It is also a disaster for good international relations and in terms of protecting the people of this country, it is downright dangerous.

How right she was. Angus Robertson framed his concern differently:

> Like most people in this country, I commend all proportionate, consistent, ethical and just efforts to combat terrorism and rogue states, but – like the majority of people – not as a pretext for war in Iraq.

The following day, Tam Dalyell was to pithily highlight the truth of the link between Iraq and Al Qaeda:

> There is a connection between Al Qaeda and Baghdad – Al Qaeda has twice tried to kill Saddam Hussein.

By 29 January, Blair had shifted, suggesting the Iraqi state had links with Al Qaeda:

However, I chose my words very carefully in front of the Liaison Committee: we do know of links between Al Qaeda and Iraq.

Repeating his line at Prime Minister's Questions on 5 February:

> . . . from intelligence submitted to me by the Joint Intelligence Committee . . . There are unquestionably links between Al Qaeda and Iraq.

He was challenged on this on BBC *Newsnight* that very evening:

> Jeremy Paxman: 'You know your defence intelligence assessment is that there is currently no link between Baghdad and Al Qaeda?'

> Tony Blair: 'It would not be correct to say there is no evidence linking Al Qaeda and Iraq.'

On the night of the Common's debate on whether or not to go to war, Blair deliberately linked Iraq and Al Qaeda to maximise the fear factor in waverers:

> Dictators like Saddam; terrorist groups like Al Qaeda threaten the very existence of such a world. That is why I have asked our troops to go into action tonight.

The politically monochrome world view of George Bush was apparent in his address officially (and, of course, erroneously) declaring the end of the war on 1 May 2003 from the USS Abraham Lincoln:

> We've removed an ally of Al Qaeda. We have not forgotten the victims of 11 September. With those attacks, the terrorists and their supporters declared war on the United States. And war is what they got.

No Iraqi was involved in 9/11; nor was the Iraq Government, nor its agents.

By 27 June, Jack Straw was defending his position and misrepresenting that of the Prime Minister, to the Foreign Affairs Committee:

> I never claimed, neither did the Prime Minister, that there was any direct linkage between Al Qaeda and the Iraq regime.

Bob Graham, reporting for the *Evening Standard* from Baghdad, graphically illustrated how Bush and Blair's propaganda had at least convinced members of the military. Quoting Specialist Corporal Michael Richardson on 30 June 2003, he wrote:

> There's a picture of the World Trade Centre hanging up by my bed and I keep one in my Kevlar. Every time I feel sorry for these people I look at that. I think: 'They hit us at home and now it's our turn'.

Yet in an article I wrote at the beginning of August, I again pointed out that the alleged link between Saddam and Al Qaeda was illusory:

> As the Foreign Affairs Select committee report point out there was no demonstrable connection between Al Qaeda and the Saddam regime . . . It has always been a fear of many of us that military action would exacerbate the problems . . . and the attacks on the United States servicemen in particular in Iraq seem to be evidence of this.

In fact, the Foreign Affairs Committee Report pointed to different conclusions to those of Blair, Bush *et al*:

> The committee cannot conclude these threats [posed by the combination of WMD and international terrorist organisations] have diminished significantly, in spite of 'regime change' in Iraq and progress in capturing some of the leaders of Al Qaeda. The war in Iraq might in fact have impeded the war against Al Qaeda . . . it might have enhanced the appeal

of Al Qaeda to Muslims living in the Gulf region and elsewhere.

The threats described (both real and imagined) by Blair were not diminished by war, but exacerbated by it. This was just months into the conflict. It is possible now to see just how wrong were the pro-war arguments.

The September report's quotation of the Joint Intelligence Committee (of September 2003) was even more pessimistic. Blair had cherry picked from their analysis, ignoring the overall message, so that he might justify his war:

> The Joint Intelligence Committee assessed that Al Qaeda and associated groups continued to represent by far the greatest terrorist threat to western interests and that threat would be heightened by military action against Iraq. The Joint Intelligence Committee assessed that any collapse of the Iraqi regime would increase the risk of chemical and biological warfare technology or agents finding their way into the hands of terrorists, not necessarily Al Qaeda.

The *Guardian* set out the harsh reality of what had been 'achieved' in an editorial piece published on 16 March 2004, tellingly entitled 'Tony Blair will not be forgiven'. This came on the back of the Madrid bombings, although before the 7/7 bombings in London. It was both true and prophetic:

> . . . we are more at risk from international terrorism than ever. The reason can be summed up in one word: Iraq . . . it is undeniable that the war itself, and the circumstances in which we went to war, raised Britain's profile as a target. This was not only predictable, but was repeatedly predicted before the war . . . 9/11 occurred on the watch of George Bush. He and his administration had a far more aggressive mindset than their predecessors. They also had an ideological bent that demanded an enemy. The coincidence of the attacks and this newly hostile approach was a recipe for disaster. None of the myths fabricated about Iraq is more relevant to recent events than the

linkage claimed with Al Qaeda. The idea that the loathsome, but secular, Saddam would entertain the fundamentalist Osama bin Laden was ludicrous, yet repeatedly made. When dissident voices argued that a war on Iraq would actually make it a hotbed for terrorists, they were dismissed . . . Similarly, when it was argued that an attack on Iraq would inflame Muslim opinion and increase the support for terrorism, that was also dismissed . . . We have now added the cause of Iraq to its [Al Qaeda's] prospectus . . . If such an attack [as Madrid's] were to take place here, the question would inevitably be whether our support for America's war against Iraq had made it more likely . . . If ever there was a case of an individual driving the nation into war then it was him [Blair]. People will inevitably link his personal crusade to any failure to forestall terrorist outrages.

By 23 March, Noam Chomsky could say in the *Toronto Star* just what a 'success' the Bush–Blair war had been:

Every act of violence increases the recruitment of terrorists. Iraq has been turned into a base of terror.

A nightmare had been created in Iraq, despite the conclusion reached by the United States' 9/11 Commission on 16 June 2004 that there was:

. . . no credible evidence that Iraq and Al Qaeda cooperated on attacks against the US.

A clear and imminent threat

Naturally, the common people don't want war; neither in Russia, nor in England, nor in America, nor in Germany. That is understood. But after all, it is the leaders of the country who determine policy, and it is always a simple matter to drag the people along, whether it is a democracy, or a fascist dictatorship, or a Parliament, or a communist dictatorship. Voice or no voice, the people can always be brought to the bidding of the leaders. That is easy. All you have to do is to tell them they are being attacked, and denounce the pacifists for lack of patriotism and exposing the country to danger. It works the same in any country.

Hermann Goering (1893–1945)

The whole thrust of British policy on Iraq post 9/11 was to portray it as a threat to Britain, and to the West generally. Some of the suggested capabilities of Saddam Hussein's Iraq were risible, but were deemed necessary to convince the British public that unlawful 'action' needed to be taken against an obdurate and dangerous dictator. Fear was to be the emotion shared by government propaganda, aided and abetted by a compliant and complicit press.

The United States Administration was to similarly inflate the potential threat of Saddam describing him as a latter day Hitler. The standard definition of a 'threat' – capability plus intent – was never seriously examined by either government in the immodest haste to attack Iraq and to effect regime change there. However, American Secretary of State, Colin Powell, initially had a less favoured view of Saddam Hussein in the first Gulf War.

Powell's view shone through in the transcript of a meeting he had had with the German Foreign Minister, Joschka Fischer, on 20 February 2001:

Containment has been a successful policy, and I think we should continue it until such time as Saddam Hussein comes into compliance with the agreements he made at the end of the [Gulf] war.

He added that Iraq:

. . . is not threatening America . . . His [Saddam Hussein's] forces are about one third their original size. They don't really possess the capability to attack their neighbours the way they did ten years ago.

He certainly did not view Saddam as an imminent threat. Just four days later, at a Cairo press conference, Powell foresaw no threat from Saddam:

He [Saddam] has not developed any significant capability with respect to WMD. He is unable to project conventional power against his neighbours.

Nothing had changed by 15 May that year. Testifying before the Senate Appropriations Sub-committee, Powell could take a sanguine view of Iraq:

The sanctions as they are called, have succeeded over the last ten years, not in deterring him from moving in that direction, but from actually being able to move in that direction. The Iraq regime . . . doesn't have the capacity it had ten or twelve years ago. It has been contained.

Even later that year, his eventual successor as Secretary of State, and then National Security Advisor, Condaleeza Rice, could confidently assert on CNN on the 29 July that:

We are able to keep arms from him [Saddam]. His military forces have not been rebuilt.

The tipping point for views on Iraq within the United States Administration was, of course, to be 9/11 and the terrorist attacks on the American mainland. Prior to this point, there was no currency in any linkages between Iraq and Al Qaeda , nor in Iraq as a real and imminent threat to anyone.

This reality was recognised by some in the British Parliament who took an interest in such matters. Thus, Malcolm Savidge could tell the House of Commons on 4 October 2001:

> Saddam Hussein may be insane, but I believe that he has a murderous obsession with self-preservation . . . I want to compare the two threats: the threat of smuggled weapons and the threat of rogue states' missiles. The first is real, immediate and high. The second may not be illusory but it is certainly distant in time and low.

This was an eminently sensible and informed analysis of the real threat which might face the West.

Presaging President Bush's infamous 'axis of evil' speech, I tried to open up the discussion as to what exactly constitutes a threat, in a Parliamentary debate on Missile Defence on 16 January 2002:

> The standard response is to counter the rogue states, which appear to be defined as those which refuse to recognise United States hegemony. Admittedly, many are nasty regimes – North Korea, Iran and Iraq, for example – but so are many American and British allies. The key might lie in what constitutes a threat. The United States Administration appears to rate as a threat those states which they know or suspect to be developing such missile technology. Traditionally, in this country and in Europe we have not restricted implied threat to capability but have linked it to intent to use the technology. Why should one of the three states that I have mentioned seek to threaten the US with an ICBM, in the knowledge that the retaliation by the US to an attack with weapons of mass destruction would be terrible and total? The events of 11 September demonstrate that there are

far more devilish ways to wreak havoc than using an ICBM, without attracting the national annihilation that would surely follow such an attack . . .

American neocon thinking had already made up its own mind on what was a threat, although their definition was meaningless in traditional terms. Thus, the President could state on the 29 January 2002:

> States like these (North Korea, Iran, Iraq) and their terrorist allies constitute an axis of evil, arming to threaten the peace of the world . . . I will not stand by, as peril draws closer and closer. The United States of America will not permit the world's most dangerous regimes to threaten us with the world's most destructive weapons.

It was clear from this State of the Union address just where neoconservative ideologues were taking the United States and the rest of the world. Tony Blair was not to be far behind in his unseemly rush to follow the American lead. In a press conference with Vice President Dick Cheney, held on 11 March 2002, the British Prime Minister could confidently declare:

> . . . that there is a threat from Saddam Hussein and the weapons of mass destruction that he has acquired is not in doubt at all.

Once again, Prime Minister Blair, whether through ignorance or conceit, brushed aside all other possibilities, expressing himself in absolutes. This reflected his repeated preference for generalisation, often extrapolating unjustifiably from narrow specifics. He showed a remarkable indifference and impatience with inconvenient hard facts. He was to continue to be uncomfortable with the necessary details of international issues. Disturbingly, although the Prime Minister dismissed doubt at the time, we now know there was much doubt at the time in the Government and military circles around him. He apparently rejected inconvenient arguments out of hand – they did not fit his preconceived and prejudiced view of the situation.

Naturally, his ministers fell into line – the way of the Blair Government – telling the Prime Minister what he wanted to hear, rather than what he ought to hear. Without any substantial case for doing so, Foreign Secretary Jack Straw could echo his master's voice in the House of Commons on the 12 March 2002:

> The Iraq regime represents a severe threat to international and regional security as a result of its continued development of weapons of mass destruction.

Tony Blair was to elaborate his distorted presentation of Iraq even further. In the House of Commons debate on war in Iraq of 18 March 2003, he could argue:

> The threat is chaos. And there are two begetters of chaos. Tyrannical regimes with WMD and extreme terrorist groups who profess a perverted and false view of Islam.

A non-too-subtle linkage of mythical WMD with terrorism – both untrue – was to be yet another device to suggest that Iraq was a 'threat' to the West generally, and to the United Kingdom specifically.
Yet this had never been the case. Note the advice of senior FCO mandarin Peter Ricketts to Jack Straw, of the 22 March 2002:

> The truth is that what has changed is not the pace of Saddam Hussein's WMD programmes, but our tolerance of them post-11 September . . . even the best survey of Iraq's WMD programmes will not show much advance in recent years on the nuclear, missile or chemical weapons/biological weapons fronts . . . United States scrambling to establish a link between Iraq and Al Qaeda is so far frankly unconvincing. To get public and Parliamentary support for military operations, we have to be convincing that: the threat is so serious/imminent that it is worth sending our troops to die for; it is qualitatively different from the threat posed by other proliferators who are closer to achieving nuclear capability [including Iran] . . . Military operations need clear and compelling military objectives . . . for

Iraq, 'regime change' does not stack up . . . Much better as you have suggested, to make the objective ending the threat to the international community from Iraqi weapons of mass destruction before Saddam uses it or gives it to the terrorists . . . another major message which the Prime Minister will want to get across: the importance of positioning Iraq as a problem for the international community as a whole and not just for the United States.

This advice, while wrong about WMD, was meant to inform the Foreign Secretary and, through him, the Prime Minister about the reality of Iraq. This leaked memo showed clearly that there was little or no substance to the case being built up for war, but helpful on the line to be taken. Presumably, Foreign Secretary Straw was as aware as Prime Minister Blair that there was no justification for war. Their dilemma was to be resolved by changing the emphasis, obfuscating the real motivations and aims, and propagandising their cause. In short, they would spin the facts to fit the policy.

Jack Straw was to be instrumental in presenting this false prospectus. For example, in an interview with David Frost on the 24 March, he blandly stated:

Iraq poses a threat to the world because of its manufacture and development of WMD.

No explanation of the nature of the 'threat' was offered and he put 'the manufacture and development of WMD' as incontestable fact. This was simply untrue.

Writing to Tony Blair on the presentational difficulties, Straw said on 25 March 2002:

I judge that there is at present no majority inside the PLP for any military action against Iraq . . . we have a long way to go to convince them as to: (a) the scale of the threat from Iraq and why this has got worse recently (b) what distinguishes the Iraqi threat from that of e.g. Iran and North Korea so as to justify military action: (c) the justification for any military action in terms of international law and d) whether the consequences of military action really would be a compliant, law-abiding replacement government . . . A legal justification is a necessary but far from sufficient precondition for military action. We have also to answer the big question – what will this action achieve? There seems to be a larger hole in this than on anything else.

No trace here of Robin Cook's ethical foreign policy. Straw simply accepts the Bush/Blair agenda, with no objections. The difficulties highlighted raise no points of principle; they are merely obstacles to be overcome. This might be said to be one example of the old adage that 'politics is the art of the possible'.

The insistence that Iraq was a threat was key to Blair's incessant campaign to convince the British Parliament and public that black was white. In the House of Commons on the 12 April 2002, he repeated:

Saddam Hussein's regime is despicable, he is developing weapons of mass destruction and we cannot leave him doing so unchecked . . . He is a threat to his own people and to the region and, if allowed to develop these weapons, a threat to us also. Doing nothing is not an option . . . Our way of proceeding should be and will be measured, calm, and thought through.

His was a simple and simplistic argument – Saddam was bad (true) and his regime was 'despicable' (also true); he had WMD (false), and he was a threat to (a) his people (true), (b) the region (false), and (c) the world (false). In short, it was a bogus case which Blair put to Parliament and people as justification for war.

Meanwhile, Bush was becoming more gung-ho about the Iraqi 'threat' almost by the day. On 1 June 2002 , he declared to a group of military academy graduates:

We must take the battle to the enemy, disrupt his plans and confront the worst threats before they emerge.

The next day, he was able to refine this pre-emptive approach:

> Our security will require all Americans . . . [to] be ready for pre-emptive action when necessary to defend our liberty and to defend our lives.

This implied an almost Manichean view of the world – a struggle between darkness and light, good and evil. There were no prizes for guessing who qualified as the 'good guys' in this titanic struggle and were entitled to act as judge, jury and executioner on the international stage.

Still, Blair needed to show some nifty footwork, given that pre-emptive war was illegal under international law, as was regime change. Asked at the House of Commons Liaison Committee of 16 July 2002, whether or not he was preparing military action against Iraq, he held no hostages to failure:

> I think they pose an enormous threat to the world. How we deal with that, however, is open to question. That is why I say consistently to people there are no decisions which have been made in relation to Iraq at all . . . No, there are no decisions which have been taken about military action.

However, the Prime Minister contemporaneously pushed the same unsubstantiated allegations to that very committee:

> As more negotiations go on and he fails to comply and you know that he is developing these weapons of mass destruction, then over a period of time you are entitled to draw the conclusion that this threat is growing not diminishing.

The US administration felt no compunctions about setting out their agenda. Cheney could confidentially tell a veterans' convention on 27 August 2002:

> The danger to America requires action on many fronts all at once . . . we realise that wars are never won on the defensive. We must take the battle to the enemy.

Blair battled on with his own line. On 3 September:

> Iraq poses a real and a unique threat to the security of the region and the rest of the world.

On 9 September, his own Joint Intelligence Committee cautioned:

> . . . the use of chemical and biological weapons prior to any military attack would boost support for US-led action.

The intelligence analysts were trying to give Blair a more sober assessment of Iraq's capabilities and intentions. They did not constitute a threat. However, the following day, speaking to the Trades Union Congress conference, the Prime Minister was ploughing a different furrow:

> So let me tell you why I say Saddam Hussein is a threat that has to be dealt with. He has twice before started wars of aggression. Over one million people died in them. When the weapons inspectors were evicted [sic] from Iraq in 1998 there were still enough chemical and biological weapons remaining to devastate the entire Gulf region.

This was alarmist and inaccurate, given the assessments given to him by his own experts. His closest advisers reflected his cynicism. In an email to John Scarlett, Chairman of the Joint Intelligence Committee, Blair's Chief of Staff Jonathan Powell said on 17 September 2002:

> The document does nothing to demonstrate a threat, let alone an imminent threat from Saddam. In other words it shows he has the means but it does not demonstrate he has the motive to attack his neighbours let alone the West. We will need to make it clear in launching the document that we do not claim that we have evidence that he is an imminent threat.

His message was clear. The dossier produced by Scarlett's team did not have the desired evidence that Saddam was a threat. It was a shameful invitation to the intelligence community to shape their analysis to meet the political exigencies created by the Prime Minister's gadarene rush to leap over the neocon cliff.

As Glen Rangwala wrote on 17 September 2002, in an article entitled *The Dishonest Case for War* in Iraq:

> There is no case for a war in Iraq. It has not threatened to attack the United States or Europe. It is not connected to Al Qaeda. There is no evidence that it has new WMD, or that it possesses the means of delivering them . . . You cannot launch a war on the basis of unconfirmed suspicions of both weapons and intentions . . . The United States and United Kingdom policy has been to provide disincentives to Iraqi compliance rather than incentives . . . If the Iraqi regime is led to believe that the United States has made an invasion inevitable, it will have no reason to cooperate with weapons inspectors . . . If the United States and the United Kingdom re-engage with the political process that was laid out in the ceasefire resolution, Iraq will once again be provided with reasons to cooperate with the weapons inspectorate.

The eventual published version of the dossier was to read:

> Intelligence indicates that as part of Iraq's military planning Saddam is willing to use chemical and biological weapons.

This was a perversion of the intelligence available to the United Kingdom Government. Other distinctions were being blurred. The Prime Minister declared on 20 September:

> Saddam Hussein is a threat that has to be dealt with . . . if we do not deal with the threat from this international outlaw and his barbaric regime it will [erupt] at some point.

Now Saddam himself was the threat, not the possession by his regime of weapons of mass destruction. This confusion of issues was a recurrent characteristic of Blair's justification for the war. Critically, he repeatedly 'passed' on a threat requiring both capability and intent.

The semantics became more complex. As he declared in his foreword to the dossier published on 24 September:

> Iraq poses a current and serious threat to the United Kingdom's interest . . . I am in no doubt that the threat is serious and current, that he has made progress on WMD, and that he has to be stopped.

The threat – however, ill-defined – became in turn 'real', 'imminent' 'current', 'serious'. Little was communicated of substance here, but a climate of crisis was created and repeatedly reinforced. He had lots of support in putting across his message, that Saddam was now the threat.

His loyal Defence Secretary told Parliament on 17 October that:

> We (the international community) are in this together and we need to act together. It is in this context that we are dealing with Saddam Hussein . . . Saddam Hussein has spent years trying to build up his stores of WMD, he certainly strives to add nuclear capabilities to that arsenal. If we cannot ensure his disarmament, he will eventually succeed. If we were to underestimate the threat and fall for more of his duplicitous trickery, or simply do nothing, we would be guilty of a profound abdication of responsibility. Saddam Hussein must disarm.

The Tory spokesman, Bernard Jenkin, went even further in the same debate:

> . . . the question is not whether pre-emption is a new concept but whether we are adjusting what we regard as an imminent threat in the new security climate.

Such arguments fitted Blair's nebulous notion that our collective psychology should have changed after 9/11, as did that of the United States. Not only did such an argument fit with his presumptions, but it appealed to his lawyerly instinct for building a case. Sadly for him, such a case was built on sand. Happily for us all, international law has not been changed to accommodate the narrowness of Bush and Blair.

In an article for BBC News Online on 12 November 2002 'Threat at Home, Not Abroad' I tried to refocus on the real threats to British security and interests:

> The threat is here in the United Kingdom from terrorist organ-isations, not from a far-away Middle East despot who has no links whatever with those groups . . . a politically manoeuvred threat without any objective evidence to support the idea that there is any immediate danger from the Iraqi dictator Saddam Hussein. To my knowledge, no one had ever said there has been any direct immediate threat to the United Kingdom from Iraq. . . There is still time for Tony Blair to re-order the Government's thinking to meet the United Kingdom's security needs rather than to fall in with American ideological imperatives . . . The national interest and security are not served by meeting the objectives of other countries such as the United States, but by meeting our own concerns.

Other politicians wanted to reduce the complicated situation to a more digestible question. Hence, Jimmy Hood put it simply in Parliament on 25 November 2002:

> There is but one question that needs to be answered, both in the House and throughout the world community. Will the world be a safer place if we go to war with Iraq? If the answer is no, we should do everything in our power to avoid such a war.

Yet as always, attractively simple questions are usually deceptive, and can still turn on a syllable. As Elfyn Llwyd pointed out in the same debate:

> . . . the imminence of the threat was a mere perception and not a reality.

He was right, of course, but that is what propaganda is all about.

Interestingly, we were to be told how many Iraqis wanted a pre-emptive war, effecting regime change. Little attention was paid to those who, whilst wishing the same ends, pointed out the fallaciousness of the arguments being employed. Haifa Zanagan, an Iraqi exile in London, stated her case on 8 December 2002, in the BBC programme *The Case Against War*:

> Even though I was imprisoned by the regime, I was tortured by the regime, I would love to see the regime changed, but still I am against the war . . . I want to get rid of Saddam but not by war . . . I witnessed the suffering of many Iraqis in exile yet I don't want Iraq to be led to another war . . . I don't think he's [Saddam] a threat to the world peace, he's not a threat to the world. He's definitely not a threat to America or Britain.

She supported much of what Blair and Bush say they wanted, but she could not put her name to the nonsense being propagated to justify those ends.

Other voices agreed, including Sir Andrew Greene, former United Kingdom Ambassador to both Syria and Saudi Arabia. In the same programme, he averred:

> I think this talk about Saddam being a threat to the West frankly is largely manufactured.

His was an authoritative voice, indeed. He was to be joined in questioning government assumptions by Tory MP, Douglas Hogg. Speaking in the House on 16 December, Hogg put his finger on the critical issue:

> Does the Right Honourable Gentleman [Hoon] not understand that while a Security Council resolution may make a policy of war legal, it does not make it wise or moral? Furthermore, does he not understand that in the absence of a grave and imminent threat to ourselves and our allies, many of us believe that war is wrong, by which I mean not morally justified, as well as politically profoundly unwise.

As the pressure for war built up, so did the opposition become more targeted on the weaknesses of the Government's case. At the beginning of January, in an article on my website, I wrote:

> With regard to Iraq . . . It is not a threat to either the United States or the United Kingdom. Indeed, it is not a threat to its own neighbours, as they themselves testify. It is not in league with Al Qaeda. No doubt to Osama bin Laden, Saddam is as abhorrent as the Great Satan itself, given the secular nature of the Iraqi state. Even if it were still developing weapons, it is not in the same league as Israel or Pakistan when it comes to WMD. In its internal repression, it is probably no worse than Saudi Arabia, or Algeria.

This was not rocket science, simply the obvious conclusion to be drawn on information readily available to us all.

Douglas Hogg was one of those who battled continuously on the floor of the House of Commons. Questioning the increasingly hapless Defence Secretary, Geoff Hoon, he asked him on 7 January 2003:

> Does he not understand that many people do not believe that the threat posed by Iraq is sufficiently imminent or grave to constitute a moral basis for war?

The public were, of course, concerned in large numbers by what looked increasingly like the inevitability of war. Indeed, the Prime Minister seemed determined to pursue the military option. At a press conference on the 13 January 2002 he said:

> Now I simply say to you, it is a matter of time unless we act and take a stand before terrorism and WMD come together, and I regard them as two sides of the same coin. And the reason why Iraq is important is Iraq is the issue around which this has come to focus.

Once again, this was untrue, not least because any focus on Iraq was contrived by Bush and Blair. It was not simply happenstance.

The Americans were also trying to reinforce the image of Saddam as a threat. The United States Ambassador to the European Union – Rockwell Schnabel – demonised him at a speech in Brussels on 20 January:

> You had Hitler in Europe and no one really did anything about him . . . We knew he could be dangerous but nothing was done. The same type of person [is in Baghdad] and it's there that our concern lies.

This kind of hyperbole convinced no one. Rather, it was counterproductive, and led to the kind of reaction exemplified by John Pilger's claim on his website, www.johnpilger.com, of 29 January, that:

> Bush's State of the Union Speech last night was reminiscent of that other great moment in 1938 when Hitler called his generals together and told them 'I must have war'. He then had it.

In increasing desperation, Tony Blair began to detach himself from reality:

> . . . the policy of containment I think only worked up to a point and was beginning to fracture very badly.

There was no evidence to support this assertion made to the House of Commons Liaison Committee on 21 January 2003, On the contrary, as we have seen, both Colin Powell and Condoleeza Rice had believed the opposite, until Bush had to have his war.

Blair's confusion did not end there. He went on:

> The problem in respect of Iraq is not the problem necessarily of proliferating the WMD, it is actually that they may use the WMD.

He seemed not to have a clear and consistent line of argument. Was the threat of Saddam using WMD, or selling them to terrorists, or both? The harsh reality was that it did not matter. It was simply a cloak for his real motivation. Nevertheless, he found his way back to his line further into his session with the Liaison Committee:

> The reason for dealing with Saddam is because of the threat that is posed, is because of the weapons of mass destruction that he is developing and is because of the United Nations resolution.

Tragically, there was no such threat; the WMD did not exist; the United Nations resolution was exploited and undermined by Bush and Blair. His argument fell apart. John Horam put Blair's problem to him bluntly:

> . . . people in this country have two very clear ideas in their mind. One is Saddam Hussein is a threat and the other is international terrorism. What they are confused about is the link between the two. They understand the threat from international terrorism, which is clearly a threat to this country, but they do not see Saddam Hussein in the same way. So far you have failed to establish the link between the two.

Meanwhile, in the main chamber of the House of Commons, the indefatigable Douglas Hogg was now confronting the Foreign Secretary:

> The Right Honourable Gentleman has characterised Iraq as the most aggressive rogue state. While that may historically be true, will he give the House what evidence he has that Iraq is now plotting aggression against its neighbours or anyone else? Why should we not be able to rely on the policies of containment and deterrence that have been effective since the last Gulf War?

Straw could only waffle in reply. In truth, ministers often went through the motions on such questions. Everyone knew Blair was set on his war despite the evidence and the arguments against such an adventure. When Paul Flynn tried to pin the Defence Secretary down:

It is acknowledged that Iraq was a danger in the 1980s and early 1990s but is now an impoverished state. Will he describe to us how Saddam Hussein might use his WMDS now against the UK?

A weary Geoff Hoon could only reply dismissively:

Last year, the Government published a detailed dossier, drawing on a number of services, about the threat that Saddam Hussein's regime in Iraq poses.

Exasperation began to set in unexpected quarters. Marsha Singh – a Sikh and a loyal Labour member – made an impassioned plea in the same debate:

I have tried, but I find no justification for a war against Iraq. I find that the Muslim world, not only part of it, is completely bemused. It asks why UN resolutions are enforced against Iraq but not against Israel: why Palestinians are not given their homeland and why that is not a priority for the international community. Muslims are asking, 'Why is Kashmir not a priority for the international community?' They are bemused and they have every right to be. Saddam Hussein has been contained since 1991. He has not posed a realistic threat to anyone since then. Apart from Kuwait, none of Saddam's neighbours has asked us to attack Iraq, or offered to help us. How is Iraq an imminent danger in this country? Will someone please answer that question? No other significant world leader backs the United States in this war. Do other leaders see something that we do not? I do not see why we should spend billions on a war that cannot be justified, when our own people have economic needs, or why we should damage our political and economic relations with the Muslim world. I cannot countenance the deaths of service people and of thousands of Iraqis in this pointless war. I see the danger of regional instability. I agree with the ordinary men and women on the streets of this country, who ask, 'What has this war got to do with us?' The best defence in the world is peace. To get peace, we need conflict resolution in the trouble spots. We need to halt the arms trade, cancel third world debt and encourage good and transparent Government. We need disarmament and we should lead by example.

Elfin Llwyd , a solicitor, searched assiduously for evidence of Iraq as a threat, to justify the Government's position; but he failed:

There is no clear or compelling evidence to suggest that the United States or the United Kingdom could invoke the self defence provisions. One would have thought that the dossier that was the subject of the recall of Parliament in September would have spelt out the case for self defence. Alas, that document did nothing of the kind. In fact, there was nothing in it that could not have been gleaned from the broadsheets and the internet. Certainly, there was no urgency in any perceived threat. If anything, the document tended to defuse the case for urgent action. The ifs, buts and suppositions in the document spoke volumes. No one could seriously allege that there is an imminent danger of attack that would legitimise an act of self defence.

Some in the fourth estate tried to give wider currency to these disturbing questions. As the redoubtable Robert Fisk wrote in the *Independent* on 27 January 2003:

From Washington's pathetic attempt to link Saddam to Al Qaeda, to Blair's childish 'dossier' on weapons of mass destruction, to the whole tragic farce of United Nations inspections, people are just no longer fooled.

Back in Parliament, on 29 January, Lynne Jones asked when and why Blair had assessed Saddam as a threat:

> Can [the Prime Minister] explain why he [Saddam] did not use those [WMD] during the Gulf war when his arsenal was massively greater than it is now? In particular, can he explain why Saddam represents a greater threat today than he did in 1997, 1998, 1999 and all his time as Prime Minister until President Bush's axis of evil speech, when apparently the situation changed?

She was right, of course. Blair simply aped many of Bush's positions when he believed it to be advantageous to do so. Not that the Prime Minister was in any way dissuaded by increasing hostility, any more than he was dissuaded by inconvenient facts. He told the House on 2 March 2003:

> Saddam's WMD and the threats that they pose for the world must be confronted. In doing so, this country and our armed forces will be helping the long-term peace and security of Britain and the world.

He went on to say:

> The evidence that Iraq is developing WMD, chemical, biological and nuclear, is there; it is documented in the United Nations inspectors report. I do not believe that the British and American intelligence agencies are not telling us the truth about these things – I think they are right – but we need not rely on that to be worried about Iraq and WMD. We need only read the reports, going back for years, about those weapons and their manufacture in Iraq, and the fact that Saddam . . . has used them against his own people and against other countries.

This shows appallingly poor judgement, and a disregard for intellectual rigor in dealing with such important matters of state. He appears dismissive of hard evidence, preferring instead to follow his own unreliable and misinformed prejudices. Lord Butler was later to question the Prime Minister's whole approach to good governance.

Two nights later on BBC *Newsnight*, he was once again pushing the canard that Iraq had WMD and was a threat to her neighbours. He shamelessly used his political capital with the British public, and his skill as a communicator, to propagandise his false prospectus to the British public:

> The (clear and imminent) danger (to this country) is that if we allow Iraq to develop chemical, biological and nuclear weapons they will threaten their own region. There is no way that we would be able to exclude ourselves from any regional conflict there was there.

Addressing the International Institute for Strategic Studies on 11 February, Jack Straw 'defined' the Saddam 'threat':

> It is this deadly combination of capability and intent which makes Saddam uniquely dangerous.

Understandably, doubt grew rather than disappeared. At Prime Minister's Questions, Tory Jonathan Sayeed asked:

> . . . is the Prime Minister certain that we are not allowing frustration and impatience to cloud our judgement, for what new threat, proven threat or imminent threat is there to justify war?

It was not our judgement which was impaired, but that of the Prime Minister and those complicit in his determination to join the American war against Iraq.

The doubts were being expressed in the surgeries of Members of Parliament:

> The Prime Minister has just told the House that everyone accepts that Iraq is a threat, but many of my constituents tell me that they are still unclear about the direct threat and risks to the United Kingdom as a result of not disarming Iraq.

Thus, Andrew Selous MP illustrated that the public were more circumspect than simply accepting the Government's assertions. They, too, wanted to know what was the nature of the 'threat' posed by Saddam.

However, there are none so blind as those who will not see. One of those was the leader of the opposition, Iain Duncan Smith, who told the House of Commons on 18 March:

> . . . the main reason why we will be voting for the motion is that it is in the British national interest. Saddam Hussein has the means, the mentality and the motive to pose a direct threat to our national security.

The Prime Minister was as one with him:

> Those two threats (terrorism and states with NBC weapons) have, of course, different motives and different origins, but they share one basic common view: they detest the freedom, democracy and tolerance that are the hallmarks of our way of life. At the moment, I accept fully that the association between the two is loose – but it is hardening. The possibility of the two coming together – of terrorist groups in possession of WMD or even of a so-called dirty radiological bomb – is now, in my judgement, a real and present danger to Britain and its national security.

With hindsight, it is astonishing that so many Members of Parliament followed Blair and Duncan Smith into the voting lobbies. Any objective assessment of their case was bound to lead to rejection of it. Since the actual war, it has been shown to have been totally groundless.

Almost immediately after the initial subjugation of Iraq, those who led us into the quagmire began to rewrite history. Blair waffled in his Sedgefield constituency on 5 March 2004:

> . . . the fundamental source of division over Iraq is not over issues of trust or integrity. The real issue . . . is not a matter of judgement . . . .the key point is that it is the threat that is the issue.'

On 14 March, on the CBS *Face the Nation* programme, Donald Rumsfeld could say with a straight face:

> You and a few other critics are the only people I've heard use the phrase 'immediate threat'. It's become a kind of folklore that that's what happened. If you have any citations, I'd like to see them.

Unsurprisingly , the reporter quoted him in reply from 19 September 2002:

> No terrorist threat poses a greater or immediate threat to the security of our people.

Blair stumbled on with the same red herring into June, 2004. On the BBC *Today* programme of 6 June he still insisted:

> What we also know is we haven't found them [WMD] in Iraq – now let the survey group complete its work and give us the report . . . They will not report that there was no threat from Saddam, I don't believe.

In a question to the Prime Minister on 14 July 2004, I reminded him:

> The Prime Minister said that everyone genuinely believed that Saddam had both strategic intent for WMD and actual weapons. That is a classic definition of a threat: capability plus intent. However, I remind him that many of us took issue with that at the time . . . The Attorney General said that there would be no justification for the use of force against Iraq on the ground of self-defence against an imminent threat.

It was another reminder that, given the opportunity, those guilty of taking the country into an illegal and immoral war, must be held to account at every opportunity for their actions.

A marriage of convenience

Wars teach us not to love our enemies, but to hate our allies.

Ulysses S. Grant (1822-1885)

There was a relatively short period of time during which members of the British establishment married members of leading American families. This in turn led to a network of relationships which were influential within the governments of both the United States and the United Kingdom. Winston Churchill was a classic example of a beneficiary of these relationships, strongly connected to the establishments on either side of the Atlantic.

This was characterised as a 'special relationship' between the two countries, and perhaps best exemplified by the close working relationship during the Second World War, of Churchill and President Franklin Delano Roosevelt. It became an article of faith in British political circles that the United Kingdom would always have a special priority in American considerations. Although it was argued to have been the case during the Falklands War, it was certainly not the case during the Suez fiasco. For much of the Cold War decades, American concerns were more focussed on Germany than they were on Britain.

The reality was more that the United Kingdom increasingly became a client state rather than a special partner; but it has suited British Prime Ministers to perpetuate the myth of the UK as uniquely placed in the American scheme of things. So it was in the build up to the Iraq war, although a pretence of independence of action was maintained, as was pointed out in the *Guardian* on 8 January 2001:

The official British line is that there are no plans to change the approach to Iraq and that British foreign policy is determined independently of the United States.

Others were already exercised by British genuflexion to Bush's 'Son of Star Wars' National Missile Defence Programme. I criticised Jack Straw's knee jerk support for it, in the *Guardian* on 27 July 2001:

I find it curious that a senior figure in the Government could so publicly embrace Bush's madcap venture. The slavish adherence to all things American flies in the face of national interest.

No-one should have been surprised. Certainly, it was no shock that on 11 September 2001, in his reaction to the terrifying attacks on New York and Washington, Prime Minister Blair responded supportively and unconditionally:

We . . . here in Britain stand shoulder to shoulder with our American friends . . . and we, like them, will not rest until this evil is driven from our world.

Thankfully, there were those who, even in American's time of trial, wanted to be a critical friend of that great nation, rather than an unquestioning one. Richard Allen told the House of Commons on 4 October 2001:

We should be that country's [United States] best friend, listening to what they say but not scared to criticise.

Sir Christopher Meyer was later to reveal that the British Prime Minister was, from the outset, in a position to be that critical friend, and restrain Bush in a variety of ways from precipitate action. However, he failed to do so. Perhaps he lacked the strength of character to stand up to the President. Nevertheless, he was forewarned by myself, among others, in the House of Commons on 15 October that year:

My greatest concern is the voice of those who wish to widen the war. The way in which elements in the American Administration have sought to shape an agenda that is dramatically different to that of the British Government is no secret.

Quoting Thucydides, I urged Blair that:

. . . slow and cautious may be seen as wise and sensible.

The American neocons were leading the way in Washington, and their views were anathema to Labour values. One would have thought that a Labour Prime Minister ought to have recognised this. How could such a leader not distance himself and his country from the delusional and dangerous approach of those like Michael A. Ledeen of the American Enterprise Institute, who said on 29 October 2001:

> This is total war. We are fighting a variety of enemies. There are lots of them out there. All this talk about first we are going to do Afghanistan, then we will do Iraq . . . that is entirely the wrong way to go about it . . . We have a winning Messianic vision because we are a Messianic country . . . If we just let our vision of the world go forth, and we embrace it entirely and we don't try to piece together clever democracy . . . but just wage a total war against these tyrants . . . our children will sing great songs about us years from now.

A Conservative dissident in such jingoistic times, Andrew Tyrie, expressed concern in the House about Blair's own 'dangerous messianic rhetoric', suggesting in November that the Prime Minister make clear:

> Nor is it our purpose to extend the war aims to Iraq.

Bush, however, spoke for himself and Blair at a press conference on 8 November 2001:

> We both recognise that we wage a fight to save civilisation, and we must prevail; and not only must prevail, we will prevail.

The American President was now taking a hyperbolic line. An anonymous military figure, having visited General Tommy Franks' military headquarters in Florida, was quoted on 2 December 2001 in the *Observer*:

> The Americans are walking on water. They think they can do anything and there is bloody nothing Tony [Blair] can do about it.

The argument put in British political circles at the time was that the United Kingdom needed to stay close to the Americans to exercise a restraining influence. Clearly, according to our military source and Sir Christopher Meyer, this was not to be the case, if indeed it ever had been. Events were to show that such a relationship never eventuated. The British – and Blair in particular – were to be a useful political crutch for the Bush Administration, no more and no less.

Menzies Campbell put the challenge directly to Blair in the House of Commons on 8 January 2002:

> Will it not be a clear indication of the United Kingdom's influence over the United States if we continue successfully to discourage the Bush administration from precipitate military action against Iraq unless there is incontrovertible evidence of Iraq involvement in terrorism, or alternatively, it becomes abundantly clear that the policy of deterrence and containment successfully followed since December 1998 . . . has ceased to be effective?

Before losing his way over the Middle East generally, Nick Cohen of the *Observer* was one of the more acute – and acerbic – observers of the special relationship. Thus, on 10 March 2002, he noted accurately:

> The greatest defeat of British foreign policy is the loss of the illusion that London influences Washington . . . a roaring, uncontrollable America sees him [Blair] as an ornamental extra; nice to have, but inessential.

Many Members of Parliament worried that the Americans would manipulate Blair, and wanted a debate to set the parameters, hopefully, for government policy over Iraq. On 12 March Douglas Hogg asked the Government to tread warily:

> Does the Right Honourable Gentleman understand that many of us are very concerned about the talk of pre-emptive military

action against Iraq? . . . Would the Right Honourable
Gentleman ensure, first, that before he has further substantial
discussions with the United States Government, he holds a full
debate in the House, so that the view of honourable Members
can be identified?

Needless to say, his request was not met until we were well down the road to
war, after the evidence had been fixed.

The junior Foreign Office Minister, Ben Bradshaw, was unconvincing when he
told the House on that day:

I do not think that it is correct to talk about Britain following
the United States. Britain will make a decision based on our
national interest.

However, as time would tell, he was correct in one sense – Blair was right
alongside Bush in his eagerness for a war in Iraq. What was not clear, and
became less so overtime, was where the British national interest was being
served. Shortly after this on 1 April 2002 – April Fool's Day – Blair visited the
President Bush's ranch in Crawford, Texas. It is widely believed that this was
Blair's Rubicon moment in committing his country to war in Iraq, alongside
the United States. As he truthfully told NBC on 4 April:

The discussion we [he and Bush] had [on Afghanistan], it
wasn't a question of restraining the president, the discussion
was what was the best way of doing it? We worked out the best
way, we did it. Now in respect of Iraq, it is exactly the same.

He was committed to supporting war from the beginning, and they certainly
worked out their political strategy to take them to the invasion of Iraq. Blair
was determined to play a full role in the planning – he was not merely a
bystander, or even a restraining influence. His vanity demanded a proactive
role in the build up to war. As he said in his speech at the George Bush Senior
Presidential Library on 7 April 2002:

> . . . when America is fighting for those values, then, however
> tough, we fight with her – no grandstanding, no offering
> implausible and impractical advice from the touchline . . .
> Britain will be at America's side doing it.

Blair seemed blinded as to where the United States Administration was
headed:

> Of course, countries want to protect their territorial integrity
> but few are into empire building.

He only needed to look at the Project for a New American Century's *Pax
Americana* blueprint to see that the present United States Administration was
one of the 'few'!

Others viewed things differently, with different possible options. I told the
Mirror on 9 April:

> I do have concerns about being seen to be tied in with some of
> the more adventurous notions of the American administra-
> tion. It's not a question of one or two powerful countries
> acting in a gung-ho way. To deal with Iraq, you need to deal
> with the United Nations, not through unilateral or bilateral
> action.

By 29 April, my frustration was showing through in the same newspaper, as I
spoke about Blair's backing of Bush's heavy-handed military tactics:

> Tony Blair seems completely out of kilter with public opinion.
> He is trapped in a downward spiral in his support for the US.

The Prime Minister was digging himself deeper and deeper into a hole, as
Bush looked to bomb Iraqi air defences – and much else – on an ever
increasing scale. Not that Blair was bothered. He was becoming more
detached from the British public's unease, telling *Newsnight* on 15 May:

I don't believe there are really significant differences [between
the way this country views the world and the way that George
Bush's administration views the world].

There were actually huge differences but he either could not, or would not,
see them. His path was decided, and by July 2002, according to James
Naughtie in his 2004 book *The Accidental American*, Blair and Bush were
agreed on attacking Iraq.

Perhaps naively, many still hoped that there could be an alternative resolution
to the differences with Iraq other than war. Harry Cohen tabled an early day
motion on 15 July 2002:

That this House notes the suggestion of Mikhail Gorbachev, at
a meeting with Parliamentarians on 10th July, that the United
States and Iraq should attempt to resolve their differences by
direct discussions between representatives of both their
countries rather than resort to war; and considers that the
United Kingdom Government should adopt this proposal as its
official policy and that an offer of a venue in London for such
talks should be made to both sides.

This reflected the overwhelming wish to find a peaceful solution. Cohen was
formally hoping that Blair would play a more constructive role. But that was
not to be. As the Prime Minister told Michael Cockerell of the BBC on 31 July:

The reason why we are with America in so many of these issues
is because it is in our interests. We do think the same, we do feel
the same [and they] need to know – are you prepared to
commit, are you prepared to be there and, when the shooting
starts, are you prepared to be there?

Another visit to Camp David in September sealed the deal with Bush.
Whatever form the 'special relationship' took in the hands of Bush and Blair,
it was not as it was being presented to the British Parliament and people. The
famous and respected Washington journalist Bob Woodward was to tell Jim

Naughtie of the BBC on 7 September about an interview he had conducted with President Bush:

> I asked the President . . . 'Did the Prime Minister say 'I will supply troops'?' And the President said 'Yes'.

Whilst there are many caveats which may be put on this reported conversation, it occurred while Blair, Straw, Hoon *et al* continued to insist that no decisions had been taken by the British Government on military action. As I reminded readers of the *Guardian* on 23 September:

> Many around the world breathed a sigh of relief when President Bush went to the United Nations recently [supposedly seeking a United Nations mandate] unaware that the approach was merely a tactic . . . Successive [United Kingdom] governments have deluded themselves that we have a 'special' relationship with the United States – special only in so far as we tend to fall in with every crazed administration notion, and ask for nothing in return. We end up as America's handrag, with diminished credibility within Europe and facing increased hostility across the globe. Is this in the British national interest? I fear not.

This was a more accurate reflection on the true nature of the special relationship in the context of Bush and Blair. Glenda Jackson had a different take on the special relationship, wondering on 17 October 2002 whether it had become a synonym for the international community:

> On the issue of a strike against Saddam Hussein, it would seem that the international community has reduced to two sovereign states, namely the United Kingdom and the United States. Is he [the Defence Secretary] saying that this now constitutes the international community and that we will engage against Iraq if the rest of what I understand to be the international community stays where it is, firmly saying no to a pre-emptive strike?

Alice Mahon brought the same debate back to consideration of the nature of the Bush-Blair deal:

> I draw the attention of the Secretary of State to a United States Congressional Budget Office document, which clearly states: 'President Bush has been guaranteed that Britain will send troops to fight a United States-led war.' It continues 'The report, finalised on September 30th, says Britain is the only country that has said it will commit troops'.

I put it another way in the *Guardian* on 7 November:

> George Bush is hell bent on war, aided and abetted by the British Prime Minister. He will get his war and he is just going through the diplomatic niceties with the French and the Russians.

On that same day, Jack Straw's sycophancy hit a new low:

> At this point, I should like to pay my own tribute to President Bush and to United States Secretary of State Colin Powell, for their great patience and great statesmanship.

Blair, too, played the role of deferential acolyte to the United States, in his address at the Lord Mayor's Banquet on Armistice Day:

> I believe . . . the world needs a broader agenda than simply terrorism and WMD. And we need full United States engagement and leadership on all of it.

It would have been preferable if he had promoted consensus at the United Nations, rather than American hegemony. Sir Andrew Green – former senior ambassador to Syria and Saudi Arabia – summed matters up well on 8 December on the BBC TV programme *The Case Against War:*

> I think the policy is misguided and misconceived . . . it will
> destabilise the Gulf and we'll have consequences that cannot be
> foreseen or indeed predicted . . . I think we've gone off the rails
> . . . I think that the British Government have effectively fallen in
> line [with American policy] and I think that's a serious mistake.

Still the Prime Minister would not own up to his personal interpretation of the special relationship. Charles Kennedy tried on 18 December to squeeze it out of him:

> If the American Government were . . . to take any kind of pre-
> emptive action in respect of Iraq, would their action have the
> backing of the British Government?

The usual evasive response from the Prime Minister was in keeping with his strategy of admitting nothing, although he had already committed the United Kingdom to the unconditional support of whatever President Bush chose to do. Welsh Nationalist Elfyn Llwyd took a different tack that same day with the Defence Secretary:

> The Secretary of State goes out of his way to say that the deploy-
> ment is routine. Does he not consider that the United Kingdom is
> now on a treadmill to war, and that, in fact, the decision to
> commit will not be made by Number 10 but by somebody else
> across the sea who has already decided that war is inevitable?

Hoon had made a statement on 'contingency preparations for a war in Iraq'. His critics knew it was window dressing – the key decisions were made. It was a matter of 'when', not 'if'.

As Jeremy Corbyn put it:

> Has the Secretary of State not just made a statement that
> softens us up for a war? He has no intention of going back to
> the UN or seeking Parliamentary approval, and is moving
> troops into the region to start a war the moment that George

Bush says so. Can he deny that carte blanche has been given to George Bush to do what he will, and that the British Government will support him?

No one with half-a-brain was fooled by the political pretence.

The war came, and its initial phase quickly passed. It was but a prologue to a longer and more bitter struggle. I set out my personal views in the *Guardian* on 18 August 2003:

> Militarily, we grow ever closer to the United States. The defence secretary . . . has acknowledged that we are to be to the United States armed forces what the sepoys were to the British Indian Army. Diplomatically, the gains of many decades have been frittered away by our blind obedience to the American administration's wars. Huge numbers of people view the British Prime Minister as Bush's poodle, and see Britain as no more than the errand boy for the American neo-conservatives . . . We have next to no influence with the United States administration . . . As America's love affair with Tony Blair blossoms, the world – and the United Kingdom's place within it – becomes less stable . . . What an ignominious way we have begun the twenty-first century – as a satrapy of the new American world order . . . The irony of our position is that, as we further alienate our friends, including those in America who look for constructive criticism rather than sycophancy, so we reinforce the prejudices of our enemies. Thus do nations dwindle into insignificance and irrelevance.

Following charges of anti-Americanism, I was again to respond in the *Guardian* on 18 November 2003:

> . . . it is not knee-jerk anti-Americanism which holds sway in the United Kingdom. It is the reaction of one old friend to another when the latter is acting wholly unreasonably and unacceptably. In such circumstances, that old friend needs to be reminded of

> his responsibility to himself and to others . . . In such a context,
> if we do not speak out to President Bush, who on earth can?

This was how a genuinely special relationship might have operated. Sadly, Blair offered all and asked for nothing in return – not even caution. He had deluded himself. He had told a convocation of British ambassadors in London on 7 January 2003:

> . . . we should remain the closest ally of the United States, and as allies influence them to continue broadening the agenda. We are the ally of the United States because we share their values . . . the United States are a force for good. The price of [British] influence is that we do not leave the United States to face the tricky issues alone.

He had no influence, nor did he necessarily represent British views in this area. That same day, he said:

> Religious extremism through the misinterpretation of Islam is a danger all over the world . . . . because it can be manipulated by small numbers of fanatics to distort the lives of ordinary people . . .

He may well have applied that thinking to the neoconservative ideologues in the American administration. He also set out his number one foreign policy priority:

> What are the principles of foreign policy that should guide us?
> . . . First, we should remain the closest ally of the US . . .

That should have been a means to other foreign policy objectives, not the end in itself which it appeared to be for the British Prime Minister.
Paul Flynn had a more honest assessment of our relationship with America, when he asked Hoon in the House of Commons on 7 January 2003:

> Can we have a vote in this House . . . to give us a chance of escaping from our present link as a junior partner with the United States in this axis of delusion?

He was followed by the persistent Douglas Hogg:

> Will the Secretary of State reflect on the fact that although a strategy of maintaining a close relationship with the United States is necessary and right, it is not a sufficient justification for United Kingdom participation in a war against Iraq?

Charles Kennedy tried it on with Blair:

> Kennedy – Under what circumstances would the United States take military action against Iraq that our country would not choose to support?

> Blair – I have made clear the circumstances in which we do support military action.

Parliamentary warhorse Dennis Skinner – who had been politically 'groomed' by Blair over a long period – weighed in at Prime Minister's Questions a week later:

> When the PM meets the American President at the end of the month, will he tell George Bush that there is almost certainly a majority of the British people against the idea of a war with Iraq?

An honest answer from the Prime Minister would have been 'No!' That same day, in a letter to *The Times*, novelist John le Carré hit the nail on the head:

> The most charitable interpretation of Tony Blair's part in all this is that he believed that, by riding the tiger, he could steer it. He can't. Instead, he gave it a phoney legitimacy, and a smooth voice. Now, I fear, the same tiger has him penned into a corner,

and he can't get out. I cringe when I hear my Prime Minister lend his head prefect's sophistries to this colonialist adventure. His very real anxieties about terror are shared by all sane men. What he can't explain is how he reconciles a global assault on Al Qaeda with a territorial assault on Iraq. We are in this war, if it takes place, to secure the fig leaf of our special relationship, to grab our share of the oil pot, and because, after all the public hand-holding in Washington and Camp David, Blair has to show up at the altar.

On the same day, in the House, I wanted to know where the Government stood up for British interests:

Does my Right Honourable Friend [Hoon] agree that his slavish devotion to American policy in this area (missile defence) adds further to global destabilisation?. . . In the Government's rush to embrace every crackpot notion foisted on us by the ideologues in Washington, I should like the Secretary of State to point out where the independence of thought and the independence of policy are in British Government interests, reflecting true British needs.'

Tony Wright requested some degree of British independence of the United States Administration at the Liaison Committee of 21 January:

I take it . . . that if the inspectors report adequate compliance, there could be no question of military action and if the Americans were to say, 'We've had enough of all this, we are just going to do it,' then we would part company?

Blair offered no hostages to fortune in reply:

The position of ourselves and America is exactly the same, that there must be findings that constitute a breach.

Richard Allan was also concerned about the British national interest:

> ... preventive military action is justified by the United States in
> respect of defending United States interests abroad. I am not
> sure that the United Kingdom has traditionally had such a
> policy. I am trying to establish whether there is a difference or
> whether it is the United Nations resolution that is the critical
> deciding factor for United Kingdom involvement as opposed to
> us saying what is in the United Kingdom interest to take action
> against Iraq.

Blair answered what he had not been asked:

> ... you are right ... that in respect of the case of Iraq the
> reason why we support the position that we do is because of the
> UN resolution.

He moved from reason to metaphysics:

> Yes... America ... is a force for good in the world. I believe ... it
> is a strong matter of principle.

Meanwhile in the main chamber of the House, members like Malcolm
Savidge were trying to deal with the practicalities of the Prime Minister's
flights of political fancy:

> I am appalled at the extent to which the simplistic ideology and
> language of the US hard right is coming to dominate this
> Government, with talk of rogue states and the pretence that the
> most likely source from which unconditional terrorists would
> obtain WMD is Iraq.

Lawyer and politician, Bob Marshall-Andrews, pointed out the paradoxes
thrown up by the Government's unconditional support for all American
notions:

> Those . . . on this side of the argument . . . do not harbour
> within us festering anti-American feelings. Our opposition is to
> the nature of the American regime . . . It is ruled, governed and
> motivated by a ghastly mixture of fundamental Christian evan-
> gelism, ruthless Zionism and the oil economy. That mix, if it is
> allowed to rule us in our international affairs, will bring us
> nothing but disaster. Those of us who oppose this war do so
> because we believe that it is ill proven and unnecessary . . . The
> motivation for this war is suspect in the extreme, and those
> outside the House know that it is so.

President Bush and his colleagues adopted a rather crude 'with us or against us' demarcation of friends and foes. Part of that was the allegation of anti-Americanism levelled both by Americans and British politicians against those who took a more thoughtful view of what was being proposed.
Colin Burgon put it well in the House on the 22 January 2003:

> As a friend of America and its people, I say that honesty is
> central to any proper friendship. If the United States has no
> better friend than the United Kingdom, we should be able to tell
> the United States if we think that it is heading in the wrong
> direction.

Prime Minister Blair was apparently incapable of doing so. At the White House on 31 January 2003, the true measure of the relationship was revealed. Blair supported Bush on his 'weeks, not months' ultimatum to Baghdad; and he failed to elicit any Bush enthusiasm for a second United Nations resolution.
Even the revered Nelson Mandela appeared to hold Blair in contempt. As Jeremy Paxman put it to the Prime Minister on *Newsnight* on 5 February 2003:

> . . . when a great world figure like Nelson Mandela calls the
> British Prime Minister the American Foreign Minister – don't
> you feel embarrassed?

Perhaps he should have approached his American partners along the lines suggested in the House on 25 February, by a former member of his cabinet, Chris Smith:

> . . . is it not the role of a true friend, in present circumstances, to be candid with the President of the US and tell him the evidence is not yet compelling, that the work of the inspectors is not yet done, and that the moral case for war – with all its consequences – has not yet been made?

Scottish Nationalist Alex Salmond took the Prime Minister to task the very next day:

> It is possible for that [pre-emptive aggressive] policy to become central to the [United States] Administration only in an atmosphere of fear. That is where the Prime Minister is heavily culpable . . . because he was in a position to put the brakes on that sort of policy . . . There is no doubt that the Prime Minister is no longer in charge of these events and that events are controlling him.

He was adumbrating the atmosphere of fear and crisis that had been encouraged in the United Kingdom, and Blair's failure to restrain Bush – not because he could not (we do not know whether that was possible) but because he would not. The British Prime Minister was rolling over before American determination. It was, as I said in the *Mirror* on 27 February, cut and dried:

> The decision was not made in Downing Street, not in the Foreign Office. It was made in the White House. The hard reality is that it is an American military campaign that is going to be fought.

That same day, I wrote in *Tribune*:

> Without the consent of his party, the British people, or Parliament – which has been denied a vote on the issue to date

– the Prime Minister has committed Britain to a United States-led war on Iraq. He hopes that the United Nations can be browbeaten into acquiescence in such a war. If not, he will certainly follow where the Americans lead . . . The truth is that he and his acolytes have boxed themselves into the American President's corner, with no obvious way out.

Chief UN Weapons Inspector Hans Blix was said to have tried to separate Blair from Bush on the timetable for war, on 28 February. If so, like everyone else, he failed to dent the Prime Minister's commitment to the President. Even when Bush offered him a way out on 9 March – an offer to keep British troops out of the impending invasion of a sovereign state – Blair resolutely declined the opportunity. He was convinced British troops ought to be shoulder-to-shoulder with American troops in the illegal invasion. After all, from his perspective on 12 March, at Prime Minister's Questions:

It's the British national interest that must be upheld at all times.

As I suggested to my local paper five days later:

This is an American war, the grounds for which have shifted time after time after time . . . .The risks are enormous. Further instability in the Middle East will occur, and more Muslims will rush to join terrorist groups. There may be huge loss of life, mainly civilians, women and children. I also expect economic fallout due to uncertainty over oil . . . Why are we in this mess? I have to conclude that Tony Blair was suckered into it. Quite simply, Iraq is no threat to us.

But the truth remained that British influence was, according to David Curry, marginal:

I have doubts about whether the policy . . . that the United Kingdom can act as influence, harness, guide and tutor to the exercise of power by the world's only superpower is, in the long term, any more than a historical intellectual conceit.

Blair could not apparently see the irony when he said on 19 March:

> The art of leadership is saying no, not yes. It is very easy to say
> yes.

Not everyone wanted to simply acquiesce in the vainglorious adventurism of the American President. Hence, in an early day motion dated 11 November 2003, Simon Thomas wanted him cross-examined in the British Parliament:

> That this House notes the visit of President Bush to the United
> Kingdom; and extends to him an invitation to address
> honourable Members and to answer questions on the reasons
> for war in Iraq, the conduct of war in Iraq, the current situation
> in Iraq, and the need for the United Nations to guide the recon-
> struction of that country.

This was not to be, of course. As time passed, British soldiers were affected by their association with the Americans. In the *Guardian* of 18 October 2004, I noted:

> We are putting our troops in harm's way and subject to the
> vagaries of how the Americans do things.

By 6 November, my focus had shifted to the Iraqi regime:

> We can't go on indefinitely propping up an American appointed
> regime. I think we ought to be saying there is an end to all this.

An anonymous respondent from Monterey in California had told James Naughtie in an online forum earlier that year:

> After 9/11 the Bush administration was drunk with a blind
> desire for revenge and their own plans to remake the world in

their image. A true friend would have taken away our keys and not allowed us to drive. Instead, Tony Blair hopped into the passenger seat and did all the talking so no one could smell George Bush's reeking breath . . . I had been counting on Blair and our other moderate allies to help us show some restraint in a modern, interconnected world. Blair's enabling stance was a betrayal to Britain, the United States and the world community.

What glorious opportunity for real moral leadership had been available to Blair; and what a cataclysmic failure of his not to grasp it. If he had done so, his much sought for legacy would have been already gift-wrapped for posterity.

The Prime Minister forged ahead, learning nothing from his mistaken course. On 18 October 2004, Llew Smith tabled an early day motion, asking the Prime Minister to heed history:

That this House recalls that the last time an American administration put pressure on a British labour Government to provide troops to back the United States' plans to escalate an ill judged war was in 1970 Vietnam: remembers that this House debated the request on 5 May 1970, on a motion proposed by a former leader of the Labour party, the then Honourable Member for Ebbw Vale, Michael Foot, who put the argument that day that the escalating events can have the gravest consequences for us all, notes that he pleaded that in his opinion it was 'sheer despair for people to say that nothing that we can do or say can have much influence on such distant occurrences and keep our mouths shut, and possibly keep our eyes closed as well.

Once again, history failed to restrain or inform either the Americans or Tony Blair – indeed, British troops took up positions which freed United States troops to invade Fallujah. As a result, thousands of innocent men and women and children died in that city.

For many, Blair had sold his political soul. The effects of this were felt in many ways. Thus, I wrote in *Tribune* on 4 February 2005:

> They [i.e. the Blairites] dream of an Americanised party, with supporters rather than members, selling whatever policies they believe will appeal to the dwindling numbers bothering to vote.

In a speech to the Blairite think tank Progress in the autumn of 2005, Blair outlined his vision of just such an Americanised party. This was not a partner of American thinking, but a disciple.

As I have already noted, Mathew D'Ancona had seen Blair's general direction back in November 2001, when he wrote:

> He [Blair] is applying precisely the techniques he has honed on the domestic front to his mission overseas. He is approaching the war on terrorism as if it were an extension of the New Labour project, the latest and greatest challenge for the arch-moderniser.

Four years later, Sir Christopher Meyer's memoirs gave an insight:

> Since the Crawford Meeting [in 2002] a question began growing in my mind. When is a condition not a condition? Had Blair said at Crawford that he would be unable to support a war unless British wishes were met? I doubted it.

Blair had failed from the outset to promote an independent view. His was a client's relationship to his patron, the American President. As I put it in *Tribune* on 12 May 2005:

> Too much time and political energy has been wasted by Labour on overseas adventures. That is not to say that we should renege on our overseas commitments. What the electorate believe is that the Government has sought out other people's battles to fight, rather than our own . . . It is also time for a Labour Government to reassess its place in the world, and the consequent priorities for the state. We are not an American satrapy;

nor do the British people wish it to be. Nor are we as yet fully integrated into the European Union. Decisions on the latter are yet to be made. What we cannot do is bestride the gulf between the Old and the New Worlds, without both exposure and embarrassment. Foreign policy – and that of defence – must be about British interests, no-one else's.

Weapons of mass delusion

Thus when we fondly flatter our desires, our best conceits do prove the greatest liars.
Michael Drayton (1563–1631)

For the British Government – and Tony Blair in particular – the possession and development of weapons of mass destruction was the *sine qua non* for hostility towards Saddam Hussein. It was presented to Parliament and people as the specific *casus belli* for the war against Iraq. These 'weapons' allegedly were a direct threat to Britons and British interests. Thus, a pre-emptive strike to remove this threat was justified in the eyes of the British Prime Minister, despite evidence to the contrary.

Back in 1995, Saddam's brother-in-law, Hussein Kamel, had testified to United Nations inspectors that:

> I ordered the destruction of all chemical weapons. All weapons – biological, chemical, missile, nuclear – were destroyed.

Tony Blair was happy to refer to Hussein Kamel's confession, but not to the substance of it. It was more difficult to ignore Scott Ritter, former head of the UNSCOM unit charged with uncovering Saddam's fabled WMD. Writing in *Arms Control Today* on 1 June 2000, Ritter declared:

> It was possible as early as 1997 to determine that, from a qualitative standpoint, Iraq had been disarmed. Iraq no longer possessed any meaningful quantities of chemical or biological agent, if it possessed any at all, and the industrial means to produce these agents had either been eliminated or were subject

to stringent monitoring. The same was true of Iraq's nuclear and ballistic missile capabilities.

Even George Tenet – then Director of the United States Central Intelligence Agency – admitted in a report to the US Congress dated 7 February 2001:

> We do not have any direct evidence that Iraq has used the period since [Operation] Desert Fox to reconstitute its WMD programmes.

Of course, this was prior to 9/11, but the consensus was clear. Iraq had no threatening WMD programme. That view was confirmed by no less a person than the Secretary of State, Colin Powell, in a *Face the Nation* interview on 11 February 2001.

> We have been able to keep weapons from going into Iraq.

The National Security Adviser, Condoleeza Rice, shared his view, telling CNN's *Late Edition* on 29 July 2001:

> We are able to keep arms from him [Saddam]. His military forces have not been rebuilt.

Then came 9/11. Tony Blair was quick to begin to unpick the previous Western position on Saddam and WMD. In an interview with Al-Jazeera on 9 October 2001, he set out his stall:

> The Iraqis want to use that money to transgress the UNSCR on developing weapons of mass destruction. That is our only quarrel with what is happening in Iraq . . . we are prepared to ease that regime provided he is prepared to give proper guarantees he won't develop those weapons of mass destruction.

No weapons of mass destruction equalled no quarrel with Saddam. Tony Blair made no reference to regime change, nor to any humanitarian or human rights issues. This was, of course, the early stages of the process of softening up public opinion. The presentational strategy, providing justification for war, was yet to be worked up between Number 10, the Foreign Office, and the Ministry of Defence.

Jack Straw was to begin his contribution to this process in an appearance before the Foreign Affairs Select Committee on 5 December 2001:

> We are very concerned about Iraq's development of these weapons and believe action must be taken.

Already, the confusion of speculation and fact had become standard practice in presenting the Government's case. Blair was to tell Australia's Channel Nine television on 3 March 2002:

> We know that they are trying to accumulate weapons of mass destruction.

'We know' became a familiar phrase to trip off the Prime Minister's lips; but, in fact, many believed that the farrago of half truths and suppositions underpinning the Government's case were highly questionable.

It was not as if Her Majesty's Loyal Opposition had anything worthwhile to say, showing great loyalty and no opposition. Their chief spokesman on defence, Michael Ancram, told the world on 4 March 2002:

> That this House welcomes the support for action against Iraq given to President Bush by the Prime Minister in interviews to the Australian media during his recent trip to that country; notes his comments that it was known that Iraq was trying to accumulate WMD and that Saddam has used them against his own people; supports his words 'This is not something that just America is talking about. This is something we have got to deal with'; and calls on him to continue to make his support clear.

Meanwhile, the supposedly objective and independent Joint Intelligence Committee began to shift its ground. It presumably had no wish to antagonise its political masters with the whole truth. An assessment of 15 March 2002 was conditional:

> Intelligence on Iraq's weapons of mass destruction and ballistic missile programmes is sporadic and patchy . . . From the evidence available to us, we believe that Iraq retains some production equipment, and some small stocks of CW [chemical weapons] agent precursors, and may have hidden small quantities of agents and weapons . . . There is no intelligence on any BW agent production facilities but one source indicates that Iraq may have developed [biological weapons] mobile production facilities.

The Joint Intelligence Committee 'believed' a proposition; the politicians metamorphosed this into 'no doubt whatsoever'. This certitude was exemplified by Blair in an interview with NBC TV on 4 April 2002:

> We know that he has stockpiles of major amounts of chemical and biological weapons, we know that he is trying to acquire nuclear capability, we know that he is trying to develop ballistic missile capability of a greater range.

We know now that the Prime Minister knew nothing of the sort. Indeed, all of the existing evidence available to him suggested the opposite to the conclusion he chose to draw. Either he misunderstood what he was being told completely (in which case he was unfit intellectually to be Prime Minister) or he cynically chose to disregard compelling evidence.

The whole question of WMD pointed up the hypocrisy of the West on the issue, summed up by the Iraqi Foreign Minister Dr Naji Sabri, in the *Mirror* on 4 April 2002:

> If the measure used by the US of making somebody part of the axis of evil is acquisition of weapons of mass destruction, then

the US is number one in this axis, number two is Israel and number three is Britain.

However, the die was cast. Blair insisted in a press conference with President Bush, on 6 April 2002:

There is a reason why weapons inspectors went in there and that is because we know he has been developing these weapons. We know that those weapons constitute a threat.

Four days later, at Prime Minister's Questions, he repeated his unsubstantiated charge on the development by Saddam of WMD:

The time for military action has not yet arisen. However, there is no doubt at all that the development of WMD by Saddam Hussein poses a severe threat not just to the region, but to the wider world. I draw the House's attention to the fact that, in my first statement to the House a few days after 11 September, I made it clear that the issue of weapons of mass destruction had to be, and should be, dealt with. How we deal with that will be a matter for deliberation and consultation in the normal way. After 11 September, we proceeded in a calm and sensible way, and we shall do so again, but we must confront the issue of weapons of mass destruction.

Again, on *Breakfast with Frost*, on 21 April 2002:

The evidence of Saddam Hussein's weapons of mass destruction is vast.

This was wholly untrue. Just four days later, rebuttal on nuclear WMD – the most obvious and feared kind – came from the prestigious International Atomic Energy Authority:

There were no indications that there remains in Iraq any

physical capability for the production of amounts of weapons-usable nuclear material of any practical significance.

Yet even opponents of the threatened war against Iraq could unwittingly suggest that Iraq might have a WMD capability, if not intent. An early day motion from Malcolm Savidge read:

That this House welcomes the clear statement by the Defence Secretary in the House on 15 July, that British Government policy has not changed since John Major, during the Gulf War, explicitly ruled out the use of British nuclear weapons against Iraq, even in reply to a chemical or biological attack on our forces, on the grounds that a proportionate response could be made using conventional weapons and that Britain would never break the Nuclear Proliferation Treaty.

This implied that Iraqi forces might use tactically the very WMD which the evidence suggested – rightly, as time would tell – did not exist.

Back in Whitehall, the Joint Intelligence Committee was still struggling to give Prime Minister Blair the ammunition which he needed. As the Butler Report was to show, by 21 August 2002, little headway had been made:

We have little intelligence on Iraq's CBW [chemical and biological weapons] doctrine and know little about Iraq's CBW work since late 1998.

Across the pond, Dick Cheney was undaunted. Speaking to the Veterans of Foreign Wars Convention [a sympathetic audience], he could declare:

Simply stated, there is no doubt that Saddam Hussein now has weapons of mass destruction.

Others, happily, were both more measured and responsible. Hans Blix – chief of the weapons inspectors – was careful in setting out his position on the apparently 'missing' weapons from the pre-1991 Iraqi inventory:

> This is not the same as saying there are weapons of mass destruction. If I had solid evidence that Iraq retained WMD or were constructing such weapons I would take it to the Security Council.

Such circumspection did not meet the requirements of President Bush, who addressed the United Nations General Assembly on the 12 September 2002:

> Right now, Iraq is expanding and improving facilities that were used for the production of biological weapons.

Tony Blair went further in the House of Commons when launching his 'dodgy dossier' on Iraq's WMD on 24 September:

> Saddam's weapons of mass destruction programme is active, detailed and growing. The policy of containment is not working. The WMD programme is not shut down. It is up and running . . . The intelligence picture (the intelligence service) paint is one accumulated over the past four years. It is extensive, detailed and authoritative. For the preparation of the dossier we had a real concern not to exaggerate the intelligence that we had received . . . we rate the credibility of what we have very highly. I say no more than that . . . It [the intelligence service] concludes that Iraq has chemical and biological weapons, that Saddam has continued to produce them, that he has existing and active military plans for the use of chemical and biological weapons, which could be activated within 45 minutes, including against his own Shia population and that he is actively trying to acquire nuclear weapons capability.

Blatantly untrue, this was the kernel of the misrepresentation of the true facts which has continued to haunt him, and will be his legacy to future generations of politicians. It was a critical point in a critical debate. It was riddled with falsehoods:

> . . . we know Saddam has been trying to buy significant quantities of uranium from Africa.

This was not the case at all. The British Government knew the alleged documentation evidencing this was forged.

> Iraq has chemical and biological agents and weapons available . . . from pre-Gulf War stocks.

Again, this went against all the evidence, including the scientific evidence concerning the challenging maintenance of notoriously unstable chemical and biological agents for twelve years.

> . . . plants formerly associated with the chemical warfare programme have been rebuilt. These include the chlorine and phenol plant at Fallujah 2 near Habbaniya.

Untrue. All eight of the sites mentioned in Blair's dossier had been visited and cleared by UN inspectors. At Fallujah 2, the inspectors reported that: 'The chlorine plant is currently inoperative.'

> According to intelligence, Iraq has retained up to 20 Al Hussein missiles . . . They could be used with conventional, chemical, or biological warheads and, with a range of up to 650k, are capable of reaching a number of countries in the region including Cyprus, Turkey, Saudi Arabia, Iran and Israel.

None of these were found. So seriously did the British Government take its own propaganda that chemical protection equipment was actually removed from 'threatened' British bases in Cyprus in the following October. And infamously:

> [Saddam Hussein's] military planning allows for some of the WMD to be ready within forty-five minutes of an order to use them.'

This was one of the more obvious 'sexed-up' claims. The alleged source for it was one individual who has never been produced – or even named – to validate the obviously preposterous claim.

Undaunted, Prime Minister Blair told the House of Commons:

> The reason [for the publication of the September dossier] is because his chemical, biological and nuclear weapons programme is not an historic leftover from 1998. His WMD programme is active, detailed and growing . . . The WMD programme is not shut down. It is up and running.

Dr Mohammed El Baradei, head of the IAEA, was to rubbish the charge to the Security Council of the United Nations the following January.

At least President Putin of Russia appeared to see through the fog of propaganda, telling a press conference he shared with an uncomfortable Tony Blair in London, on 11 October 2002:

> Russia does not have in its possession any trustworthy data which would support the existence of nuclear weapons or any weapons of mass destruction in Iraq and we have not received from our partners such information.

Blair kept up the farce into November, telling Parliament:

> Conflict is not inevitable. Disarmament is . . . My message to [Saddam] is this: disarm or you face force.

How could Iraq disarm itself of weapons it did not have? The inspectors were there, and were confirming that fact. Saddam couldn't win, as American spokesman Ari Fleischer made clear in a press briefing on 2 December 2002:

> If he declares he has none, then we will know that Saddam Hussein is once again misleading the world.

Despite Iraq's submission of a 12,000 page declaration to the UN that they had no WMD, the United States and United Kingdom governments rejected the suggestion of no WMD out of hand. Western governments had provided some of the material for WMD to Saddam. I questioned the Foreign Secretary on 10 March 2003:

> Will he [the Foreign Secretary] also confirm, given his comments on anthrax as an alleged biological weapon in Iraq, that the anthrax was provided by the US, as set out in Senator Riegle's report?

Such questions were minor irritants to the British Government. Geoff Hoon, Defence Secretary, repeated the Government case in Parliament on 7 January 2003:

> . . . the key reason for continuing concern about Saddam Hussein and the Iraqi regime is their possession of WMD. It is crucial that they should be disarmed of those weapons.

Two days later, Ari Fleischer repeated this in Washington:

> We know for a fact that there are weapons there.

Although Dr El-Baradei reported otherwise that day to the UN Security Council:

> . . . no evidence of ongoing prohibited nuclear or nuclear-related activities has been detected.

There was no stopping Tony Blair. On 21 January 2003, he told the House of Commons Liaison Committee:

> What we are sure of is chemical and biological weapons. What we believe they are doing is trying to reconstitute their nuclear programme . . .we cannot be sure how far along the

path of the nuclear weapons programme they are. What we believe is that they are trying to reconstitute it. On the chemical and biological side we believe they have still got weapons that they can use. They have also got the missile capability of firing them a significant distance . . . what we believe . . . is that they are being dispersed to different parts of the country.

His belief was no substitute for hard evidence. It was in stark contrast to the measured views of Hans Blix, expressed in his interim report to the United Nations:

In the fields of missiles and biotechnology, the declaration contains a good deal of new material and information covering the period from 1998 and onward. This is welcome.

He was seeking a constructive engagement with the Iraqis, to establish the truth, unlike President Bush who declared on 28 January 2003:

The UN concluded that Saddam Hussein had materials sufficient to produce more than 38,000 litres of botulinum toxin.

In fact the UN inspectors reported:

It seems unlikely that significant undeclared quantities of botulinum toxin could have been produced.

What was the word of mere experts who had actually inspected sites and inventories in Iraq? President Bush could tell the American people in his State of the Union address:

Our intelligence officials estimate that Saddam Hussein had the materials to produce as much as 500 tons of sarin, mustard and VX nerve agent.

Many British backbenchers remained unimpressed by the barrage of propaganda emanating from both Downing Street and the White House. Paul Flynn tabled the following early day motion on 23 January 2003:

> That this House notes that all the sites listed in the United Kingdom dossier on Iraq of 24 September 2002 have subsequently been inspected by UNMOVIC and IAEA inspectors who report that they have not discovered 'any signs of weapons of mass destruction or any programmes for their production'; recalls that some of the sites visited on the day of the publication of the dossier it is claimed that 'Iraq consistently refused to allow UNSCOM inspectors access to any of the presidential sites'; but that the UNSCOM document S/1998/326 reports that 'The initial entry to the eight presidential sites in Iraq was performed by mission UNSCOM 243 during the period from 25th March to 4th April 1998 . . . Cooperation from Iraqi counterparts was satisfactory'; believes that the intelligence provided for the dossier has proved to be unreliable and inaccurate; urges that no future intelligence claims should be accepted until it has been meticulously verified; and notes with alarm the prospect that similar uncorroborated claims could be used as a pretext to send British soldiers into battle to kill and be killed.

This highlighted the ever-decreasing credibility of the Government's case, and its contentious dossier in particular. Blair remained unmoved in his argument. At Prime Minister's Questions on 5 February 2003, he insisted:

> I believe that our case on WMD is very clear indeed. It is perfectly obvious that Saddam has them.

What he believed was neither obvious nor demonstrable. The Anglo-American plot thickened when Colin Powell told the United Nations Security Council on that same day:

By 1998, United Nations experts agreed that the Iraqis had perfected drying techniques for their biological weapons programmes.

This was to be specifically contradicted by the United Nations inspectors in March:

It has no evidence that drying of anthrax or any other agent in bulk was conducted.

Again, Powell told the international body that:

Saddam Hussein . . . has the wherewithal to develop smallpox.

But in March, the United Nations inspectors were to record:

There is no evidence that Iraq had been actively engaged in smallpox research.

Yet again, Powell was to make false accusations about terrorism and WMD in Iraq:

When our coalition ousted the Taliban, the Zarqawi network helped establish another poison and explosive training centre camp, and this camp is located in north eastern Iraq. You see a picture of this camp.

Eventually, when the camp was 'liberated', an embedded ABC journalist who entered the camp with United States forces was to report:

They . . . found nothing.

Finally, Powell was to join Bush and Blair in presenting as fact what Blair and Bush wanted to be the case, although there was no evidence to support the absolute position of Bush and Blair on Saddam's possession of WMD:

> We know that Saddam Hussein is determined to keep his weapons of mass destruction, is determined to make more.

They knew nothing of the sort, and, accordingly, a fascinating alternative scenario was presented by Blair on BBC's *Newsnight*, also on 5 February:

> ... it is absolutely clear what has been happening over the past few months, which is of course, I mean the moment we mentioned those (WMD) in our intelligence reports we were aware of the fact the Iraqis would then have a significant period of time in which to conceal these weapons.

Having his cake and eating it, he answered a question put by a member of the audience on that same programme:

> Question –What are we going to accomplish with this war?

> Blair –Disarmament of Iraq of the weapons of mass destruction.

Bush tolerated no restraints on his imagination, either, telling a radio audience on 8 February:

> We have sources that tell us that Saddam Hussein recently authorised Iraqi field commanders to use chemical weapons – the very weapons the dictator tells us he does not have.

No evidence, no information, pure invention.
As Hans Blix pointed out to the United Nations Security Council on 14 February:

> ... many proscribed weapons and items are not accounted for
> ... One must not jump to the conclusion that they exist.'

Bush and Blair had added one and one together, and got three; added a number of unverified and unverifiable allegations from dissident Iraqis; mixed the result in with their own wish list; and came up with wholly unsustainable positions. Blair ploughed on in the House of Commons on 25 February. He obviously felt he had an audience to frighten into support:

> The intelligence is clear: [Saddam] continues to believe his WMD programme is essential both for internal repression and external aggression . . . The biological agents we believe Iraq can produce include anthrax, botulinum toxin, aflatoxin and ricin. All eventually result in excruciatingly painful death.

After all, he argued:

> I have always said that the purpose of any action has got to be the disarmament of Iraq of WMD.

And opposition spokesman, Michael Ancram, supported him:

> Everything that we are being asked to support is on the basis of the existence of WMD.

Despite this abdication of the responsibility to oppose, the Liberal Democrats did their best. Patsy Calton told the House of Commons:

> I am disgusted – I know that my constituents are too – by the propagandist manoeuvrings to which we as a people and as a Parliament have been subjected. It does not matter how often the Prime Minister, the Secretary of State for Defence and the Foreign Secretary mouth the words 'WMD', 'anthrax', and 'VX': so far, none has been found and no intent to use them has been displayed.

Still the Prime Minister persisted with his untruths. He told the *Independent on Sunday* on 2 March:

The UN inspectors found no trace at all of Saddam's offensive biological weapons programme – which he claimed didn't exist – until his lies were revealed by his son-in-law.

This was a pure invention. The UN inspectors had determined that Iraq had had a biological weapons programme months before Hussein Kamel defected. The UN had secured Iraqi admission to this programme on 1 July 1995. Kamel defected on 7 August 1995.

Blair went on:

> Only then (after Kamel's defection) did the inspectors find over 8,000 litres of concentrated anthrax and other biological weapons, and a factory to make more.

Anthrax has not been found in Iraq to this day. Iraq claimed its stocks – bought, ironically, from the United States – were destroyed in 1991. The fact that the United States – and its British puppets – employed double standards was pointed up by my Parliamentary question on 10 March:

> . . . the forged evidence on uranium purchases that was submitted to the IAEA was provided by the United Kingdom. Will he also confirm, given his comments on anthrax as an alleged biological weapon in Iraq, that the anthrax was provided by the United States, as set out in Senator Riegle's report?

As the truth was being revealed to those who chose to examine the details of the Iraq issue, the conspirators in the plot to attack Iraq were undeterred. In the United States, Dick Cheney told NBC's *Meet the Press*:

> We believe he [Saddam Hussein] has reconstituted nuclear weapons.

On the same day, 16 March, in his Azores summit speech, Blair complemented Cheney's attack on truth:

Still no proper production off evidence of the destruction of, just to take one example, the ten thousand litres of anthrax that the inspectors just a week ago said was unaccounted for.

The following day, Blair's point man, Jack Straw, could assert in Parliament:

We know that this man [Saddam] has got weapons of mass destruction. That sounds like a slightly abstract phrase, but what we are talking about is chemical weapons, biological weapons, viruses, bacilli and anthrax – 10,000 litres of anthrax – that he has. We know that he has it, Dr Blix points that out and he has failed to account for that.

This was categorically untrue, unfounded and inaccurate as was known from the United Nations inspectors' reports. Straw went further:

If we allow these weapons to remain in possession of Saddam Hussein and do nothing about it, we cannot complain when the regime becomes further empowered to act in a tyrannical way with his neighbours and also if such weaponry finds its way into the hands of other rogue states or terrorist groups and then inflicts destruction very much nearer home.

By the 18 March, Parliament was to make a decision on war – a unique situation given the British constitution, and the absence of anything remotely analogous to the United States War Powers Act. Tony Blair was unrepentant:

We are asked now seriously to accept that in the last few years – contrary to all intelligence – Saddam decided unilaterally to destroy those weapons. I say that such a claim is palpably absurd.

He went on:

> This House recognises that Iraq's WMD and long range missiles and its continuing non-compliance with Security Council resolutions, pose a threat to international peace and security.

How does he justify those words now? At the time, he was singing from the same hymn sheet as the White House. Ari Fleischer told the press on 21 March:

> Well, there is no question that we have evidence and information that Iraq has weapons of mass destruction, biological and chemical particularly . . . all this will be made clear in the course of the operation, for whatever duration it takes.

General Tommy Franks made his thoughtful contribution on cue the following day:

> There is no doubt that the regime of Saddam Hussein possesses weapons of mass destruction. And . . . as this operation continues those weapons will be identified, found, along with the people who have produced them and who guard them.

Blair completed the virtuous circle at a press conference on 25 March:

> We have absolutely no doubt at all that those WMD exist.

Continuing:

> Our aim has not been regime change, our aim has been the elimination of weapons of mass destruction.

Weapons inspectors had reported Iraq's 'proactive' co-operation, reporting that Iraq could be declared as fully disarmed within three months if that co-operation continued. Why, therefore, should the inspections programme be terminated?

Donald Rumsfeld, in his usual *gauche* way, told ABC TV on 30 March that:

> We know where they are. They're in the area around Tikrit and
> Baghdad and east, west, south and north somewhat.

Prime Minister Blair also remained adamant on WMD, telling Abu Dhabi TV
on 4 April:

> We have got absolutely no doubt that those weapons exist ...
> I have got no doubt that we will find them.

Reinforcing his message with:

> I have got absolutely no doubt that those weapons are there ...
> once we have the co-operation of the scientists and the experts,
> I have got no doubt that we will find them.

Three days later, Defence Secretary Hoon was still chanting the mantra:

> The destruction of WMD continues to be our priority.

The leading players in Washington and in London stuck to the agreed line,
despite all of the evidence to the contrary. As Blair told a joint press conference with Bush on 8 April:

> On WMD, we know that the regime has them, we know that as
> the regime collapses we will be led to them. We pledge to
> disarm Iraq of WMD and we will keep to that commitment.

It is worthwhile recalling journalist Glen Rangwalla's pithy observation that:

> the only reliable signs of illicit weapons that have been found in
> Iraq are the cluster bombs that were dropped from United
> States and United Kingdom jets.

Increasingly, backbench Members of Parliament were picking out the inconsistencies in the Government's fabricated case for war. Hence, David Chaytor
could table an amendment to an early day motion on 9 April, pointing out the
fallacy of a nuclear armed Iraq:

> . . . but notes Dr El Baradei's 7 March report to the United
> Nations Security Council which concluded that there was 'no
> evidence or plausible indication of the revival of a nuclear
> weapons programme in Iraq'.

In a thoughtful article for *Labour Left Briefing* entitled 'Chasing Phantoms?'
of 9 April, Rangwala again dryly observed:

> Without independent verification from UN inspection teams
> that Iraq did retain prohibited weapons, the US and UK alike
> will be judged as having launched a war on the basis of deceit.
> If this war was for the disarmament of Iraq, as Blair told us,
> then unless prohibited weapons are found and destroyed, it can
> only be judged a failure.

Still, Fleischer pressed on. He had no choice, given the line:

> . . . but make no mistake . . . we have high confidence that they
> have WMD. That is what this was about and it is about. And we
> have high confidence it will be found.

By 14 April, however, hesitancy entered Blair's deliveries on the subject:

> . . . progress [in finding WMD] is found to be slow.

WMD had slipped to third place on the Blair agenda and it did not go
unnoticed. I was just one of those playing hard ball with a mendacious
executive, tabling an early day motion on the 30 April:

> That this House, recognising that the principle justification for

British involvement in the Anglo-American invasion of Iraq was the latter's alleged possession of, and intention to use, weapons of mass destruction, and given that, to date, no evidence of that country's contemporary capability or intent with regard to such weapons has been found, calls upon the Government to publish in full both the evidence it holds, and its sources, for its assertions used in support of pre-emptive war, in order to pre-empt the charge that this House has been misled by those assertions.

As ever, President Bush was perhaps one of the last to get the message, telling reporters on 3 May:

We'll find them. It'll be a matter of time to do so.

Colin Powell followed up with the 'give us time' theme the following day:

I'm absolutely sure that there are weapons of mass destruction there and the evidence will be forthcoming. We're just getting it just now.

By 12 May, Condoleeza Rice opened up a fresh direction on the hackneyed WMD justification:

United States officials never expected that 'we were going to open garages and find' weapons of mass destruction.

Two days later, Jack Straw was changing tack on BBC Radio 4:

I hope there will be further evidence of literal finds . . . It certainly did exist. There is no question about that, and the Blix reported suggested that it still existed. . . . It's not crucially important for this reason (of the need to find WMD) . . . The evidence in respect of Iraq was so strong that the Security Council on the 8th November said unanimously that Iraq's proliferation and possession of the weapons of mass destruction and unlawful missile systems, as well as its defiance of the United Nations, pose – and I quote – 'a threat to international peace and security'.

He could not go unchallenged. As I put it in the *Independent* that same day:

> Jack Straw is trying to reinvent history. All these claims about WMD are built on sand. If they do not find these weapons, it takes away the only conceivable justification for conducting this war . . . It shows the real reasons for this war: the superpower flexing its muscles and looking after resources in this petroleum rich country.

Meanwhile senior figures in the Bush Administration were increasingly at odds. Rumsfeld told the Senate Appropriations sub-committee on Defence on 14 May:

> I don't believe anyone that I know in the administration ever said that Iraq had nuclear weapons.

He was plainly unaware of Cheney's comment to NBC's *Meet the Press* of 16 March 2003:

> We believe he has, in fact, reconstituted nuclear weapons.

One man whose integrity was not in question was Hans Blix. He said on 23 May:

> I am obviously very interested in the question of whether or not there were WMD and I am beginning to suspect there possibly were not.

But many still clung to the WMD argument. Hence, United States General Richard Myers could tell the NBC TV programme *Today* on 26 May that:

> Given time, given the numbers of prisoners that we're now

interrogating, I'm confident that we're going to find weapons of mass destructions.

Within two days, US Deputy Defence Secretary and arch-neoconservative, Paul Wolfowitz, was rowing back:

> For reasons that have a lot to do with the US Government bureaucracy, we settled on the one issue everyone could agree on, which was WMD.

His interview with *Vanity Fair* magazine was critical. It was official confirmation that the WMD argument for war against Iraq was a convenient pretext for the invasion of Iraq, not an unyielding principle.
Blair was still plugging the WMD line two days later. Clearly he was not yet up to speed on the global dimension of political sophistry:

> There is no doubt about the chemical programme, the biological programme, indeed the nuclear weapons programme. All that is well documented with the United Nations.

He could actually plead defensively at a press conference in Poland on 30 May that:

> We have already found two trailers, both of which we believe were used for the production of biological weapons.

This 'evidence' was the misrepresentation of trailers used for producing hydrogen for artillery guidance balloons. Ironically, this equipment had been sold to Iraq by the United Kingdom nearly twenty years earlier.
The truth began to ooze out of occupied Iraq. As US Lt. General James Conway said in a press interview on 30 May:

> It was a surprise to me then – it remains a surprise to me now – that we have not uncovered weapons, as you say, in some of the forward dispersal sites. Believe me, it's not for lack of trying.

We've been to virtually every ammunition supply point between the Kuwaiti border and Baghdad, but they're simply not there.

Blair also went on the back foot, telling journalists:

It [finding WMD] is not the most urgent priority now for us since Saddam has gone. So you are just going to have to have a little patience.

Untrue, and heralding a long period of obfuscation on his previous certainties. Thus, he hoped that a wholly biased Iraq Survey Group would bail him out:

There are literally thousands of sites. As I was told in Iraq, information is coming in the entire time but it is only now that the Iraq Survey Group has been put together that a dedicated team of people, which includes former UN inspectors, scientists and experts, will be able to go in and do the job properly . . . As I have said throughout, I have no doubt that they will find the clearest possible evidence of Saddam's weapons of mass destruction.

A none-too-subtle dig at the United Nations inspectors, but the truth could not be stemmed. Chair of the Pentagon's Defense Review Board, Richard Perle, speaking in Moscow on 22 July, said:

We don't know where to look for them and we never did know where to look for them.

Cheney did a somersault to NBC's *Meet the Press* on 14 September:

Yeah. I did misspeak . . . We never had any evidence that he had acquired a nuclear weapon.

In the British Parliament, other inconsistencies emerged. Alex Salmond could reveal in an early day motion:

That this House notes the published diary extracts of the Right Honourable Member for Livingston, in which he records that the Prime Minister admitted before the start of the conflict in Iraq that he knew that the Iraqi regime did not possess WMD that could be fired within forty five minutes of order; and calls on the Prime Minister to make a statement to the House in order to explain his version of events.

This became a totemic issue for the deliberate distortion of the facts by the Prime Minister, designed to create unwarranted alarm. Not that Tony Blair was fazed by this pressure in any way. He could blithely insist on 16 December 2003 in a radio interview that:

The Iraq Survey Group has already found massive evidence of a huge system of clandestine laboratories, workings by scientists, plans to develop long range ballistic missiles.

Furthermore, he told the BBC's Arabic Service on the same day:

I don't think it's surprising we will have to look for them. I'm confident that when the Iraq Survey Group has done its work we will find what's happened to those weapons because he had them.

This was a consistent and sustained campaign to sell internationally, a false justification for a war on Iraq. As I put it to PeaceUK.net on that same day, speaking after the capture of Saddam Hussein:

I don't think this [the capture of Saddam Hussein] makes a difference for us because the war was about WMD and the threat from them. It might make a difference in America where the war was personalised. They said they would find weapons immediately after the war. I doubt he has in his memory banks the location of all his weapons. But if they have him under lock and key and they can still not find his weapons, it will show that the whole thing was a sham.

The real villains on Iraq and WMD were set out in an early day motion tabled by Austin Mitchell on 16 December 2003:

> That this House notes that the Biological and Toxin Weapons Convention (BTWC) binds signatories not to transfer to any nation any agents, toxins, weapons and equipment of biological and toxin warfare and provides that any nation finding another signatory in breach of this undertaking may lodge a complaint to the Security Council; understands that the Riegle Report to the United States Senate has published evidence that the United States sold biological materials including Bacillus Anthracis, Clostridium Botulinum, Histoplasma Capsulatum, Brucella, Melitensis and Clostridium Perfringens to various agencies of the Iraqi Government pursuant to export licenses issued by the United States Department of Commerce, in quantities set out in the Report and at the time when the United States was fully aware of the Iraqi biological warfare programme and that these exports have been fully documented and are also set out in the 23rd September 2002 edition of Newsweek and by Senator Robert Byrd in speeches to the Senate on 20th and 26th September 2002; requests the Government to exercise its power to report these sales to the Security Council of the United Nations in the light of its commitment in the April 2002 Green Paper 'Strengthening the Biological and Toxin Weapons Convention' that those at every level responsible for any breach of international law relating to the use of such weapons will be held personally accountable because compliance with the BTWC is an issue the international community cannot avoid; and urges the Prime Minister either to lodge the necessary complaint with the Security Council of the United Nations or change his stated policy after an appropriate public announcement and discussion.

The denial of reality by the senior proponents of the Iraq war continues to the present day. Once the Iraq Survey Group had reported no WMD in Iraq, I told the *Mirror* in October 2003:

The Prime Minister and Foreign Secretary are in deep denial of reality.

In January of 2004, Blair was still using scare tactics over WMD, despite the comment of Charles Duelfer of the Iraq Survey Group that:

The prospects of finding existing weapons are just about nil.

Lynne Jones tabled a comprehensive early day motion on 8 January 2004:

That this House expresses concern that according to its most recent quarterly report, the United Nations Monitoring, Verification and Inspection Commission (UNMOVIC), which conducted weapons inspections in Iraq prior to Operation Iraqi Freedom, is not being permitted to verify WMD related claims made by the United States Iraq Survey Group weapons inspectors now operating in Iraq; notes that in October 2003, Mr David Kay testified before the United States Congress that the ISG had not found evidence of Iraqi WMD stockpiles, nor had it found evidence of actual biological weapons production or active chemical and nuclear weapons programmes; further notes that Mr Kay did not testify that the ISG had found dozens of WMD related programme activities and significant amounts of equipment that had been concealed from UNMOVIC inspectors, but that despite these claims UNMOVIC has so far received no information on ISG activities other than Mr Kay's publicly available testimony before Congress; questions the reasons for withholding access to UNMOVIC to the full ICG progress report and the findings, documents, interviews and materials supporting and underlying the report; and calls on the United Kingdom Government to press for this material to be released to UNMOVIC immediately.

Weapons inspector David Kay was moved to admit to the US Armed Services Committee:

> We were almost all wrong . . . it is highly unlikely that there were large stockpiles of deployed militarised chemical and biological weapons there.

This was 28 January 2004. Neither Bush nor Blair could resile from the testimony of a hand-picked investigator. Desperation crept in, as was implied in the early day motion of 24 February, posted by war critic Llew Smith:

> That this House notes that on 11 February this year the US Central Intelligence Agency (CIA) posted on the Iraqi Rewards Programme section of its web site details of rewards that will be available for specific and verifiable information on the location of stacks of recently made chemical and biological weapons munitions, missiles, unmanned aerial vehicles, or their component parts, the location of chemical or biological laboratories and factories, development and production sites, and test sites associated with WMD or sites where these materials were secretly disposed of, weapons systems plans, military orders, or other relevant documents about biological and chemical weapons, missiles, or unmanned aerial vehicles, and Iraqis who are able and willing to provide detailed information on Iraq's WMD programmes and efforts to hide them, recalls how on 5 February 2003 United States Secretary of State, Colin Powell, addressed the United Nations Security Council on Iraq's weapons of mass destruction programme saying his purpose was 'to provide you with additional information to share with you what the United States knows about Iraq's WMD', adding 'indeed, the facts and Iraq's behaviour show that Saddam Hussein and his regime are concealing their efforts to produce more WMD; and believes that the Government should authorise the Secret Intelligence Service (MI6) to back their United States counterparts, the CIA, to support this latest attempt to find the missing Iraqi weapons of mass destruction.

By May Day that year, an anonymous Cheney aide was being quoted in *Vanity Fair*:

> The imminence of the threat from Iraq's WMD was never the real issue . . . WMD were on our minds but they weren't the key thing. What was really driving us was our overall view of terrorism and the strategic conditions of the Middle East.

In short, the Bush Administration was following the blueprint of the Project for a New American Century. WMD was simply a pretext for the war.
Blair was forced into an implicit admission that WMD would not be found. He was careful, however, to canvass every possibility, assuming that they had been in Iraq. On 6 July 2004, he just could not admit to the House of Council Liaison Committee that he had been wrong:

> I have to accept we haven't found them [WMD] and may never find them. We don't know what has happened to them. They could have been removed. They could have been hidden. They could have been destroyed.

Even the Iraq Survey Group had to conclude that there was no evidence of WMD in Iraq. I and others welcomed the conclusions published in their report of 6 October, and called upon the Government to come clean in an early day motion put down on 11 October:

> That this House welcomes the report of the Iraq Survey Group; notes the exhaustive work of the group and its United Nations predecessors; finds its considered view that Saddam Hussein had destroyed his weapons of mass destruction a decade ago to be conclusive, and calls upon the Government to recognise that the United Kingdom was led into war on a false premise.

Two days later, Glenda Jackson, focussed directly on the Prime Minister:

> That this House notes that on 4 June 2003, Official Report, column 161, the Prime Minister stated, in respect of those expressing doubt over his certainty that Iraq possessed WMD, that when a series of allegations are made, all described by the Prime Minister as untrue, that it was important, if people had evidence to justify such allegations, that that evidence be given; further notes that he stated that he had no doubt that the Iraq Survey Group would find the clearest possible evidence of WMD; further notes that the Iraq Survey Group has delivered its final report and has found no WMD; and therefore calls upon the Prime Minister to follow his own prescription and provide the House with the evidence upon which he based his allegations regarding Iraqi WMD.

It was not until 12 January 2005 that the United States Government formally announced that no WMD had been found in Iraq, and that the search for them was over. Tam Dalyell made a final attempt to call the British Government to account for their role in the ISG and WMD fiascos:

> That this House calls on the Government to provide an explanation for the wind-up of the Iraq Survey Group.

What possible answer could Her Majesty's Government give?

Plus ça change

You can no more win a war than you can win an earthquake.
Homer (c.800BC– c.700BC) from *The Iliad*

One of the more vexatious issues which faced the British Government in the run up to the war on Iraq, was the question of 'regime change'. Quite apart from the issue of legality, the small matter of the politics needed to be addressed. Very early on in this saga, the journalist Feargal Keane expressed his own take on the issue in the *Independent* of 29 December 2001:

> I suspect the Americans will launch some form of military action against Iraq . . . The war will be about getting rid of Saddam . . . An attack on Iraq will shatter what remains of the coalition against terror but the US will be willing to live with that . . . Britain will take on the role of getting food to the hungry, rebuilding roads and bridges. If Saddam is toppled, expect Britain to offer help to the inevitable security force deployed afterwards. The problem for Mr Blair could lie with British public opinion if the impression gains hold that we are picking up the pieces for America to deal with the humanitarian consequences of military action.

This was an accurate synopsis of a generally-held view at the time. However, there was an implied trust of Prime Minister Blair and his Government, in their motives and their approach.

The Americans showed no caution – they were typically robust in stating their case. As was Colin Powell when he addressed the Senate Budget Committee on 12 February 2002:

> With respect to Iraq it has long been . . . a policy of the United
> States Government that regime change would be in the best
> interests of the region, the best interests of the Iraqi people . . .
> and we are looking into a variety of options that would bring
> that about.

It took the United Kingdom a little longer to broach what would prove to be a legally contentious issue. Advice from Downing Street to ministers at the beginning of March 2002 implied acceptance of the American objective of regime change:

> . . . the re-integration of a law abiding Iraq, which does not
> possess weapons of mass destruction or threaten its neighbours,
> into the international community. Implicitly, this cannot occur
> with Saddam in power.

It went on:

> In sum, despite considerable difficulties, the use of overriding
> force in a ground campaign is the only option that we can be
> confident will remove Saddam and bring Iraq back into the
> international community.

In a briefing to the Prime Minister, dated 4 March 2002, his foreign policy adviser David Manning reported on a meeting he had had with United States National Security Adviser, Condoleeza Rice:

> I said that you would not budge in your support for regime
> change but that you had to manage a press, a Parliament and a
> public opinion that was very different than that in the States.
> And you would not budge either on your insistence that, if we
> pursued regime change, it must be very carefully done and
> produce the right result. Failure was not an option.

Regime change, of course, is illegal as a war aim in international law. Blair knew this, but was typically more concerned with the presentation of an illegal policy rather than with its probity. As his Attorney General, Lord Goldsmith, was to say on 7 March 2003:

> Regime change cannot be the objective of military action.

This was never far from Blair's mind. It was why he was to stress regime change as a means rather than the end of his policy towards Iraq. Nevertheless, it was pure sophistry to argue other than that he was determined to join Bush in his illegal war.

At least Bush was open in his intentions. As he told ITV's Trevor McDonald on 4 April 2002:

> I made up my mind that Saddam needs to go ... I'm confident
> that we can lead a coalition to pressure Saddam Hussein and to
> deal with Saddam Hussein.

He could not have been clearer. Tony Blair knew this. His dilemma was in unequivocally supporting the American objective without publicly declaring his commitment to illegality. Inevitably, he needed to construct a different case to justify his war. As each unsustainable position on the war collapsed, he was to shift to another justification for British involvement in this primarily American adventure. It was little wonder that politicians, jurists, soldiers, and commentators were to form an unlikely chorus of inquisitors on the Prime Minister's real motives for standing 'shoulder to shoulder' with President Bush:

> I can say that any sensible person looking at the position of
> Saddam Hussein and asking the question – would the region,
> the world, and not least, the ordinary Iraqi people be better off
> without the regime of Saddam Hussein? The only answer
> anyone could give to that question would be yes ... You know
> it has always been our policy that Iraq would be a better place
> without Saddam ... how we now proceed in this situation, how

we make sure that this threat that is posed by WMD is dealt with, that is a matter that is open. And when the time comes for taking those decisions we will tell people about those decisions.

It was a fine line to walk, balancing his commitment to Bush's cause, with the political exigency of assuaging his domestic critics. His 'get out of jail free' card remained the removal of the fabled weapons of mass destruction.
Bush was at least honest on this occasion, even managing some self-deprecating humour:

> Maybe I should be a little less direct and be a little more nuanced and say we support regime change.

He went on to tell his audience that he had left the apparently powerless Blair in no doubt as to American intentions:

> I explained to the Prime Minister that the policy of my Government is the removal of Saddam and that all options are on the table.

The following Wednesday, at Prime Minister's Questions in the House of Commons, Blair was asked whether he could confirm that getting rid of Saddam Hussein may now be an objective of the Government. His answer was classically evasive, and opened the way for the responsibility (and the blame?) to be passed to the House of Commons. After all, the Prime Minister knew that there was a huge amount of agitprop to be employed, to win over Parliament and public to his tarnished cause:

> There is no doubt at all that the world, and the region, would be a better place without Saddam Hussein . . . However, the method of achieving that is . . . open to consultation and deliberation. When the judgements are made, I have no doubt at all that this House – indeed, the whole country – will want to debate the issue thoroughly.

His concern was in finding a formula enabling him to subscribe to regime change without alienating support. WMD remained, in his view, the key. The Liberal Democrat spokesman Menzies Campbell put the question directly to Jack Straw on 16 April 2002:

> . . . can the foreign Secretary confirm that, unlike others, it is not the policy of HM Government to seek to replace Saddam Hussein through the use of military action.

A simple 'yes' or 'no' would have sufficed; but evasion was the order of the day.
Campbell persisted:

> As neither the charter of the UN, nor indeed any other principle of international law, nor even the ceasefire resolutions which affect Iraq, authorise regime change, can the Foreign Secretary confirm that, unlike others, it is not the policy of Her Majesty's Government to seek to replace Saddam Hussein through the use of military action?

Still, there was no definitive reply. The writing was on the wall for all to see. What was truly amazing was just how many Parliamentarians refused to see what was being done in their name. What was even more alarming was the number of Members of Parliament who knew fully what lay ahead but who chose, presumably for careerist reasons, to support the Blairist line. The Prime Minister himself was always careful to leave his options open. Thus, speaking to BBC TV's *Newsnight* on 15 May:

> I certainly believe that getting rid of Saddam would be highly desirable. It's always been the American policy to get rid of Saddam Hussein. That isn't to say they're about to launch military action.

There remained little doubt, however, as to what he really believed, as he continued:

'I certainly endorse the [US] policy of doing everything we can to get rid of Saddam Hussein if at all possible.

Later that year, he was piously to turn truth on its head, arrogating for himself the role of spokesman and servant of the international community, on BBC World Service on 9 October:

... the international community's will has been expressed in relation to the disarmament of that regime rather than regime change itself ... our purpose in the action that we are taking is to make sure that the will of the international community and the United Nations is upheld.

The Tories, bereft of any ethical or innovative thinking, echoed the Prime Minister's lead. Their spokesman Bernard Jenkin intoned in Parliament on 17 October 2002:

Of course, the long term objective in Iraq is disarmament. If that means regime change, our objective must be to create a stable and safe Iraq ... The Prime Minister himself said that he heartily desired regime change.

Thankfully, there remained consistent and targeted opposition. As Neil Gerrard put it in a debate on 25 November:

We all know that [Saddam] is an evil dictator, but he was an evil dictator when Donald Rumsfeld was shaking his hand and when this country was supplying him with arms. Anyway, we are told that this is not about regime change.

He knew that it was about regime change, as did I, speaking in the House of Commons on 18 December:

Recalling AJP Taylor's theory on mobilisation, is not there a certain inevitability about military action given the Americans' stated intention of regime change in Iraq?

I knew, too, that the decision had long been taken to effect regime change by force of arms. I was to remind others later (in the *Guardian* on 15 October 2003) that the whole objective of the war was regime change, not WMD:

> The arrest [of Saddam Hussein] puts the focus back on regime change, which was not the reason we went to war. We went to war over the supposed threat from weapons of mass destruction.

Long before this, Harry Cohen had illustrated the paradoxical nature of the Government's case, when he said in the House of Commons on 7 January 2003:

> Was he [the Lord Chancellor] correct in saying that war could be averted either by Iraq disarming or, separately, Saddam Hussein standing down? In the latter instance, why would WMD not be a factor that warrants war? Why and when did regime change become a purpose of the Government's war preparations?'

John le Carré, himself a master of fiction, found himself moved to write to *The Times* on 15 January 2003:

> I'm dead against Bush, but I would love to see Saddam's downfall – just not on Bush's terms and not by his methods - and not under the banner of such outrageous hypocrisy. The religious cant that will send American troops into battle is perhaps the most sickening aspect of this surreal war-to-be.

Blair was unmoved before the House of Commons Liaison Committee of 21 January 2003:

> Obviously, the region, Iraq, will be a better place without Saddam.

It might have read 'would' instead of 'will', but the issue was cut and dried for the Prime Minister – a telling slip in his usual conditional language. He went on:

> I think what is important is if we do end up having to change
> the regime in Iraq as the only way of disarming Iraq of WMD,
> it is important we then cooperate and help the Iraqi people in
> the long term . . . You do not engage in military conflict that
> may produce regime change unless you are prepared to follow
> through and work in the aftermath of that regime change to
> ensure the country is stable and the people are properly looked
> after . . . if we come to changing the regime, if we come to
> removing Saddam as the only way of dealing with the issue of
> WMD, then I think it is extremely important that we make the
> most detailed preparations and work within the international
> community as to what happens afterwards.

This personalisation of a broader problem, identifying it solely with the then leader (reprehensible although his reign was) seems weak ground on which to base a war. As the aftermath of the invasion has shown, neither Bush nor Blair thought through the implications of their onslaught on Iraq.

The very next day, Defence Secretary Hoon was also to emphasise, in a circumlocutory fashion, the issue of regime change:

> My Right Honourable Friend [Straw] said specifically that one of
> those objectives [of our policy on Iraq] was to restore a represen-
> tative Government in Iraq, which I consider a proper policy
> objective.

Blair kept up the propaganda message on *Newsnight* on 5 February:

> Look, let's leave aside what's been happening in the last few
> months and all the debate about whether we have a war in Iraq
> or not. I mean, you wouldn't dispute with me that this is a
> barbaric and appalling regime.

That was true; but so were many regimes, some of them our friends and allies. The choice now facing the American and British leaders involved saving face, as Tony Wright explained to the House of Commons, on 26 February:

> Is it not the case . . . that if the UN process was to work, the
> crisis was to be resolved and Saddam was to be disarmed...it
> would be a humiliation and failure for the American President,
> because it would subvert the whole strategy of regime change
> that has been put in place? Is not that why, whatever we say or
> do today, there is going to be war?

In that same debate, Andrew Robathan gave the Government a chance to come clean:

> Is it not a fact that our objective is, and has to be, regime change
> in Iraq?

Needless to say, the Government could not be frank, unlike President Bush, speaking on the same day to the American Enterprise Institute:

> . . . we will ensure that one brutal dictator is not replaced by
> another.

In the great debate in the British Parliament, held on 18 March, Prime Minister Blair remained defensive:

> I have never put the justification for action as regime change.

This was true – he had studiously avoided doing so. Yet all of his actions and statements suggested inevitably that regime change was his objective. It merely remained unstated. That is, until the very next day, in Prime Minister's Questions:

> It is the case that if the only means of achieving the disarma-
> ment of Iraq of WMD is the removal of the regime, then the
> removal of the regime of course has to be our objective.

Even here, it was qualified. He became bolder by 20 March. In his declaration of war, regime change became the prime objective, no longer the removal of

WMD, now a secondary objective:

> Their [the British troops'] mission: to remove Saddam Hussein
> from power, and disarm Iraq of its weapons of mass destruction.

By 25 March, Blair was telling journalists that regime change was a precondition for rooting out Saddam's stockpile of WMD:

> I have always said to people that our aim has not been regime
> change, our aim has been the elimination of WMD. The idea
> that we can suddenly discover this stuff is a lot more difficult in
> a country the size of Iraq, but of course once the regime is out
> then there will be all sorts of people willing to give us the infor-
> mation that we seek.

This was not to be, because there were no WMD. We had gone to war on a false premise, for which no one has, to the time of writing, been held to account. Despite the loss of up to 650,000 Iraqi lives (according to the *Lancet*), there has never been any admission of fault by either Tony Blair personally, or his Government.

Blair persisted in saying what Bush wanted to hear. Their joint press conferences were exercises in delusion. On 27 March, Blair could say:

> Saddam Hussein and his hateful regime will be removed from
> power. Iraq will be disarmed of weapons of mass destruction
> and the Iraqi people will be free . . . though of course our aim
> is to rid Iraq of weapons of mass destruction and make our
> world more secure, the justice of our cause lies in the liberation
> of the Iraqi people.

The only correct item in this wish list is that the regime has been changed. Blair patronised the Arab press with an article on 30 March 2003:

> This is not a war of conquest but of liberation.

That would not resonate with the families of the dead. Nevertheless, hints of Blair's triumphalism began to appear, lauding regime change, on Abu Dhabi TV on 4 April:

> . . . it is the regime that has got to go.

There were also significant if small shifts in the arguments put by Blair to justify the war. As he told the BBC World Service on 4 April:

> It is a war against Saddam because of the weapons of mass destruction that he has, and it is a war against Saddam because of what he has done to the Iraqi people.

As time has revealed, the Iraqi people have been increasingly worse off under the occupation. Still, Blair had the confidence to tell them on 8 April:

> This is a campaign against Saddam's regime.

The sub-text was: 'We are not against you, the ordinary people. We are about changing your leadership – that is, regime change.' As he continued at that press conference with President Bush:

> The power of Saddam is ending and our enemy in this conflict has always been Saddam and his regime.

By 14 April, he was telling the House of Commons:

> . . . the regime of Saddam is gone, the bulk of Iraq is under coalition control and the vast majority of Iraqis are rejoicing at Saddam's departure . . . We took the decision that to leave Iraq in its brutalised state under Saddam was wrong.

This is effectively a *post facto* recognition of regime change as the war aim, a position to be echoed repeatedly by Government spokesmen. Hence, on 14 May, Jack Straw could tell BBC Radio 4:

> You see these pictures in newspapers about the discovery of 15,000 or so mass graves . . . Anybody who had any doubt about the rightness of our actions should just draw their own attention to the venality of the Saddam regime, which thankfully has now been removed.

It was difficult to keep up with the Government's change of direction. The justification for the war was no longer WMD, but regime change – illegal although it would have been. There was a temptation to believe that the inner cabal of the Blair Government was making it up as they went along. Either way, their credibility was evaporating in the face of fierce and widespread scrutiny.

Some of this obviously got to the Prime Minister. He responded at a press conference in Poland on 30 May:

> I have just caught up overnight with some of the allegations that have been made . . . what is happening here is that people who have opposed this action throughout are now trying to find a fresh reason for saying why it wasn't the right thing to do . . . There is no doubt about the chemical programme, the biological programme, indeed the nuclear weapons programme. All that is well documented by the United Nations. Now, our priority, having got rid of Saddam, is to rebuild the country . . . The threat from WMD, obviously with Saddam out, is not immediate any more. It [the WMD investigation process] is not the most urgent priority now for us since Saddam has gone.

He had tried to haul it back from regime change. The only problem was that no evidence was to be found of WMD. Nevertheless, by the end of 2003, Tony Blair was feeling almost cocky. As he told the *News of the World* on 16 November:

> But for this military action, Saddam Hussein and his sons would still be in absolute control . . . free to continue the repression and butchery of their people.

Once more, Blair mixed fact and speculation. He was to be further boosted with the December capture of Saddam. Yet his critics persisted. By 5 March 2004, he had shifted yet again, telling his Sedgefield constituency:

> I accept ... that ... regime change alone could not be and was not our justification for war. Our primary purpose was to enforce UN resolutions over Iraq and WMD.

We were back to WMD – and acting as the United Nation's policeman! Later that year, he was to come as close as he has to apologising for taking the United Kingdom to war on a false prospectus. Addressing the Labour Party Conference, he declared:

> The evidence about Saddam having actual biological and chemical weapons, as opposed to the capability to develop them, has turned out to be wrong. I acknowledge that and accept it. I simply point out, such evidence was agreed by the whole international community, not least because Saddam had used such weapons against his own people and neighbouring countries. And the problem is, I can apologise for the information that turned out to be wrong, but I can't sincerely at least, apologise for removing Saddam ... The world is a better place with Saddam in prison not in power.

He is arguing that the 'end' – removing Saddam – justified the 'means' – the war. However, that was never the case he put before Parliament and people. He still fails to see that one cannot retrospectively change the justification for going to war. Until he declares his true motives for his course of action, we can only speculate as to what his intentions were. We do know that what he said and what was the case, were entirely different.

Llew Smith picked up on the meandering reasoning of the Prime Minister in an early day motion table 11 January 2005:

> That this House notes that on Breakfast with Frost, broadcast on 9 January, the Prime Minister described the invasion of Iraq

in 2003 as 'that war to remove Saddam Hussein'; recalls a memo dated 14 March 2002, and published in full in the Daily Telegraph on 18 September 2004, written by the Prime Minister's then personal foreign policy advisor, Sir David Manning, who recorded that Mr Blair privately supported a policy of regime change in Iraq; contrasts this with what the Prime Minister told this House on 24 September 2002 ([Official Report, column 17], namely that 'regime change in Iraq would be a wonderful thing. That is not the purpose of our action; our purpose is to disarm Iraq of WMD'; and thus believes the Prime Minister should make a further statement to the House to clarify why he supported and helped orchestrate the invasion of Iraq.

We still await that further statement. Was it even the case that regime change had the fabulous benefits claimed for it anyway? Not according to an Iraqi shopkeeper – Mohammed Kubaissy – interviewed on 4 January 2005 on Independent Radio News:

I am still searching for what they have been calling democracy.

A just war

> *Quite often, as life goes on, when we feel completely secure as we go on our way, we suddenly notice that we are trapped in error, that we have allowed ourselves to be taken in by individuals, by objects, have dreamt up an affinity with them which immediately vanishes before our waking eyes: and yet we cannot tear ourselves away, held fast by some power that seems incomprehensible to us. Sometimes, however, we become fully aware and realise that error as well as truth can move and spur us on to action.*
>
> Goethe (1749–1832)

For many people, the question of a legal war is, at best, an arcane question best left to lawyers and philosophers; at worst, it is a total irrelevance. The Prime Minister, himself a lawyer and ever conscious of the judgement of history, initially took a proper view, conceding the need for legal authority behind any military action against Saddam. As early as 17 December 1998, he could tell the House of Commons:

> Whatever the risks we face today, they are as nothing compared to the risks if we do not halt Saddam Hussein's programme of developing chemical and biological weapons of mass destruction . . . Even if there were legal authority to do so, removing Saddam through military action would require the insertion of ground troops on a massive scale . . . Even then, there would be no absolute guarantee of success. I cannot make that commitment responsibly.

Once the tragedy of 9/11 unfolded, it became even more necessary to remember the legal, as I reminded the *Guardian* readership on 23 September 2001:

> These atrocities [9/11 and terrorism generally] have to be dealt with on the basis of evidence and the rule of law.

Tony Blair apparently agreed, telling the House on 4 October of that year:

> In respect of Iraq it is important that we act on the basis of evidence.

The ever-faithful Jack Straw expanded upon the legalistic argument that same day:

> The basis for international law of the whole world is the United Nations Charter.

But experienced Parliamentary hands already had their doubts. Former Foreign Office Minister Tony Lloyd, conscious of Blair's propensity to act first and think later, questioned the Government:

> Will my Right Honourable Friend confirm that under international law and the aegis of the United Nations, action has to be, in the Prime Minister's words, proportionate, and that we cannot sanction action going beyond what is legitimate and proportionate.

In the same debate, Liberal Democrat Paul Keetch went further, already conscious of Blair's eagerness to comply with any American request:

> The aim of any action must be clearly stated and the scale of the operations must be directed towards achieving that aim. In short, such action must be targeted, based on sound intelligence and fall within the boundaries of international law . . . One

does not start a military campaign by saying to a close ally – however close that ally may be – that one will do whatever it wants.

By March 2002, the Whitehall machine was fully cranked up, producing advice and papers. On 8 March, the *Iraq: Options Paper* was circulated. Produced by the Defence and Overseas Secretariat of the Cabinet Office, the doubts were there for ministers to see:

> . . . our intelligence is poor . . ..there is no greater threat now than in recent years that Saddam will use weapons of mass destruction . . . The United States administration has lost faith in containment and is now considering regime change . . . A legal justification would be needed. Subject to Law Officers' advice, none currently exists . . . In the judgement of the Joint Intelligence Committee there is no recent evidence of Iraq complicity with international terrorism . . . [the United Nations Security Council] would need to be convinced that Iraq was in breach of its obligations regarding WMD, and ballistic missiles. Such proof would need to be incontrovertible and of large-scale activity. Current intelligence is insufficiently robust to meet this criterion . . . If an invasion is contemplated this autumn, then a decision will need to be taken in principle six months in advance.

Blair was to turn these 'doubts' into 'challenges' to be overcome in his quest for war. The suggestion is that, despite his repeated denials, his mind was already made up. What he needed was time to fit up the case for war. He had, after all, not only to overcome the internal objections of the Cabinet Office, but also those of the Foreign and Commonwealth Office. Their annex to the *Options Paper* – 'Iraq: Legal Background' – agreed that to construct a legal case for such a war was highly problematic, if not impossible.

The ever flexible Jack Straw could report to the Commons on 12 March 2002, that:

I strongly accept that we do not take military action without clear and compelling evidence . . . and take it only wherein it is clear that it is, as it were, a last resort.

Because, in his view (of course, that of another lawyer):

. . . what lies at the heart of this issue is the rule of international law.

Right up to the great debate the following year, Tony Blair appeared to agree, telling the Commons on 18 March:

I have never put our justification for action as regime change. We have to act within the terms of Resolution 1441. That is our legal base.

That was consistent with what he had told the House during Prime Minister's Questions on 17 April 2002:

. . . .we will proceed carefully and deliberately, not precipitately, and . . . we will ensure that the House is properly consulted . . . we will make sure that whatever we do – as I say constantly, no decisions have yet been taken – should be in accordance with international law.

Legal experts were, however, expressing their own doubts. Hence, Professor Colin Warbrick, quoted in a Parliamentary debate on 30 October 2002, could argue:

I am particularly sceptical of claims that the failure of diplomacy justifies resort to force 'as a last resort'.

Rabinder Singh QC set out an opinion, commissioned by CND, on 15 November:

> The use of force against Iraq would not be justified unless (a)
> Iraq mounted a direct attack on the United Kingdom or one of
> its allies and that ally requested the United Kingdom's assis-
> tance or (b) an attack by Iraq on the United Kingdom or one of
> its allies was imminent and could be diverted in no other way
> than by the use of force or (c) the United Nations Security
> Council authorised the use of force in clear terms . . . United
> Nations Security Council resolution does not authorise the use
> of force by member states of the United Nations . . . the United
> Kingdom would be in breach of international law if it were to
> use force against Iraq on reliance on resolution 1441 without a
> further security council resolution.

The legal storm was gathering force. One might have thought that lawyers
like Blair, Straw and Hoon would have taken notice of their expert professional peers.

Lynne Jones tried to pin down the terms under which a legal war might be
waged on Iraq, in the debate on the United Nations Security Council resolution, held in the House of Commons on 25 November 2002:

> The only grounds on which an individual member state could
> take military action against Iraq would be under the right to self
> defence or in taking humanitarian action. I cannot see that such
> a situation applies to this country.

Jack Straw chose his response carefully:

> If force becomes necessary, any decisions made by Her
> Majesty's Government will be careful, proportionate and
> consistent with our obligations in international law.

Even supportive clergymen expressed concern. On the BBC's *The Case
Against War*, on 8 December, Bishop Harris retreated from his hitherto loyal
support:

I've supported every war this country has been engaged in over the last twenty years, but on the evidence at present available to us, I can't support a military action against Iraq . . . because I simply don't think the traditional 'just war' criteria have been met . . . In order for a war to count as just, there must be just cause, and it would be a just cause if the threat posed by Saddam Hussein was immediate and serious, but the threat is not immediate and serious. He is a long term worry, but the policy of containment and deterrence has worked for the last ten years . . . Nothing new has come on the scene to force us to cross this terrible threshold of a war.

Critically, the armed forces expressed concern. The Chief of Defence Staff, James Boyce, was to insist on further legal advice before committing forces to the war. Perhaps the former commander of the 7th Armoured Brigade during the first Gulf war – Major General Patrick Cordingley – had it spot on in the same programme as Bishop Harris:

At the moment I don't believe the case has been made for another war . . . My reservations are all to do with the numbers of Iraqis that might be killed, you could argue, unnecessarily.

Ultimately, of course, the Government had its way, and war was declared. The legal issue, however, has never died. On 6 December 2003, with no WMD in sight, I sought the legal justification for the war through the columns of the *Mirror*:

If Saddam did not have WMD and our leaders knew, why did we go to war?

This was not an academic question, given the repeated assurances from ministers that they were acting within the law. For example, on 7 January 2003 Geoff Hoon told the House:

This issue is not simply whether there is a moral basis for war, but whether there is a legal basis for it. The Government have consistently made it clear that we will take decisions based on the appropriate international legal position.

Even that was insufficient for Tony Lloyd:

I am intrigued by my Right Honourable Friend's view that there is a need only for a legal basis for action, not a moral basis.

Another lawyer, Elfyn Llwyd put his point to the Prime Minister on 15 November 2003:

The Prime Minister often says that he likes to do things because they are right. How could it possibly be right to risk the lives of young British service men and women on a venture in Iraq that does not have the backing of international law, or the support of the majority of British people?

There was no direct response to his question. Even the relatively docile Liaison Committee woke up to the radical nature of what was being proposed. On 21 January 2004, Graham Allen asked:

Does the United Kingdom have a policy now of supporting pre-emptive military action against states that pose a potential future threat?

The Prime Minister replied 'No.'
Allen continued:

They [public and politicians] feel the current strategy somehow falls outside the criteria of a just war . . . a suggestion that one takes military action against a fairly vague threat is not seen as justified whereas military action against a very clear and present danger is justified.

The Prime Minister responded:

> It is a judgement obviously as to whether Iraq constitutes a threat . . . people recognise that Iraq, if it were out to rebuild these weapons, would constitute a threat.

He further ventured:

> I do think it is very important that the United States is engaged with the international community and obviously it should act in accordance with international law, as we all should.

Significantly, the question he had been asked was:

> Since that superpower [the United States] has espoused the policy of regime change, of first strike and not allowing any other power to challenge its supremacy, is it not important for the long term that the Americans show as early as possible an absolute commitment to international law?

He did not dispute the assertions within the question. Perhaps he just no longer cared. It certainly seemed to be the case given the increasing Parliamentary and public concern. Bill Tynan, perhaps naively, put the question to Jack Straw:

> Does he [Straw] not accept that the majority of the people of this country do not accept, and are not convinced at this time, that there is a justification to declare war on Iraq?

The following day, the hapless Hoon was to make a bizarre case for pre-emption as self-defence:

> . . . it has always seemed to me . . . that pre-emption is simply a form of self-defence, and that is the basis on which it could be and would be justifiable in international law.

It was left to the redoubtable Alice Mahon to sum up the situation in a Parliamentary debate on 22 January 2004:

> Resolution 1441 is not a resolution for war. It does not authorise military action and the Government know that it does not. It does not contain the automatic trigger that the United States wanted: it simply requires that the SC must meet if a breach is thought to have taken place. From the moment that resolution 1441 was passed, both the United States and our Government have sought to interpret it as a vote to make war possible, and not a vote for peace. It has not brought the United States back under the umbrella of international law, as many hoped it would, and the central issue remains will the British Government defend international law, and by that I mean the charter – not a resolution that has been arrived at by arm twisting, by bribing, by intimidation – which says that when we are not being threatened we should not pre-emptively attack? Or will that fall as a result of United States muscle? Throughout all this, the Government have refused to recognise the dangers inherent in allowing an unchecked United States superpower to set the international agenda . . . The Government knows that they are prepared to take Britain into a war with Iraq if, or should I say when, President Bush decides to go, and they are prepared to do so regardless of the United Nations. I believe that when the Prime Minister visited the ranch in Texas he promised that he would give support. A deception has been carried on for months.

Falklands War hero Simon Weston spoke for many when he was interviewed by the *Mirror* on that same day. He could see what our political leaders could – or would – not see:

> Saddam may well have these weapons but where's the proof? Where's the evidence? At the moment Blair hasn't given us any, just trite statements asking us to believe him . . . . There is no

heart for this one. There is no belief . . . .If we do go in, we have
to have unequivocal proof sanctioned by the United Nations for
doing so. Get this wrong and we'll just create yet another generation of hatred . . . If the United States, Britain and their allies
do not remove him with lawful world authority . . . we'd be no
better than Saddam when he invaded Kuwait. We'd be invading
a sovereign state, no matter how much we dislike it. We need a
world licence to do this.

A million demonstrators could not move Blair, nor could commentators like
Malcolm Harrison in a piece published online in 1 February 2003:

Blair has moved the goal posts – from 'a war against terrorism' to
'Saddam Hussein's connection with Al Qaeda' to 'the removal of
weapons of mass destruction [that seem impossible to find] and
then to 'a moral duty to remove a brutal despot [there is ample
proof that Saddam was a brutal despot a decade ago]' . . . If all
those reasons were mutable and therefore not the real reason for a
historically significant pre-emptive strike on Iraq, then what is the
real reason? This invasion has every sign of being one with a very
powerful hidden agenda, and the propaganda is just a smoke
screen to make us equally culpable in the murder of innocents.

He accurately pointed to the illegality and immorality of the war:

The need to reduce terrorism is not a justifiable reason for the
US to sweep away all moral constraints and make a pre-emptive
strike on Iraq. It gives licence to any nation to take out its
neighbour if it imagines it to be a threat . . . [it is] an immoral
war dressed up as a crusade.'

Blair remained slippery on *Newsnight* on 5 February:

Paxman – Do you consider this a just war do you?
Blair – I wouldn't go to war if I didn't consider it right.

Some political lawyers saw the need for more specific justification than Tony Blair's convictions or hunches. Thus, Douglas Hogg put down an early day motion on 11 February:

> That this House does not believe that British forces should be required to participate in a war against Iraq unless all of the following conditions are met (a) that there is clear evidence that Iraq poses an imminent threat to peace (b) that there is a substantive motion of this House authorising military action (c) that there is an express resolution of the Security Council of the United Nations authorising the use of military force against Iraq and (d) that all other policy options have been exhausted.

The following day, Liberal Democrat Leader Charles Kennedy reminded the Prime Minister that his case had not convinced the jury of public opinion:

> . . . every measure of public opinion shows that people are not persuaded of the case for the course of action being followed.

Blair did now accept – at least publicly – that there was a moral dimension to the issue:

> When we look at the issue and the moral background to the decisions that have to be taken, I agree that, before we take the decision to go to war, the morality of that should weigh heavily on our conscience.

However, his sincerity on this has to be questioned. It is often thought Mr Blair has the ability to hold contemporaneously that two contradictory propositions are true.

The pressure continued. Michael Moore told the House on 26 February:

> International law is clear that war can only ever be justified as a last resort. In upholding it, we must show conclusively that that is so and that we will go to war only if all other diplomatic

and political options have been exhausted. That is far from being the case at this point.

The formidable Ken Clarke was unequivocal in the same debate:

> The resolution turns on the question whether a material breach has occurred. Although other concerns cannot be brushed aside, the revolting nature of the Iraqi regime and its cruelty, much though we deplore it, is not a legal basis for war. We must concentrate on whether there are WMD, whether disarmament can be induced and, if not, whether force will be used to effect it.

Equally resolute was the *Guardian* editorial of that day:

> To go to war now would be to act without the freely given consent of the vast majority of nations: without the support of key allies: without a legally unambiguous mandate: without just cause and against the wishes of the people of the west and the Muslim world.

An unbending Tony Blair told the Commons on 5 March:

> . . . we will always act in accordance with international law.

Lynne Jones clearly took a sceptical view of the Prime Minister's undertakings, tabling an EDM that same day:

> That this House notes that the United Nations Charter allows for military forces to be used only as an exception and in two sets of circumstances, in self defence or as expressly authorised by the Security Council under Chapter VII; further notes that, in previous crises, the United Nations has always used the term 'all necessary means' when authorising military action and this phrase is absent from Resolution 1441 and the Draft Resolution proposed by the United States, the United

Kingdom and Spain; further notes that on 5 March, the Prime Minister did not answer the question put to him by the Honourable Member for Birmingham Selly Oak as to whether nine affirmative votes for the Draft Resolution in the Security Council would give clear legal authority for war against Iraq; further notes the current legal opinion by Rabinder Singh QC and Charlotte Kilroy of Matrix Chambers, that neither Resolution 1441 nor the Draft Resolution individually or together, provide authorisation for Member States to use force against Iraq and that, as a consequence, the United Kingdom would be acting in violation of international law if it were to join in any attack on Iraq in reliance on either or both of these resolutions; likewise is concerned that the escalation of the bombings by the United States and the United Kingdom in the no-fly zones does not obey United Nations rules on the use of military force, and therefore calls on the Government to amend its policy on Iraq in line with the United Nations Charter and international law.

Government law officer Peter Goldsmith was obviously uneasy. His opinion of 7 March was clear:

I remain of the opinion that the safest legal course would be to secure the adoption of a further resolution to authorise the use of force . . . I must stress that the lawfulness of military action depends not only on the existence of a legal basis, but also on the question of proportionality . . . regime change cannot be the objective of military action.

Blair was to quixotically interpret this very differently, as he commented more than two years later, on the 25 April 2005:

It's not a question of changing his mind. The legal advice of the Attorney General was very clear.

Goldsmith had changed his mind: but Blair was right to say his advice was clear – and clearly ignored. Charles Kennedy had put this to the Prime Minister at Prime Minister's Questions on 12 March 2003:

> Kennedy – Has the Attorney General advised the Prime Minister that a war on Iraq in the absence of a second United Nations resolution authorising force would be legal?

> Prime Minister – . . . we as a country would not do anything that did not have a proper legal basis to it

> Kennedy – United Nations Secretary General Kofi Annan has said that in the absence of a second United Nations resolution we would be acting in a way that breached the UN Charter.

We were to discover that Goldsmith had been pressured by both Downing Street and the Americans, before changing his mind. Naturally, Blair rejected Kofi Annan's allegations of illegality. He insisted:

> As the Foreign Secretary has pointed out, resolution 1441 gives the legal basis for this war.

By 17 March Goldsmith accepted the line peddled by Number 10:

> The United Nations decided in Resolution 1441 that, if Iraq failed at any time to comply with and cooperate fully with the implementation of Resolution 1441, that would constitute a further material breach. It is plain that Iraq has failed so to comply and therefore Iraq was at the time of Resolution 1441 and continues to be in material breach.

His private advice ten days earlier had been rather different, as a leaked memo illustrated:

The language of Resolution 1441 leaves the position unclear, and the statements made on adoption of the resolution suggest that there were differences of view within the Council as to the legal effect of the resolution.

The official, published advice also counselled that:

Resolution 1441 would in terms have provided that a further decision of the Security Council to sanction force was required – if that had been intended . . . Thus, all that Resolution 1441 requires is reporting to and discussion by the Security Council of Iraq's failures, but not an express further decision to authorise force.

The private advice had warned:

The argument that Resolution 1441 alone has revived the authorisation to use force in Resolution 678 will only be sustainable if there are strong factual grounds for concluding that Iraq failed to take the final opportunity . . . In other words, we would need to be able to demonstrate hard evidence of non-compliance and non-cooperation.

Finally, from the official advice:

The Security Council in Resolution 1441 gave Iraq 'a final opportunity to comply with its disarmament allegations' and warned Iraq of the 'serious consequences' if it did not . . . It is plain that Iraq has failed to comply and therefore Iraq was at the time of Resolution 1441 and continues to be in material breach.

The private advice had said:

In the light of the latest reporting by UNMOVIC, you will need to consider very carefully whether the evidence of non cooperation and non compliance by Iraq is sufficiently compelling to justify the conclusion that Iraq has failed to take its final opportunity.

Robin Cook put the enormity of what was being done into his resignation speech to Parliament:

> ... at no time have we signed up even the minimum necessary to carry a second resolution ... Our interests are best protected not by unilateral action but by multilateral agreement and a world order governed by rules . . . Our difficulty in getting support this time is that neither the international community nor the British public is persuaded that there is an urgent and compelling reason for this military action in Iraq.

The Deputy Legal Adviser to the Foreign and Commonwealth Office – Elizabeth Wilmhurst, a loyal and expert civil servant and legal counsel – felt moved to resign on 18 March:

> I regret that I cannot agree that it is legal to use force against Iraq without a second Security Council resolution to revive the authorisation given in SCR 678 . . . My views accord with the advice that has been given consistently in this office before and after the adoption of United Nations Security Council Resolution 1441 and with what the Attorney General gave us to understand was his view prior to his letter of 7 March . . . I cannot in conscience go along with the advice . . . which asserts the legitimacy of military action without such a resolution, particularly since an unlawful use of force on such a scale amounts to the crime of aggression, nor can I agree with such action in circumstances which are so detrimental to the international order and the rule of law.

The choice facing Parliament was stark and I set it out when I moved an amendment to the Government's motion for war:

Military action against Iraq would be illegal, immoral and illogical. The Government will tell us that the selected evidence from the Attorney General that has been published has satisfied the Government and ought to satisfy the House, but I prefer to take the views of the many eminent jurists who have reached very different conclusion. And yes, I also accept the view set out by Kofi Annan that the international community needed a second resolution. I am satisfied that, without the second resolution, we are getting into extremely dangerous ground and setting extremely dangerous precedents . . . we are going after the wrong enemy at the wrong time and in the wrong way. I do not believe that Saddam Hussein has been anything other than contained. I do not believe any assertion that is made without the evidence being provided that there are linkages between him and Al Qaeda. I do not believe that he has had the wherewithal, or would have it, to be able to attack the United Kingdom directly.

Others took a different view in the debate, including Bruce George, Chairman of the Defence Select Committee:

I support the Government because the Attorney General said yesterday that there was a legal basis for the war.

Internationally, there was perhaps predictable dissent from China, via the Xinhua News Agency:

[Military Action] violated the United Nations Charter and the basic norms of international law.

Vladimir Putin was quoted in *The Times* on 22 March. It was, he said:

'a big political error' . . . .'unjustified' . . . . [danger of international law being replaced by] ' the rule of the fist.'

President Assad of Syria weighed in on 22 March, on Syrian Radio. According to him it represented:

> . . . barbaric aggression . . . [a] flagrant violation of the principles of international law, in breach of international legitimacy, and condemned by all the people on earth.

Two days later, I asked

> . . . what advice the Attorney General has given the Government on war with Iraq without explicit United Nations authorisation.

It appeared that the Attorney General had verbally 'briefed' Cabinet, instead of making his complete, written advice available. This was unprecedented. Members of the Government were unable to make full and informed decisions on Iraq, if they had only been partially or selectively or politically briefed. Nothing would put the question of legality to bed. The Foreign Affairs Select Committee Report into Iraq took evidence from the Archbishop of Southwark (on behalf of the Church of England's Public Affairs Unit) on 17 June 2003. He opined:

> Pre-emptive action can itself be stabilising to and a breach of international peace. As a result, it is crucial that states considering pre-emptive action have more than probable cause to believe they must attack. Otherwise, questions will always be asked as to whether a pre-emptive attack was itself never more than an act of aggression.

Robin Cook fingered the Government's quandary in a letter to the same inquiry:

> The Attorney General's legal advice is founded entirely on the failure of Saddam to comply with the obligations on Iraq to eliminate its WMD. I am no lawyer, but it does appear arguable that if Iraq had no WMD there could in logic be no legal basis for a war to eliminate them.

By 2 February 2004, the NGOs were beginning to report their experiences of Iraq post the invasion. Harry Cohen tabled an early day motion:

> That this House notes that Human Rights Watch has stated that the United States and Britain had no justification for invading Iraq on a humanitarian mission; that, according to its executive director, Mr Kenneth Roth, such interventions should be reserved for stopping an imminent or ongoing slaughter and not to address atrocities that were ignored in the past; that there were no mass killings going on; that war was not the only option as legal, economic and political measures could have been taken; that there was no evidence that humanitarian purpose was the main one for launching the invasion; that the attack did not have the backing of the UN or any other multi-national body; and that the situation in the country has not got better.

Later that year, on the 15 September, Kofi Annan was to bluntly tell a BBC interviewer that the war was:

> From our view point and the United Nations Charter point of view . . . illegal.

Once more, Blair was to brush aside inconvenient opinions, telling BBC's Today programme:

> That is his view – it is not ours . . . The view we took at the time – and we take it now – is that the war was justified legally because he [Saddam Hussein] remained in breach of United Nations resolutions.

Blair's detachment from reality was almost sublime. In his world, virtually everyone else was out of step but him. As he preached in the *Washington Post* of 6 March 2005:

As a matter of law, the breach of United Nations resolutions was critical ... But sometimes there is a false distinction in this. As I said in February 2003 ... the nature of the regime is immensely important in determining how serious a view we should take of the breach of United Nations resolutions. WMD issues with a benign regime is a completely different manner of problem than WMD issues with a regime that is thoroughly evil and wicked, as this one was.

It was as if nothing had impacted on his first, prejudiced views on Iraq. He was unyielding, and ignored discomforting truths, as laid out in an EDM of Llew Smith:

That this House notes that Sir Stephen Wall, who was appointed by the Prime Minister as European Policy Adviser to the Prime Minister in June 2000, told the BBC Panorama programme 'Iraq, Tony and the Truth on the build up to the invasion of Iraq', broadcast on 20 March, that in respect of the legality of the invasion, 'We stretched the legal argument to breaking point in my view and the fact that we didn't have that authority, I think does set a dangerous precedent'; further notes that he added, 'I regret that I didn't speak my mind to Tony Blair on it'; agrees with Sir Stephen's conclusions that going to war is about the most serious thing that can be done in international affairs and 'that if people's lives are to be put at risk apart from the civilians in the country being attacked, it does have to be the last resort and you do actually need some international authority to do it; believes Sir Stephen's career curriculum vitae including posts as Private Secretary to the Foreign Secretary from 1988 to 1990 and to the Prime Minister from 1991 to 1993, and heading the foreign Office EU Department between 1983 and 1988, demonstrates the esteem with which his wise counsel was appreciated by senior Ministers across several governments; and therefore calls on the Prime Minister to release the full legal opinion prepared by the Attorney General, Lord

Goldsmith, on the legality or otherwise of taking military action against Iraq in March 2003

Was it any wonder that Ali Fadhil, a medical professional keeping a diary in Iraq for the use of Channel 4 and the *Guardian*, could describe the experience of a housewife – Nihida Kadhim – living in Fallujah:

> On her mirror she pointed to a message that had been written in her lipstick: 'FUCK IRAQ AND EVERY IRAQI IN IT.'

This message, written by an American soldier, might have been the slogan of the British and American leaders, given their cavalier disregard for anything and everything to do with the welfare of the Iraqis themselves.

United Nations endorsement

Since wars begin in the minds of men, it is in the minds of men that the defences of peace must be constructed.
UNESCO Constitution (1945)

One of the central planks of the British Government's strategy in the build up to war in Iraq, was the quest for unequivocal United Nations support. This was to be in accord with the opening preamble of the United Nations charter – adopted on 26 June, 1945:

> We the people of the United Nations determine to save succeeding generations from the scourge of war, which twice in our lifetime has brought untold sorrow to mankind and to reaffirm faith in fundamental human rights, in the dignity and worth of the human person, in the equal rights of men and women and of nations large and small, and to establish conditions under which justice and respect for obligations arising from treaties and other sources of international law can be maintained, and to promote social progress and better standards of life in larger freedom, and for these ends, to practise tolerance and live together in peace with one another as good neighbours, and to unite our strength to maintain international peace and security, and to ensure, by the acceptance of principles and the institution of methods, that armed force shall not be used, save in the common interest, and to employ international machinery for the promotion of the economic and social advancement of all peoples.

In the context of Iraq, Tony Blair went on the record early within his Prime Ministership (24 February 1998) in invoking the authority of the United Nations in aid of his attitude towards Saddam Hussein:

> We should never forget that, if we do not stop Saddam Hussein acting in breach of his agreement on WMD, the losers will be not just those threatened by him but the authority and standing of the UN itself.

Post 9/11, Gerald Kaufman, a senior backbencher, perhaps inadvertently raised the dilemma which was to face the Bush-Blair axis, in a verbal shot at his old political foe, Tony Benn. On 4 October 2001, he told the House:

> . . . it is not so much use people asking for United Nations authority for action and then opposing the action all the same. That happened in Iraq when Mr Benn demanded a United Nations Security Council resolution, got it and then opposed the action.

It remains a question upon which history will pronounce. Did Bush and Blair undermine irreparably the United Nations by ignoring its view when they could not get the decision they wanted?
The general view of the Commons was reflected in the same debate by Jeremy Corbyn:

> I do not believe that the Pentagon or NATO can administer world justice. The UN provides the basis and principle that are needed.

Even the normally compliant chair of the Foreign Affairs Select Committee, Donald Anderson, was alarmed by the threat of unilateral or bilateral military action:

> If we want to put countries such as Iraq into the frame, we must remember that there are more effective weapons such as the

smarter sanctions and the spirit of the draft Security Council resolution that was being discussed in early July . . . Such measures are far more effective than military action.

Members had watched what had already been done in Iraq by the Americans and British in the name of the United Nations. As Alan Simpson said on 18 December 2001 in an early day motion:

That this House believes that it is now time for the international community to end the ten year war and sanctions against Iraq; notes that the United Nations Humanitarian co-coordinator Hans von Sponeck has directly attributed over three hundred and fifty civilian deaths and a thousand civilian casualties to United States and United Kingdom bombing of Iraq over the last two years; recognises that security and stability in the region will be found through inclusion and negotiations rather than by bombing, and calls on the United Nations to launch a new diplomatic initiative on Iraq based on openness, tolerance and reconstruction.

In another motion tabled the same day, Simpson extended his case:

That this House strongly believes that an inability to find Osama bin Laden must not be used as a pretext to extend the war against Afghanistan into other countries; knows that military action against Iraq, Somalia, Sudan and any of the 60 countries in America's target list, would see the international coalition against terrorism torn apart in the pursuit of vengeance rather than justice; recognises that a United Nations - led agenda of development, democracy and social justice offers the only long-term prospect of international stability; and calls upon the United Kingdom Government to lead this initiative within the international community.

Tam Dalyell asked the Government to do the obvious in the House on 8 January 2002:

> Would it not at least be prudent to talk to Hans von Sponeck and Dennis Halliday ... before getting involved in the precipitate and disastrous folly of attacking Iraq?

In the minds of many – myself included – the chances of the Bush Administration seeking international consensus were remote, to put it mildly:

> Is it not ironic that while we discuss with the United States Administration the non-proliferation of weapons of mass destruction that Administration seems hell bent on delaying, inhibiting or destroying every international agreement and convention that underpins non-proliferation? Is it not true that the present Administration of the United States, and the right wing ideologues who control them, do not give a tinker's cuss about international cooperation or international opinion when it comes to these issues, unless they meet their own immediate political objectives?

Fanatically pro-American Foreign Office Minister Dennis MacShane missed the point:

> It is no secret in the House that Her Majesty's Government do not share the approach of the United States when it comes to strengthening international conventions and agreements to reduce proliferation, but the dialogue must continue. We welcome the fact that, although it was not possible to reach a conclusion at the fifth review conference on the biological and toxin weapon convention in Geneva last year, we are engaged in a dialogue to achieve that final agreement. Events in the United States – not least the anthrax scare – have reinforced public

opinion in America as to the importance of national and international agreements in this important field.

He went on:

> ... the United Kingdom and the United States are committed to securing full Iraq compliance with its United Nations disarmament obligations.

As time was to show, Iraq could not comply with impossible US/UK demands. They were an interpretation of Iraq's 'compliance with its United Nations disarmament obligations' not shared by the majority of the United Nations. The truth was – as Angus Robertson expressed in an early day motion of 7 March 2002:

> That this House believes that any international offensive military action against Iraq can only be morally justified if it carries a new and specific mandate from the United Nations Security Council.

Referring none too obliquely to Israel, Menzies Campbell highlighted how partial Bush and Blair were being. Speaking in the House on 12 March, he remarked:

> ... there is a strong sense among Arab governments that we are inconsistent in our determination to apply some United Nations resolutions, but not all, and that there are other countries in the region that would well be taken to task for their failure to implement United Nations resolutions . . . Does he agree that military action and the abandonment of the strategy of containment and deterrence can be contemplated only after all other reasonable alternatives have been explored, and with a proper understanding of the possible political and military consequences.

Having been asked at Prime Minister's Questions on 13 March:

> Does the Prime Minister agree that if the serious concerns about Iraqi WMD are borne out by further information, the United Nations should be the first port of call for raising the problem so that we get the broadest possible coalition to counter the threat, the Prime Minister set out his stall:

> Of course it is to the United Nations that we have constantly gone because of the problems of Iraq acquiring weapons of mass destruction. It is for that reason that many, many United Nations Security Council resolutions call on Iraq to destroy those weapons and to let the inspectors back into the country to ensure that they are destroyed. For that reason, we will continue to put maximum pressure on Iraq to come back into line with international law and United Nations Security Council resolutions.

The fact that Iraq did comply 'with international law and United Nations Security Council resolutions' was neither here nor there. As David Manning's memo of 14 March was to imply, manipulation was perhaps more important than truth:

> It must be very carefully done and failure was not an option.

Many thought that the Prime Minister was in line with public opinion when he told the House on 10 April 2002:

> It is important that we act without double standards . . . The resolution of this issue will require a massive collaborative effort on the part of the international community.

Others were far more sceptical about the Government's real intentions in partnership with the Bush Administration. I asked Jack Straw:

> . . . if the Foreign Secretary will not confirm that Paul
> Wolfowitz directed the CIA to subvert the position of Chief
> United Nations weapons inspector Hans Blix, will he confirm
> that ironically the CIA found that Mr Blix was guilty of nothing
> more than acting within the parameters set out for him?

A confident Foreign Secretary's rejoinder was:

> I am responsible for a great deal, but happily I am responsible
> neither for Mr Wolfowitz, nor the CIA.

There were, however, more thoughtful voices in America. As John Newhouse,
an acknowledged American expert on arms control and diplomacy, accurately
stated in the *World Policy Journal* on 30 July 2002:

> Nothing less than sustained multilateralism will enable major
> powers to neutralise the interactive problems of terrorism and
> WMD.

Nevertheless, the neoconservative chorus remained undimmed, as John
Bolton (eventually to become, improbably, the American ambassador to the
United Nations) declared on the BBC *Today* programme on 3 August:

> . . . let there be no mistake . . . our policy insists on regime
> change in Baghdad and that policy will not be altered whether
> the inspectors go in or not . . .

The honesty of these hawks, if frightening in its rigidity, was far more
admirable than the evasion and obfuscation of British representatives. Almost
from the outset, this dichotomy between the two principal parties in 'the
coalition of the willing' was to be a major political weakness.
Their honesty was, at times, brutal. Former chairman of the Pentagon's
Defense Policy Board– Richard Perle – told ABCs *This Week* on 18 August
2002:

Our European allies are just not relevant to this. And the one of some importance, the United Kingdom, is, I believe, going to be with us.

After all, as Dick Cheney told the Veterans of Foreign Wars convention on 27 August 2002:

> . . . a person would be right to question any suggestion that we should just get inspectors back into Iraq, and then our worries will be over . . . A return of inspectors would provide no assurance whatsoever of his compliance with UN resolutions. On the contrary, there is a great danger that it would prove false comfort that Saddam was somehow 'back in his box'.

I told the *Guardian* on 13 September:

> Bush was telling the United Nations 'I would like to have your support, but we are going to go ahead anyway.' He has made sure he has not tied his hands.

The following month, Blair prepared his party conference for 'defending' the United Nation's good standing:

> The Iraqis don't have the same tradition of political freedom. No they don't but I bet they'd like to . . . I know the worry over Iraq. People accept Saddam is bad. But they fear it's being done for the wrong motives. They fear us acting alone. So the United Nations route. Let us lay down the ultimatum. Let Saddam comply with the will of the United Nations . . . If he doesn't comply then consider. If at this moment having found the collective will to recognise the danger, we lose our collective will to deal with it, then we will destroy not the authority of America or Britain but of the United Nations itself . . . Sometimes, and in particular dealing with a dictator, the only chance of peace is a readiness for war.

On the BBC World Service on 10 October 2002, Blair told a wider audience that, with or without the United Nations, Saddam would be dealt with:

> But it is best dealt with through the United Nations, through the international community making its will clear, and Saddam complying with that will. That's our preference, but nobody should be in any doubt that if it isn't dealt with in that way it has got to be dealt with differently.

On 16 October, at Prime Minister's Questions, the Prime Minister seemed to pull back a little:

> I am not going to speculate on the basis on which we will or will not support military action in Iraq . . . I want this to proceed on the broadest possible basis of consent . . . the United Nations has to be the way of dealing with this issue . . . I certainly understand the concerns that people have about unilateral action.

Mohammed Sarwar was not fooled by the Prime Minister's hyperbole, telling the House on 17 October:

> Now is the right time to stop using the words 'international community' because only three heads of state support this war; Ariel Sharon and President Bush, supported by our Prime Minister.

Tony Blair could not evade facing up to a key choice, put to him at Prime Minister's Questions on 23 October by Andrew George:

> If the Prime Minister agrees that, to combat international terrorism, the United Kingdom should support actions that make it less likely rather than more likely, will he tell the House which he thinks would command more support at home and at the United Nations; the unilateral option of President Bush or the multilateral approach of President Chirac?

These were increasingly pressurised times for Blair. He seemed to be going in a number of directions at once, looking for a way out of an untenable position. Thus, he floated the view at a Lord Mayor's Banquet on 11 November that 'we' needed to keep the United States on board and in the lead in a much broader sense than Iraq:

> I believe . . . the world needs a broader agenda than simply terrorism and WMD. And we need full United States engagement and leadership on all of it.

This was not a new perspective, but an insufficient justification in many eyes, for going with the American agenda in Iraq. He had told the same City function:

> Last Friday . . . the United Nations came together and made its will plain. Saddam now has to decide; he can either disarm voluntarily . . . accepting the unanimous decision of the United Nations Security Council; or he can defy the world, in which case he will be disarmed by force.

He had interpreted, unlike many other world leaders, 'serious consequences' in United Nations Security Council Resolution 1441 as 'disarmed by force'.

A week later, United Nations inspectors re-entered Iraq for the first time in nearly four years. (It had been repeatedly said by the British Government that Saddam had thrown the inspectors out. This was untrue – they had been withdrawn by the United Nations for their own safety when Anglo–American bombing was intensified.) It was argued that the inspectors would need a realistic timeframe within which they might do their work. Four months later, the British Government held the vote on going to war.

The truth was apparent early on to those who chose to look seriously at American intentions. As Alan Simpson said in the House on 25 November:

. . . there are large elements within the American Administration who intend to bomb the living daylights out of Iraq, with or without a United Nations resolution.

Jack Straw incredibly asserted:

There is still an air of disbelief as to whether we will maintain our faith in the Security Council. We will do so.

Neil Gerrard gave him a reality check:

Much of (the) debate has taken place . . . as if enormous pressure has not been exerted by the United States, with the threat that it would take unilateral action if the United Nations did not act. That comes from a country that has routinely chosen to ignore United Nations resolutions in the past, and did not pay its subscriptions for much of that time.

Jeremy Corbyn remarked acerbically:

It seems to be okay for us to go to the United Nations so long as there is no danger of someone disagreeing with us.

The same day, the Prime Minister reported to Parliament on the NATO summit held in Prague:

It linked very clearly − and, I believe, rightly − terrorism and WMD . . . There was complete unanimity round the table that the choice for war or peace lies with Saddam, and that if he breaches the will of the United Nations, the United Nations will have to act. There was strong support for multilateralism and for the decision of President Bush to go through the United Nations, but equally strong insistence that multilateralism and the United Nations be seen to work . . . the ultimate message from the NATO summit was far more powerful than discussion of capabilities or formal structures. It was that, if we care about those values of freedom, the rule of law and democracy, we should not flinch from the fight in defending them.

Note the throwaway dismissal of 'formal structures'. A lawyer might be expected to take more note of why formal structures are important; a statesman even more so.

Former Defence Minister Doug Henderson was direct:

Does my Right Honourable Friend [the Prime Minister] acknowledge that if military action is taken against Iraq by America, or by America and Britain, without the express authority of the United Nations it will lack international political legitimacy? Does he agree that that would severely damage not only the United Nations but NATO?

Blair equivocated:

It will all depend on the circumstances.

Liberal Democrat leader Charles Kennedy again tried to pin down the Prime Minister on the essentiality of United Nations authority with reference to Iraq, on 11 December:

Will the Prime Minister take this opportunity to reaffirm that the perception should be that the United Nations is the sovereign authority in all this business, and that that underpins the international coalition of interest against WMD and terrorism in general? If that perception becomes misguided or misinformed internationally, it is the worse for all of us.

Blair could only say that it was 'important' – whatever he meant by that in a world of elastic meaning:

It is, of course, important that in all circumstances the integrity
of the United Nations is upheld.

By mid-December, many, like Alice Mahon, had already made up their minds:

It seems to some of us that it is absolutely clear that we will
support the Bush war on Iraq regardless of the United Nations.

As the New Year was ushered in, public opinion was not with the
Government, it seemed. One poll showed that only thirteen per cent of the
British electorate would support a war on Iraq with United Nations authorisation. This view was not in accord with that of the Prime Minister; hence,
he ignored it. On 7 January 2003 Geoff Hoon announced – to the alarm of
many – contingency preparations for war:
John Lyons asked him:

If the United Nations decides to take no military action against
Iraq, will British troops join American troops in invading Iraq?

Hoon sidestepped, only to be met by Neil Gerrard:

Will he [Hoon] name one other country that is taking steps
similar to those that he has announced today?

Hoon's vague response was:

I assure my Honourable Friend that a number of countries are
offering assistance in different ways to the United States.

He was massively wrong to tell the House:

I am confident that there is an overwhelming consensus in support
of the Government's policy on Iraq . . . I do not believe that there
is any inevitability about conflict, not least involving the United
States, because it is in no different position from that of the United

Kingdom in that it agreed to the United Nations process and it wants that process to be properly implemented and enforced.

He was wrong about the inevitability of conflict; or the position of the United States *vis-à-vis* that of the United Kingdom.

Patsy Calton took the question of public support back to the Prime Minister the following day:

Is the Prime Minister engaging in dangerous brinkmanship with Saddam Hussein or is he seriously telling us that he intends to commit British troops when an overwhelming majority of the public are against this?

A week later, it was the turn of Mohammed Sarwar to try to elicit a full and honest reply from the Prime Minister:

Does he [the Prime Minister] agree that a breach of United Nations Security Council Resolution 1441 should be a matter for the weapons inspectors and the Security Council, not President Bush and the American Administration? Does he also agree that if President Bush takes unilateral action against Iraq, he will be defying the United Nations?

Sarwar did not succeed. What was amazing was the number of gullible Members of Parliament who swallowed the Government's hogwash. Alice Mahon was not one of them. She forcefully made her point on 20 January:

I am deeply concerned that ever more of our troops are being deployed. Whenever the Government say that no decision has been taken to join Bush in his war against Iraq, many of us remain deeply sceptical. Given the demonstrations all over the world this weekend, I think that the people of this country do also. Does the Secretary of State accept that the United Nations Charter as it is currently constituted does not allow for a pre-emptive or offensive strike against another United Nations country that is not threatening anybody? No matter how many resolutions the United States bullies and intimidates other countries into supporting, that remains the case. Will the Secretary of State accept that his Government have not made the case for war against Iraq?

Douglas Hogg had rather a different take:

> May I say to the Right Honourable Gentleman that he should be careful not to invest the Security Council with undue moral authority. The Security Council is but a political institution, and resolutions of the Security Council are but political statements by a political institution. While it is perfectly true that such resolutions are a necessary precondition to war, they cannot make just or moral a war which otherwise is not.

He was not simply making an academic point. As the Government shifted its case for war, Saddam's alleged non-compliance with United Nations Security Council Resolution 1441 became critical as a trigger for war. However, this was seen as a pretext for war. In reality, it was believed by many that there was no regard for the United Nations and its authority. Had Britain and America honoured its processes, the war that eventuated would have been legally and morally more sound.

Government ministers continued to evade direct answers to straightforward questions which demanded honest answers. In the House on 30 January, John Lyons asked Geoff Hoon:

> If the United Nations Security Council decides not to take military action over Iraq, will it [i.e. the Government] accept that decision?

Hoon's response?

> That is a matter for the United Nations Security Council and its
> individual members. That decision has yet to be taken.

This was wrong on both counts. It was not for the United Nations Security
Council to agonise over whether the British Government accepted its
decisions. It was clearly a British Government decision whether or not it
accepted the view of the United Nations Security Council. On the second
count, the decision had been taken long before by two of its members – the
United States and the United Kingdom – to go to war.
Notwithstanding what we now know to have been the reality, the Prime
Minister could tell the Liaison Committee the following day:

> I think America has accepted that it is best dealt with through
> the United Nations.

He may well have believed that to be the case but it did not mean that any
attack was subject to United Nations approval if the best option was through
the United Nations; there were certainly backup options. That is why the
contingency preparations were underway for military action. He confirmed
this later in his submission:

> Of course I accept it is going to be more difficult without a
> United Nations resolution. That is the point I have accepted
> throughout, that is why I say it is desirable to have one.
> However, I do believe that if the inspectors find the information
> that allows the Security Council to judge there is a breach
> people will accept it in those circumstances; otherwise the will
> of the United Nations is absolutely set at nought. If the United
> Nations comes together and says it is vital for international
> security that Saddam disarms himself of WMD and he does not
> do so and the Security Council then says 'We are not going to
> do anything about it', it would be disastrous.

Portentously, he went on to open the debate about Iraq post the impending conflict. Unfortunately, he did not see the sorry mess which he and Bush were about to foster:

> I think it is important that if we do get to the stage of military conflict we are very clear with people in Iraq about exactly how we see the future of Iraq. That is something for the international community, incidentally, not simply the United States or the United Kingdom.

In the Chamber that day, voices of caution were heard. Michael Moore asked the Foreign Secretary:

> Does he [Straw] agree that the process should not be prejudged by impatient or precipitate moves towards war by any Security Council members?

Other consistent critics continued to pick at the Government's leaky case for war, emphasising our commitment to the United Nations. On 22 January, Alice Mahon asked:

> The Government are a member of the United Nations, and the United Nations specifically prohibits pre-emptive and defensive strikes against countries that are not threatening us. What is the threat from Iraq?

And again:

> The truth is that the United States, being the only superpower, is corrupting the one international organisation that we should all be protecting. We should be honest about the United Nations Charter: it does not provide for pre-emptive attacks.

For the American President, this was Prime Minister Blair's problem. The United Nations was irrelevant to his agenda as he made clear in his State of the Union address of 28 January 2003:

> Yet the course of this nation does not depend on the decisions of others [...] We will consult. But let there be no misunderstanding. If Saddam Hussein does not fully disarm, for the safety of our people and for the peace of the world, we will lead a coalition to disarm him.

With or without a United Nations mandate, he was ready to attack Iraq. The United Nations Security Council itself saw no 'immediate' threat from Iraq. For most of its members, containment was working.

Presumably, Tony Blair still believed that he could obtain the second United Nations resolution, which would provide the legalistic cover for an attack on Iraq. As he told the House on 3 February 2003:

> I continue to believe that the United Nations is the right way to proceed.

He continued:

> Should Dr Blix continue to report Iraqi non-compliance, a second resolution should be passed confirming such a material breach . . . I continue to believe that the United Nations is the right way to proceed . . . .I am working on the basis that people hold to both the spirit and the letter of Resolution 1441 . . . .My Right Honourable Friend [Derek Foster] is absolutely right ['Would it not have profound implications for the long term peace and security of the world if the United States took international law into its own hands?'] . . . I do not agree ['that a resolution of the Security Council, or even the discovery of WMD, do not of themselves, standing alone, constitute a moral justification for war']. It is justified to enforce the will of the United Nations. Even if, as he says,

there is no immediate threat to this country, I believe that there is undoubtedly a threat to the security of the world arising from the proliferation of WMD.

As arguments arose about French intentions to veto such a second resolution, Neil Gerrard asked in the House on 6 February:

Where in the United Nations Charter is there provision for any member state to choose to ignore a veto?

Four days later, Gerrard picked up on Blair's expressed intention to ignore any veto on his cherished second resolution:

That this House notes that the Prime Minister has said that he and President Bush will not be bound by the unreasonable use of the veto by another country on a further resolution concerning Iraq at the United Nations Security Council; notes that within the Charter of the United Nations the veto is available to the five permanent members of the Security Council and that there is no provision for it be ignored; and considers that claiming the right to ignore the veto if this would lead to an unacceptable outcome for the United Kingdom and the United States governments, whether such an action is taken or not, undermines the United Nations and means there is no reason for any other country on this or other issues in the future to respect the use of the veto by this country or the United States of America.

The following day, Jack Straw was to effectively blame Iraq for the damage being done to the UN by the British and American governments:

Over the past 12 years, the Iraqi regime has done great harm to the UN's credibility.

Blair was to tell the House on 25 February:

> If the United Nations cannot be the way of resolving this issue,
> that is a dangerous moment for our world.

This was just weeks before precipitating this 'dangerous moment' by ignoring the will of the United Nations. As Chris Smith put it in a debate the following day:

> Strength does not lie simply in military might. Strength lies in making the right moral choices. It lies in maintaining the pressure, and it lies in securing the fullest possible international agreement.

It certainly did not lie in trying to bully and twist the United Nations to the hegemonic will of one superpower and its ever-faithful ally. There were still other options open, as Ken Clarke reminded the House:

> Today's debate is the time to put down a marker to say that the other approaches – the diplomatic, deterrent policy and the use of threat in order to get compliance – have not yet been exhausted.

Alan Simpson had given up on the United States:

> It is clear that the United States view of the United Nations is that it is simply a body to be bought or bypassed.

With regard to the British Government, something had changed, but Tony Lloyd – a former minister – did not know what, exactly:

> Not many years ago, the Foreign Office and Downing Street, now briefing on the need for action, were briefing ministers . . . on the success of weapons inspections and our ability through containment and deterrence to maintain downward pressure on Saddam and Baghdad. We need to know when and why that advice changed, as it is fundamental to the reasons why we are threatening to go to war against Iraq.

Others – like Alistair Carmichael – were exercised by the double-standards being exhibited:

> In his speech today, the Foreign Secretary spoke at some length about twelve years of United Nations resolutions on Iraq . . . but he did not say much about United Nations resolutions (in Israel and Palestine). I remind the House that it is thirty-six years since the first such resolution – 242, which called on Israel to relinquish control of territories occupied in the war of 1967 – was passed. The Government will have to explain why we are prepared to value some United Nations resolutions so much more highly than others.

All of this was so much wind to President Bush, who told a press conference on 6 March:

> We will act . . . and we really do not need the United Nation's approval to do so.

Prime Minister Blair told MTV the next day:

> Military action is to uphold the authority of the United Nations and make sure Saddam is disarmed.

Alarm bells had long been ringing at the United Nations, leaving Kofi Annan to warn in a speech in The Hague on 10 March:

> The legitimacy and support for any such action will be seriously impaired [in the absence of a further explicit United Nations resolution]. If the United States of America and others go outside the Council and take military action it will not be in conformity with the Charter.

The Prime Minister had warned of the impending 'dangerous moment' pregnant with possibilities. Peter Bradley raised it at Prime Minister's Questions on 12 March:

Which is the lesser threat to global security; allowing more time for Iraq's disarmament or, in disarming Iraq – particularly in view of the French President's commitment to exercise his veto – dividing the international community? Will the Prime Minister give an assurance to the House that so long as there is a prospect of rebuilding an international coalition under the authority of the United Nations, he will resist United States pressure for precipitate action?

The Prime Minster's line was unchanged:

I will certainly do everything I can to make sure that the international community stays united at this time and that we achieve a second United Nations resolution . . . it is our intention to put a vote to the United Nations on a second resolution. We continue to work for that, flat out.

Four days later, the Chancellor of the Exchequer broke his brooding silence on Iraq. Strangely, he was to raise a resolution concerning the forced removal of Iraqi forces from Kuwait, entirely irrelevant to the disarmament of Iraq, a subject which only came before the United Nations Security Council four months after the said resolution (678) was passed:

. . . Resolution 678 (which) says that the international community should take all necessary means to uphold security and peace. In other words, that Saddam Hussein should disarm.

A more insightful comment came from Robin Cook in his resignation statement:

. . . a war that has neither international agreement nor domestic support . . . The reality is that Britain is being asked to embark on a war without agreement in any of the international bodies of which we are a leading partner – not NATO, not the European Union and, now not the Security Council.

Elaborating on this theme, he declared:

> I have been frank about my concern over embarking on military
> action in the absence of multilateral support . . . the evident impor-
> tance that we attached to a second resolution makes it all the more
> difficult now to proceed without one, and without agreement in
> any other international forum . . . I am dismayed that once again
> Britain is divided from our major European neighbours.

The following day, the House of Commons had its climactic debate on war in
Iraq. Opponents of the war moved an amendment which, in part, specifically
stated that they:

> . . . believe that the case for war against Iraq has not been estab-
> lished, especially given the absence of specific United Nations
> authorisation.

John Denham, another honourable minister who resigned over the war, spelt
out the dangers of isolation from our international partners:

> The action against Iraq is, I believe, pre-emptive, and therefore
> demands even greater international support and consensus than
> other sorts of intervention. We do not have it. Such isolation
> entails a genuine cost and danger. It undermines the legitimacy
> that we must maintain to tackle the many threats to global
> security. It fuels the movements that are antipathetic to our
> values and way of life, and the view, which is probably the
> reality, that in an interdependent world, one nation reserves the
> right to determine which of the world's problems should be
> tackled, when, where and in what way.

Joyce Quinn would not be bullied into unilateralism:

> My Right Honourable Friend the Prime Minister said that if we
> did not support the United States now, they would be tempted

in future down the unilateral route. That worries me, as I do not want to feel intimidated into supporting action on that basis.

Alex Salmond pointed out the hollowness of Government claims to be supporting the United Nations:

> . . . when the Secretary-General of the United Nations doubts the authorisation of military action without a second resolution, people can say many things about that action, but they cannot say that it is being taken in the name of the United Nations.

Denham accurately described the overt contempt of the neoconservatives for the United Nations and the international community:

> The United States Administration appear at times to delight in stressing their disdain for international opinion and in asserting their right to determine not only the target but the means and the timetable, their gratuitous actions apparently designed to make a common voice impossible, not least here in Europe. That has made the international coming together that we need impossible to achieve.

Blair could only lamely concede an auxiliary role for the United Nations:

> The United Nations should have a key role in administering the delivery of humanitarian aid.

The next day, Lynne Jones asked at Prime Minister's Questions:

> . . . what is [the Prime Minister's] strategy for a return to a world order in which decisions are taken lawfully through the United Nations, rather than by the world's superpower? Or is it too late? With his help, has the foundation stone for the Pax Americana already been laid?

It was not just backbenchers lamenting this rejection of the United Nations. The *Financial Times* quoted Jacques Chirac on 21 March:

> France regrets this action taken without the approval of the United Nations.

France was not alone in this view – they spoke for the majority in the family of nations.

Back in the House of Commons, some members began to salvage what they could. Ian Lucas tabled an early day motion on 25 March, saying:

> That this House believes that the post-war reconstruction of Iraq must be built upon the broadest possible foundation of international support; reaffirms that such a foundation is best built at the United Nations; and calls upon Her Majesty's Government to work with all permanent members of the United Nations Security Council to achieve consensus to address the urgent problems of delivering humanitarian aid to Iraq and establishing a government in Iraq that acts for the benefit of its own people.

Blair clung to his fig leaf of legitimacy for the war, although majority opinion amongst other states was against him. He told Abu Dhabi TV on 4 April:

> . . . we believe it was (a legitimate war) but you will never get the international community to agree on that, I am afraid.

Jack Straw must have been off message on 25 April, when he was asked:

> Should the United Nations have a vital role to play in respect of weapons of mass destruction?

'Yes', Straw replied – unlike Donald Rumsfeld who in answer to the same question said that there would be no role for the United Nations inspectors 'for the foreseeable future'.

Still, British backbenchers demanded a role for the United Nations. For example, Llew Smith, a Stakhanovite of early day motions, tabled one on 19 May:

> That this House agrees with the comments made by the Secretary of State for Wales to the Sunday Telegraph, published on 6th April that in respect of Iraq 'What is crucial is that the United Nations is put in charge after the interim transitional arrangements'; notes that in the draft resolution proposed by the United Kingdom, the United States and Spain to the United Nations Security Council on 9th May it suggests only a coordinating role for the United Nations, and instead proposes to create a new Iraq Authority comprising the United Kingdom and the United States as conquering powers following their invasion of Iraq; and asks that the Welsh Secretary clarify his position on the draft resolution in light of his earlier contradictory remarks.

Not that this had any effect on the Government. The Prime Minister became increasingly taken with specific issues far from Iraq, and far from an over-arching vision for Britain's role in the world, other than as a support for American policy. By 5 March, he could tell his Sedgefield constituents:

> The doctrine of international community is no longer a vision of idealism.

If that is true, it is in no small part due to his actions. He certainly had helped damage the standing of the United Nations. In the House on 19 April 2004 I bemoaned the fact that:

> ... post 30 June, heavy-handed American military activity will determine the future of Iraq, and certainly not the United Nations.

The outcome of that is distressingly clear for all to see. The tragedy for Britain's standing in the world was to be put into perspective on BBC's

Panorama programme on 20 March 2005, when Hans Blix remarked:

> I think that's an absurdity that here a minority of the council goes to war to uphold the authority of a majority that is against it.

How right he was.

United Nations Security Council Resolution 1441

One day President Roosevelt told me he was asking publicly for
suggestions about what the war should be called. I said at once
'The Unnecessary War.'

Sir Winston Churchill (1847–1965)

In the build-up to the Iraq War – and even in the protracted and uncom-
pleted post mortem on the war – United Nations Security Council
Resolution 1441 rivalled the illusory 'weapons of mass destruction' in the
amount of verbiage written, and hot air expired, by both proponents and
opponents of the war.

On 8 October 1997, the International Atomic Energy Authority (IAEA)
described to the Security Council, the account given by Iraq of its previous
nuclear projects as 'full, final and complete'. As far as the IAEA was
concerned, there was no indication of any prohibited activity by, or within,
Iraq. That is, it was known that Iraq did not have the weapons or the capability with which they were to be charged.

Tony Blair, however, could even sound bellicose then, saying after talks with
President Clinton on 5 February 1998:

> We want a diplomatic solution to the crisis [alleged Iraq
> hampering of United Nations weapons inspections] but the
> success or failure of diplomacy rests on Saddam. If he fails to
> respond then he knows the threat of force is there and it is real.

Even more alarmingly, he told the House of Commons on 16 November that
year that:

> We know . . . that under the threat of force, we can make him
> [Saddam] move. If he again obstructs the inspectors' work we
> will strike . . . There will be no warnings, no wrangling, no
> negotiation and no last minute letters. The next time coopera-
> tion is withdrawn, he will be hit.

By that time pressure was being cranked up for war. We can, therefore, take as read two strands in the complicated arguments over the war – firstly, that there was credible evidence to refute the Anglo-American clause on Iraqi WMD; and secondly, that a belligerent Blair had already thrown down a military gauntlet to Saddam. However, he needed United Nations support to make his case watertight. That was why he told the Lord Mayor's banquet of 12 November 2001:

> On Iraq, the time has come for a new United Nations resolution
> to provide for the arms inspectors to return and for the Saddam-
> induced suffering of the Iraqi people to be ended.

As the *Observer* noted on 2 December 2001, Bush did not necessarily agree:

> . . . the US is believed to be planning to exploit existing United
> Nations resolutions on Iraqi weapons programmes to set the
> action off.

Blair was to adopt that view as his fallback position. If he could get a new resolution, that would be well and good. If not, he would join America in making the best of what was already approved by the United Nations. At Prime Minister's Questions on 6 March 2002, he said:

> Of course, were we ever to take action in respect of Iraq there
> should be an opportunity for the House to express its view . . .
> However . . . no decisions have yet been taken about any
> possible action in respect of Iraq . . . .Iraq is plainly in breach
> of the UN Security Council resolutions on the accumulation of

weapons and we must deal with that. How we do so is a matter for discussion and consultation.

This was the week after he had told Cabinet that he was supporting Bush (and, therefore, Bush's weapons which were well under way). One has to question the sincerity of the Prime Minister's assurances.

On 18 March 2002, Sir Christopher Meyer, British Ambassador in Washington, sent a note to David Manning (Blair's foreign policy adviser) of a meeting with Rumsfeld's deputy, Paul Wolfowitz:

> We backed regime change, but the plan had to be clever and failure was not an option. It would be a tough sell for us domestically, and probably tougher elsewhere in Europe ... I then went through the need to wrongfoot Saddam on the inspectors and the United Nations Security Council resolutions and the critical importance of the MEPP [Middle East Peace Plan] as an integral part of the anti Saddam strategy ... If the UK were to join the United States in any operation against Saddam, we would have to be able to take a critical mass of Parliamentary and public opinion with us.

This left little doubt about either the determination or the duplicity of the British Government with regard to Saddam. Meyer showed no concern about the policies, ethical or moral dimensions of what was being engineered. It was simply a cynical plot to set up Saddam for military action, regardless of the United Nations or anyone else.

A game was played, even involving supportive Members of Parliament like George Howarth, a close political confederate of Jack Straw. At Prime Minister's Questions on 10 April 2002, Howarth asked the Prime Minister:

> Will he [the Prime Minister] give the assurance that before any military action that may eventually become necessary is contemplated, Saddam Hussein will be given every opportunity to comply with those resolutions?

This was a repeated question, and one fed to supportive back-benchers by whips, and one which was regularly answered obliquely so as to give the impression of a government led by reasonable men with open minds. As Jack Straw told the BBC on 15 September 2002:

> If the Iraqi regime re-admits weapons inspectors to Iraq, the case
> for military action recedes to the point almost of invisibility.

This was to prove wholly untrue, as was the Prime Minister's claim to the House on 24 September:

> Conflict is not inevitable. Disarmament is.

Iraqi Foreign Minister – Naji Sabri – had already written to Kofi Annan on 16 September:

> I am pleased to inform you of the decision of the Government
> of the Republic of Iraq to allow the return of UN weapons
> inspectors to Iraq without conditions.

The British Government was playing an elaborate charade, disguising – or so they thought – their real intentions. Clive Efford made a forlorn gesture to formalise the British Government's theoretical flexibility, with an early day motion on 24 September:

> That this House endorsed the Prime Minister's commitment to
> seeking a new United Nations resolution and mandate to
> enforce the process of inspecting and disabling any Iraqi WMD;
> recognises that Iraq has indicated that it will comply with
> existing United Nations resolutions; notes that Hans Blix has
> indicated that weapons inspectors could be ready to enter Iraq
> early in October and believes that no military action should be
> taken while arrangements are being made for this to take place;
> further believes that in the event of Iraq's failure to cooperate
> with the United Nations inspectors that no military action be
> taken without a mandate from the United Nations and a vote in

the House; expresses continuing concern about the wider implications of any military action not specifically approved by the United Nations; and urges maximum effort towards the renewal of the Middle East peace process as an essential precondition towards stability and peace in the region.

A few weeks later, the reality would emerge. As Glen Rangwala noted on 18 October in his article US Raises the Hurdles, speaking of Anglo-American drafts of resolutions:

The new draft supported by the British Government (therefore) undermines the very United Nations resolution that it claims to be acting in order to uphold. It goes much further . . . a string of demands are made of Iraq that it knows that Iraq could never consent to.

The Prime Minister's evasions at Prime Minister's Questions on 30 October only made critics more suspicious:

It is best not to speculate on what might happen if we do not [get a new United Nations resolution] . . . I am sure that the House will have the fullest possible chance to debate that issue.

Blair had more than speculated – he had made plans; but these were not to be shared with Parliament, nor with most of his government.

Ultimately, UNSCR 1441 was passed unanimously on All Souls Day 2002. Weapons inspectors were to return to Iraq. Depending on whether one took a Bush perspective or a Blair perspective, this either delayed the inevitable, or it bought time to sell the inevitable.

Other machinations within the United Nations were not ignored by British backbenchers. Hence, Jeremy Corbyn asked Jack Straw on Guy Fawkes Night in the Commons:

Will (the Secretary of State) explain why Britain and the United States seem to be pursuing a resolution in the United Nations that will give President Bush the sole power of decision making and veto over the future of any weapons inspectorate or any bombing or invasion of Iraq?

Many could see just how the United Nations was under the cosh from President Bush – with the support of Her Majesty's Government. The machinations of the latter became clearer almost daily. Jack Straw told the House on 7 November that:

> Although we would much prefer decisions to be taken within the Security Council, we have always made it clear that within international law we have to reserve our right to take military action, if that is required, within the existing charter and the existing body of United Nations Security Council resolutions, if, for example, a subsequent resolution were to be vetoed.

No longer was the Security Council route essential; it was merely preferred, and a veto was no barrier to military action. The formidable Alice Mahon's unambiguous riposte was in sharp distinction to the cloudiness of the Government's approach:

> It is clear to many commentators . . . .that this is a war resolution. The United States with the help of our Government, shamefully, appears to have bullied and intimidated people coming on line, and, perhaps, also promised the spoils of war – oil. The resolution is mined with the trip wires to trigger a war. It should be named after the film Wag the Dog because if Iraq does not trip up soon, I am pretty certain that the United States will make sure that it does.

Straw replied:

> There are no trip wires in the resolution, we have been extremely careful to ensure that there is none.

This was certainly not the case. Many felt that the vague wording of UNSCR 1441 was open to interpretation, and, therefore, exploitation.

Indignant, I wanted Straw to dissociate the United Kingdom from what I saw as the 'bully boy' tactics of the American Administration at the United Nations:

> . . . the Foreign Secretary said that, internationally, we are all equal. I do not doubt, however, that some are more equal than others. Given the atrocious nature of the regime in Baghdad – but also given what many believe to be the incontrovertible fact that the United States Administration had browbeaten the United Nations in an unedifying spectacle, on the basis that might is right – can the Foreign Secretary explain to me and to people of like mind how it serves our wider national interest to be associated with such diplomatic tactics?

Straw's terse response offered no relief, disputing the assumption behind the question saying it was 'simply untrue'. Unbelievably, the Foreign Secretary told his colleagues in the House that, with regard to the draft Resolution 1441:

> I do not believe that if the resolution is passed it will advance the prospect of war. I think that the prospect of military action will recede.

Naturally, it was a claim intended for the moment for the audience of professional sceptics and cynics in the House of Commons. The next day, UNSCR 1441 was passed unanimously. The 'coalition' now had the resolution they wanted to legitimise their war. It was now simply a matter of Iraq not complying. They were not to be allowed to comply. As Tony Blair said in his statement on the adoption of UNSCR 1441:

> In the event of Saddam refusing to cooperate or being in breach, there will be a further United Nations discussion, as we always said there would be. To those who fear this resolution is just an automatic trigger point, without any further discussion,

paragraph twelve of the resolution makes it clear this is not the case.

Two steps forward; one step back. We must bear in mind Christopher Meyer's telling note to David Manning earlier in March, referring to:

> The need to wrongfoot Saddam on the inspectors and the United Nations Security Council resolution.

Now the Prime Minister could shift responsibility for war onto Saddam, as he did at the Lord Mayor's Banquet:

> The dispute is with Saddam. It is now up to him as to how it is resolved by peace or by conflict.

Speaking to the Security Council on Resolution 1441, the British Ambassador to the United Nations – Jeremy Greenstock – was untypically direct:

> There is no 'automaticity' in this resolution. If there is a further Iraqi breach of its disarmament obligations, the matter will return to the Council for discussion.

Tony Blair was unrelenting in using the name of the United Nations in support of his case, as at Prime Minister's Questions on 20 November:

> That cooperation has . . . got to be a full and honest declaration on his part of the WMD that he has. If he cooperates fully with the inspection team, mandated by the United Nations, there will be a peaceful resolution to this dispute.

One had the impression that the process adopted by Bush and Blair marked Saddam down as guilty until proven innocent. They – not the United Nations, not any principles of natural justice – would determine guilt or innocence in Iraq. This was despite the concerns of a 'stacked deck' as expressed by Anne Campbell in the House on 25 November:

My constituents are concerned that the resolution deliberately makes it difficult and potentially impossible for Iraq to comply.

A prudent argument was put in that debate by David Heath:

> There is a world of difference . . . between a material breach as defined by one or two members of the Security Council and an action agreed by all. Members of the Security Council have passed a unanimous resolution, which they believe re-establishes the primacy of international law and the United Nations. That is important . . . it is clear that the SC supported the resolution on the basis of no automaticity. The understanding was that the issue would return to the Security Council . . . It is also clear that they received assurances to that effect from the British and American representatives . . . It is no good the Americans or anyone else getting impatient with the process if it does not provide them with the evidence to which they think they are entitled. It is clear that the process must be: first, to receive reports from the independent inspectors; secondly, to have an assessment by the Security Council; and thirdly, to make a decision on the correct course of action.

Des Turner referred to neoconservative thinkers, and urged caution:

> We can all think of commentators close to the American President who do not believe that Saddam will conform and who probably do not want Saddam to conform. They will gladly seize on any excuse to say that he has substantially breached the resolution and use that as an opportunity for promoting unilateral action. That would be extremely reprehensible. It would be taking a match to the powder keg that is the Middle East. Should that happen, Britain must have no part of it.

For once, Tory spokesman Bernard Jenkin showed an independent streak, volunteering the observation that:

'It is perfectly clear from the resolution that that [who should determine what is a serious breach] is entirely a matter for the weapons inspection team and Hans Blix.'

This was a vital point: who would ultimately decide if there had been a breach by Saddam – the inspectors, the Security Council, or individual members of it?

Defence Secretary Hoon tried to assuage the doubts of backbenchers:

Neither Britain nor the United States is looking for a pretext for military action . . . which will certainly be a last resort.

Reporting back to the House on the Prague NATO summit, Blair was to partially answer Jenkin – or so it seemed at the time:

It will be for weapons inspectors to say whether there is a breach [of UNSCR 1441] and there will then be discussion about the seriousness of that breach. We have undertaken to take the matter back to the Security Council.

This did not happen – did he mean to do so, but was, for some unfathomable reasonable, unable to; or did he mislead the House of Commons?

As Christmas 2002 approached, those of an optimistic bent took some succour from junior minister Mike O'Brien's report back to Parliament on 10 December:

Inspection activity in Iraq . . . resumed on the 27th. To date, there have been no reports of serious or deliberate obstruction of the inspection teams.

Although O'Brien hedged his bets on longer terms options:

Resolution 1441 does not stipulate that . . . there needs to be a second resolution to authorise military action.

Elfyn Llwyd remained unimpressed:

> . . . many in the US administration view Resolution 1441 as the pathway to war, not to peace.

I also remained unimpressed, speaking to *The Times* the next day:

> America is duping the world into believing it supports these inspections. President Bush intends to go to war even if inspectors find nothing. This makes a mockery of the whole process and exposes America's real determination to bomb Iraq.

Geoff Hoon lost his script on 18 December. Asked whether the United Nations Security Council would be the final judge on whether military action against Iraq was necessary, he gave an unequivocal 'No'. The Defence Secretary was in no mood for protracted argument or explanation. When asked on the same day by Glenda Jackson:

> If war is inevitable only if Iraq fails to comply with SCR 1441, will all members of the Security Council be furnished with the American analysis of the Iraq document? Given the somewhat intemperate statements of Secretary Powell, who rushed to judgement on the document's veracity, will such an analysis be verified by United Nations inspectors before any decision is made by the Security Council, or is the will of the international community reduced to that of the United States?

His reply was laconic:

> . . . the answer is a matter for the United States.

The reality was spelt out by Colin Powell on 20 December, in a statement on Iraq's weapons of mass destruction:

> The burden remains on Iraq to cooperate fully and for Iraq to prove to the international community whether it does or does not have WMD. We are convinced they do until they prove to us otherwise.

This was the crunch. Saddam had to prove himself innocent, and the United States would be the judge of that.

The British fell publicly into line through Hoon on 7 January, in the Commons:

> Iraq's declaration of its WMD programmes fails to give a satisfactory account of Iraq's activities in this area . . . UNMOVIC and the IAEA will next report formally to the Security Council on 27 January. That is not necessarily a decision point on Iraqi compliance . . . None of that means that the use of force is inevitable . . . it remains the case that no decision has been taken to commit those forces to action.

All options were being kept open as every contingency was explored, and as all of the necessary military, economic, political and diplomatic preparations were made.

The somewhat naïve Jenkin tried to question Hoon on his statement:

> Why . . . do they [the Government] appear to be delaying decisions about deployments and playing down our military commitment?...If the weapons inspectors find nothing and the United States decides to go ahead with military action in any case, what will be the Government's policy?

Poor Jenkin was clearly not up to speed on what was being done in our country's name by the Government, with the eager support of the Official Opposition – including himself!

Hoon appeared almost magnanimous:

> It is important that we take time to assess properly the [Iraqi regime's] declaration's contents.

A preliminary assessment was made, but was never followed up by a full and conclusive one. Presumably, it was not seen to be congruent with the Anglo-American gameplan, and so was tossed aside.

Richard Burden expressed the anxiety of many when he questioned Hoon:

> What reassurance can [Hoon] give me on others using the need to keep pressure on Saddam as a pretext and a cover to get to 27 January and then to call time on the weapons inspectors in support of adopting pre-emptive strikes, to which this House has not signed up?

There was no reassurance forthcoming.

John Pugh returned to the vexed question of who would judge on alleged breaches:

> Given the degree of scepticism world wide and in the House, who in the view of the Government is now the ultimate judge of whether Saddam Hussein has complied with Resolution 1441?

Hoon had to concede a role for the Security Council.

Terry Davies put a similar question to the Prime Minister at Prime Minister's Questions the following day:

> Who is better placed to decide whether Saddam Hussein has WMD, President Bush or Hans Blix?

The Prime Minister once more slipped out of a direct answer, although he was almost astonishingly accommodating at the Liaison Committee on 21 January. Asked 'What if the weapons inspectors ask for more time?' he replied:

Let us wait and see what actually happens . . . I have said that they should be given time to do the job, and I am sure they will be . . . the weapons inspectors should be allowed to do their job properly.

At the same meeting, he was asked:

If the weapons inspectors say 'We would like some more time either to establish a degree of cooperation or to find out why things are not in their report which we think ought to have been in their report' or instead to discover things, will it not be politically necessary in order to grant some additional time in order to maintain as great a consensus as possible in a very divisive world opinion for whatever action is ultimately necessary?

His reply once more appeared to defer to the Security Council:

Of course that is a judgement the Security Council has got to make and will make that judgement on the basis of what the inspectors say to us . . . if I am sometimes coy about speculating what happens after the 27 January or if the inspectors say this or say that, it is because I do not want to do anything that weakens that enormous pressure coming to bear on the regime either to cooperate, or, frankly, to crumble.

It was self-evidently true when he told them:

When I say the preference is for a United Nations resolution, it is easier in every respect if there is one.

After all, he went on:

. . . all I am doing is just being open with people because I do not think these circumstances [not having a second resolution] will arise.

Whether he was being honest or disingenuous is a matter of opinion. What is undeniable is that his Foreign Secretary was practising the 'hard sell' that same day in the Chamber:

> The words 'serious consequences' have only one meaning – the use of force.

Under United Nations convention, that was just not true – the phrase does not have only one meaning. Nor was the backbench resistance to war diminished. Glenda Jackson asked Straw:

> Only last week, my Right Honourable Friend stated that 27 January should not be regarded as a deadline. Having worked so hard to get the United Nations weapons inspectors back into Iraq, why does there now seem to be such a rush to get them out of Iraq and to make a decision even before they have had any chance genuinely to search that country to see whether there are any weapons?

The question of timing – or, at least, of undue haste – was more than simply a debating point. Members of the House and of the general public wanted to know why there were illogical time constraints placed on the inspectors' work. It was to meet military logistical needs, and political ones, rather than to facilitate an adequate inspection regime. This was despite the Prime Minister's claim at Prime Minister's Questions on 22 January 2003:

> I have always made it clear, that it is important that the weapons inspectors can do their job and have the time to do it.

Denzil Davies raised a general concern of those unhappy with the dash to war:

> . . . some of us . . . remain concerned about some of the statements coming out of Washington that seem to seek justification for military intervention that is way outside the ambit of UNSCR 1441.

Peter Pike raised the whole question of British autonomy in our policy towards Iraq:

> If the weapons inspectors find no weapons of mass destruction in Iraq and want more time to look, and if [the Prime Minister] is agreeable to giving more time but President Bush is not, who will make the final decision? If they go to bomb, where will they bomb if they do not know where the WMD are?

The Prime Minister qualified Iraq's ability to meet the Anglo-American demands with the highly subjective test of 'cooperation':

> . . . it is not just a question of the inspectors finding the weapons, it is a question of the duty of cooperation.

Elfyn Llwyd made clear to the House that key international players were at odds with us over the meaning of UNSCR 1441:

> It was known that the United Kingdom and the United States sought an express authorisation but such authorisation is manifestly lacking in the final wording. Security Council permanent members, Russia, France and China, made their position crystal clear: they did not want the resolution to authorise force.

George Bush had his own interpretation, as he declared on 31 January:

> 1441 gives us the authority to move without any second resolution, and Saddam Hussein must understand that if he does not disarm for the sake of peace, we along with others will go and disarm Saddam Hussein.

At the beginning of February, the British Government published another dossier of 'evidence' of Saddam's wilfulness. It claimed:

Escorts are trained, for example, to start long arguments with other Iraqi officials on behalf of UNMOVIC while any incriminating evidence is hastily being hidden behind the scenes . . . Journeys are monitored by security officers stationed on the route if they have prior intelligence. Any changes of destination are notified ahead by telephone or radio so that arrival is anticipated. The welcoming party is a giveaway.

Fortunately for truth in politics, a fortnight later, Hans Blix told the Security Council:

Since we arrived in Iraq, we have conducted more than 400 inspections covering more than 300 sites. All inspections were performed without notice, and access was almost always provided promptly . . . we note that access to sites has so far been without problems . . . In no case have we seen convincing evidence that the Iraqi side knew in advance that the inspectors were coming.

In a statement to the House on 3 February, the Prime Minister set down his own interpretation of UNSCR 1441:

. . . if he [Saddam Hussein] rejects the peaceful route – he must be disarmed by force.

But also said that:

If Iraq is not fully complying, having been given a final opportunity, a fresh resolution should issue.

On 5 February, Colin Powell addressed the Security Council. Hans Blix had suggested in December 2002, that Iraq should give, in stages, the names of Iraqi scientists with expertise in weapons of mass destruction:

Iraq may proceed in pyramid fashion, starting from the leadership in programmes, going down to management, scientists,
engineers and technicians but excluding the basic layer of
workers.

This appears to have been done by Iraq. Lists were provided of 117 persons
for the chemical weapons sector; 120 in the area of biological weapons; and
156 involved in missile technology. These were given at the end of December
and more names had since been added. Yet Powell declared to the Security
Council:

Iraq did not meet its obligations under 1441 to provide a
comprehensive list of scientists associated with its WMD
programme.

On that same day, Tony Blair told *Newsnight*:

. . . although they're allowing the inspectors access to the sites
they're not actually fully cooperating with inspectors. For
example, they're not allowing the experts that worked on these
programmes to be interviewed properly by the inspectors.

When asked in the interview 'How much time do the inspectors need?' Blair
replied:

The time to make a judgement as to whether Iraq is cooperating
or not.

Under pressure ('Are you saying there's already an authorisation [in UNSCR
1441] for war?') Blair replied defensively 'No', but continued:

. . . the clear understanding was that if the inspectors do say
that Iraq is not complying and there is a breach of that resolution, then we have to act.

Clarifying the vital question of who was to say that a veto – perhaps by the French – on further action was unreasonable, the Prime Minister replied:

> You say that if in circumstances where the inspectors – not us – have come back to the United Nations and said we can't do our job.

And then came the reason why he was keen on a second resolution:

> I think if there were a second United Nations resolution then I think people would be behind me.

A week later, Blair was again pushing the cooperation line, while simultaneously appearing to concede that the Security Council would decide on this:

> . . . the judgement that has to be made in the end is one by the Security Council as to whether there is full and complete cooperation by Iraq.

But he still clung to the hope that he would have the further validation of a second resolution:

> I still believe that it is possible that we shall attain a second resolution in the United Nations. I believe that the matter should be resolved through the United Nations.

Many in the House were still unsure, if not suspicious, of Blair's attitude towards the United Nations. Thus Menzies Campbell on 18 February called for a further debate:

> That this House calls on Her Majesty's Government to hold a debate prior to the tabling of any further United Nations Security Council resolutions relating to Iraq so that Parliament

can consider Her Majesty's Government's position in relation to any such resolution and express a view.

Later that same day, Jack Straw maintained his hard line:

> Resolution 1441 warns Iraq to expect 'serious consequences' . . . By now, even Saddam Hussein must be under no illusions. That can only mean disarmament by force.

Alan Duncan picked up on a difference between the Foreign Secretary and the Prime Minister:

> A fortnight ago, a second United Nations resolution seemed a dead cert, but now it seems touch and go. The Foreign Secretary made no mention at all of a second resolution in his statement.

No longer was it 'a dead cert'; merely a possibility now – or as Straw put it:

> It is our decision as to whether or not we move a second resolution and of course one remains in prospect.

He further emphasised the Government's preferred approach:

> . . . let it be clear that 1441 is a sufficient mandate . . . for military action.

The next day Hans Blix reported to the Security Council:

> Inspections are effectively helping to bridge the gap in knowledge that arose due to the absence of inspections between December 1998 and November 2002.

This was not in the interests of the coalition who began to undermine Blix. Meanwhile, back benchers like Hilton Dawson continued to whistle in the wind:

That this House welcomes the progress that has been made to implement United Nations Resolution 1441; recognises that the realistic threat of overwhelming military force has been a key element in securing the return of United Nations weapons inspectors; considers that they still have a great deal of important work to do; urges the Government of Iraq to comply with every requirement of Resolution 1441; continues to believe that there can be a peaceful and effective resolution of this crisis and recommends to the United Nations that it will enhance its standing and the solidarity of nations by exercising humanity and firm principle without rushing to war.

Dr Blix was able to report increased Iraqi cooperation to the Security Council:

Three persons that had previously refused interviews on UNMOVIC's terms, subsequently accepted such interviews just prior to our talks in Baghdad on 8 and 9 February. These interviews proved informative.

This positive tone was reinforced by Dr El Baradei of the International Atomic Energy Authority:

The IAEA has continued to interview key Iraqi personnel. We have recently been able to conduct four interviews in private – that is, without the presence of an Iraqi observer. The interviewees, however, have tape recorded their interviews ... I should note that, during our recent meeting in Baghdad, Iraq reconfirmed its commitment to encourage its citizens to accept interviews in private, both inside and outside Iraq.

These positive reports were underlined by other signs of progress. For example, Iraq began destroying its Al Samoud 2 missiles in March 2003. Notwithstanding these encouraging moves, the draft second resolution before the Security Council read:

Iraq has failed to take the final opportunity afforded to it in
Resolution 1441.

It suggested that it was now time to authorise military force against Iraq.
Incredibly, the next day – 23 February – Blair told the House of Commons:

Is it not reasonable that Saddam provides evidence of destruction of the biological and chemical weapons and agents the
United Nations proved he had in 1999? So far he has provided
none.

There was no proof of whatever he was supposed to have had in 1999;
Saddam had provided Blix with the documentation requested; and 1441 was
being implemented.
In an attempt to head off conflict, France, Germany and Russia – each of
whom knew a thing or two about the horrors of war – submitted informally
a counter resolution to the United Nations Security Council. It suggested
intensified and extended inspections as a solution to the crisis, in the hope
that:

The military option should only be a last resort.

It was Hans Blix who pithily pointed out the irrationality of the Anglo-
American view in *Time* magazine:

Eight years of inspections, four of no inspections, then eleven
weeks, and call it a day? It's a little short.

Blair ignored the good sense of Blix:

After twelve years is it not reasonable that the United Nations
inspectors have unrestricted access to Iraqi scientists – that
means no tape recorders, no minders, no intimidation, interviews outside Iraq as provided for by Resolution 1441? So far
this simply isn't happening.

Yet it was happening, as confirmed by both Blix and El Baradei. Charles Kennedy asked the Prime Minister on 26 February:

> Will the Prime Minister acknowledge that, unless the United Nations weapons inspectorate were to conclude that the inspection process itself had failed, it would be quite wrong for this country to participate in pre-emptive military action against Iraq . . . Is not the greater consequence and danger that the international coalition against terrorism on which he and everybody else lay such rightful importance would itself be shattered?

Blair ignored this obvious truth. His only limp argument was that:

> Passive rather than active cooperation will not do.

A fortnight later, Hans Blix was to report to the contrary, that there was 'active' or even 'proactive' cooperation. In the debate on 26 February, I gave my view on who could be trusted to make judgements on Iraq:

> We should leave it to Hans Blix and El Baradei to make the definitive statement on WMD and let the United Nations decide whether a material breach has taken place.

Gavin Strang, a former minister, agreed the case for caution:

> The truth is that the weapons inspections process has far from outlived its usefulness. Weapons inspections are still a viable alternative to military action, and the process should be pursued until either it is concluded successfully or it is clear that the inspections cannot usefully continue.

In line with the instructions under UNSCR 1441, ordering the destruction of Al Samoud 2 missiles, Iraq began that destruction. This was further evidence of their compliance with the demands of the Security Council. It appeared, however, to have little effect on Tony Blair, who told the *Independent* on 2 March:

> The United Nations has tried unsuccessfully for twelve years to get Saddam to disarm peacefully.

The Security Council had concluded back in 1999 that:

> Although important elements still have to be resolved, the bulk of Iraq's proscribed weapons programmes has been eliminated.

On 6 March, the inspectors again reported positively to the Security Council:

> No proscribed activities, or the result of such activities from the period of 1998–2002 have, so far, been detected through inspections.

On 7 March, with an eye on the increasingly shrill calls for war from Washington and London, Blix called for more time to verify Iraqi disarmament compliance. The United States responded with a deadline of St Patrick's Day – 17 March.
Colin Powell told the Security Council:

> So has the strategic decision been made to disarm Iraq of its WMD by the leadership in Baghdad? . . . I think our judgement has to be clearly not.

This was not the view of the inspectors. Hans Blix reported that same day:

> In this [investigation into bomb sites] as in other matters, inspection work is moving on and may yield results.

Furthermore, it was the case that:

> More papers on anthrax . . . have recently been provided . . .

> Iraq proposed an investigation using advanced technology to quantify the amount of unilaterally destroyed anthrax dumped at a site . . . the numerous initiatives, which are now taken by the Iraqi side with a view to resolving some longstanding open disarmament issues, can be seen as 'active' or even 'proactive'.

This was steady progress, in line with SCR 1441; but the Americans and the British were not listening, even when Blix told them:

> It is our intention to request . . . interviews [outside the country] shortly . . . the Iraqi side seems to have encouraged interviewees not to request the presence of Iraqi officials [so called minders] or the taping of interviews.

And Dr El Baradei could report at the same time:

> There is no indication of resumed nuclear activities in those buildings that were identified through the use of satellite imagery as being reconstructed or newly erected since 1998 nor any indication of nuclear based prohibited activities at any inspected sites.

The Coalition simply did not want to know. War was their preferred and – in truth – only option.
President Chirac of France recognised that the inspectors were being hog-tied. He said that he was minded to veto a second resolution until circumstances changed:

> My position is that, regardless of the circumstances, France will vote 'no' . . . because she considers this evening that there are no grounds for waging war in order to achieve the goal we have set ourselves, i.e. to disarm Iraq . . . In that case it will be for the Security Council – and it alone – to decide the right thing to do. But in that case, of course, regrettably, the war would become inevitable. It isn't today.

This was not an indefinite veto, nor an unconditional one, that was being proposed; nor did he use it. The United Kingdom and the United States simply abandoned any idea of a second resolution, so Chirac was not put to the test. He did not rule out war – he only said that, at that point, no grounds existed for waging war against Iraq.

This mattered little to the Coalition, other than as the excuse for the cheapest exhibition of Francophobia. Jack Straw, in an excellent attempt at pots calling kettles black, ignored the inspectors as he damned Iraq. Commenting on the UNMOVIC report of 7 March, he concluded:

> It is a chilling catalogue of evasion, deceit and feigning cooperation while in reality pursuing concealment.

On 11 March, Blair could tell MTV that:

> There is no rush [to war].

There was no rush now – all the preparations were in place.

The clueless leader of the opposition – Iain Duncan Smith – could only witter on about Clare Short speaking off message:

> The Secretary of State for International Development said that she would not support military action without a second resolution.

This was after a question to Blair on 12 March:

> . . . he [the Prime Minister] has confirmed in that answer that he keeps the option of committing British troops to war with or without a second resolution. Does the doctrine of Cabinet collective responsibility therefore apply to that position?

The Prime Minister replied:

> Yes, of course it does.

Was that the case, given that (a) there was no real cabinet discussion or consultation, and (b) when it was discussed, members of that cabinet were either not briefed at all, or only inadequately and partially briefed? Of course, members of the cabinet could have objected to this sorry state of affairs, or even resigned, as Robin Cook did.

The Prime Minister soldiered on at Prime Minister's Questions on 12 March. Questioned by Elfyn Llwyd:

> When will this House have a vote on whether to commit troops to war in Iraq? Does the Prime Minister agree with his Defence Minister who said yesterday that was 'pretty damn inevitable'? If so, why?

Blair followed his usual practice, and answered a question not asked:

> I think what [he] said was that, if Saddam Hussein refuses to disarm voluntarily, conflict becomes inevitable.

Meanwhile, there were the Government's own law officers to be suborned. A letter from Downing Street to the Attorney General on 15 March set the tone:

> It is indeed the Prime Minister's unequivocal view that Iraq is in further material breach [of UNSCR 1441].

Contemporaneously, Bush and Blair were bullying the United Nations, giving it on 16 March, a 24 hour ultimatum to enforce its demands on Iraq, or face war anyway within days. This was refined by Bush the next day, when he gave Saddam 48 hours to leave Iraq, or an attack would begin. One day later, Blair put forward his own ambiguous reasoning:

> The United Kingdom must uphold the authority of the United Nations as set out in Resolution 1441 and many resolutions preceding it, and therefore should use all means necessary to ensure the disarmament of Iraq's weapons of mass destruction.

He claimed that France blocked a diplomatic solution:

> On Monday night, France said it would veto a second resolution whatever the circumstances.

That was not the case. Chirac had said France would veto any resolution that authorised force while inspections were still working.
Another difficulty for Blair was that Lord Goldsmith's advice had been in line with Chirac's thinking. Further:

> There are no grounds for arguing that an 'unreasonable' veto would entitle us to proceed on the basis of a presumed Security Council authorisation . . . If world opinion remains opposed to military action, it is likely to be difficult on the facts to categorise a French veto as 'unreasonable'.

In his desperation to win the Commons vote, Blair was wholly at odds with other Security Council members. He said on 18 March:

> We very nearly had the majority agreement [on a second resolution].

The Mexican Ambassador to the United Nations – Adolfo Zinsen, disagreed, telling the BBC:

> No, we were never close to have a majority win, never.

The Prime Minister changed with the wind on Iraq. As Alex Salmond observed in the Commons debate of 18 March:

> The Prime Minister says that the French have changed position, but surely the French, Russians and Chinese always made it clear that they would oppose a second resolution that led automatically to war. Well they published that view at the time of Resolution 1441. Is it not the Prime Minister who has changed

his position? A month ago, he said that the only circumstances in which he would go to war without a second resolution was if the inspectors concluded that there had been no progress, which they have not; if there were a majority on the Security Council, which there is not; and if there were an unreasonable veto from one country, but there are three permanent members opposed to the Prime Minister's policy. When did he change his position, and why?

The inconsistencies of Tony Blair's case were laid out for all to see – assuming all wanted to see the truth. The vote in the House of Commons was won by the Government with the support of the Official Opposition. Two days later, Hans Blix lamented to the BBC's *Today* programme:

> . . .we had begun about three and a half months ago (ie: inspections) and I think we had made a very rapid start . . . I think that . . . now we call it a day and close the door . . . The impatience took over . . . If they don't find something then you have sent 250,000 men to wage war in order to find nothing.

Still Blair persisted in contradicting the man on the spot, telling Abu Dhabi TV on 4 April:

> The reason why the inspectors couldn't do their job in the end was that Saddam wouldn't co-operate.

Remember the comments of Blix to the Security Council on the previous 7 March:

> The numerous initiatives, which are now taken by the Iraqi side with a view to resolving some long-standing open disarmament issues, can be seen as 'active', or even 'proactive'.

Remember, too, the experience of Katherine Gunn. She highlighted the request to the National Security Agency for the 'aggressive' bugging of members of the United Nations Security Council. The Mexican Ambassador had also claimed that illegally elicited information had been used to torpedo any possible deal on a second resolution on Iraq.

Analysts will continue to ponder over two connected issues. Was UNSCR 1441 deliberately vague to allow for misinterpretation by the Coalition? Was there ever a serious intention to seek a further resolution on Iraq? If the former was the case, the latter was academic. It served only to act as legal window-dressing for an attack about which a decision had long been taken. Lord Goldsmith's initial agonising had been in vain, and his later support was simply intended to provide legal credibility to the Government's case. It ultimately failed to do so.

Two lords revealing . . .

Lord Hutton

Oh what a tangled web we weave, when first we practise to deceive.

Sir Walter Scott (1771–1832)

The suicide of Dr David Kelly was the event which provided perhaps the greatest public concern about the whole Iraq mess. It was a human tragedy which reduced the complexities of the many facets of the Iraq War to digestible concerns. His death encapsulated many public worries about the Blair Government, and its unseemly and – in the eyes of so many – unjustified rush to war. I put it this way on my website on 1 August 2003:

> How did the vital, but obscure, expert on WMD find himself in the media and political spotlight? Was he being offered as a sacrificial lamb on behalf of more prominent figures and organisations? What internal dilemmas was Dr Kelly unable, at the end, to reconcile within himself? . . . There is no more difficult subject for him [Blair] than questions about how we came to be involved in Iraq. We were told it was because of an imminent threat from WMD. That theory has been shown to be palpable nonsense. Desperation has become the hallmark of Number 10 . . . Attempts to deflect attention from this key issue just will not wash . . . My view is that the media not only has the right to seek the truth on this seminal issue for the Government, but – like Parliamentarians – has a responsibility to doggedly pursue it.

This was a response to the establishment of Lord Hutton's enquiry, formed with narrow terms of reference to consider the events and circumstances surrounding the death of Dr Kelly. To many, it was a stacked deck, intended to be a whitewash. Many believed that Lord Hutton himself was handpicked as an establishment man, whose record suggested he was possibly the legal figure least likely to rock the Government's boat.

Immediately the inquiry was set up, darker forces began their nefarious work, which included discrediting the recently deceased Dr Kelly. As the *Guardian*'s highly regarded defence correspondent, Richard Norton-Taylor, wrote on 7 August:

> Perhaps, as the former defence minister Peter Kilfoyle suggests, it [Tom Kelly's jibe branding Dr David Kelly as a Walter Mitty fantasist] merely reflected the culture that has infected 10 Downing Street, its smearing and spinning department in particular.

Dr Kelly was no Walter Mitty – he was an expert in his field; one who, ironically, shared the suspicions of his political masters about Saddam Hussein's stockpile of weapons of mass destruction. I sought to set out the reality in an article in the *Independent* on 10 August:

> What culminated with Dr David Kelly's death began with a massive government effort to shift the public focus away from the contemporaneous public demand for evidence that the war against Iraq was justified. You will recall that the principal casus belli set down by the Prime Minister was that there was an imminent threat to the United Kingdom, and its interests, from Iraqi WMD . . . Increasing numbers of people on both sides of the Atlantic were realising that our leaders had misled our countries, having taken us into war on a false pretext.

I went on to point out the background to the Hutton Inquiry. The Government's own inept handling of the worsening political arguments around the war – and particularly, the astonishing behaviour of the Prime

Minister's official spokesman, Alistair Campbell – initiated a chain reaction of events leading directly to the Hutton Inquiry. In an article in the *Mirror* on 13 August, 'We may never know why we were misled' I wrote:

> Remember that there would be no Hutton Inquiry if it had not been for the argument between the Government and the BBC. The argument was itself a diversion from the prime question – why did we go to war with Iraq? We had been told there was an imminent threat from WMD. We now know that to be untrue. Hard questions are being asked in America and we should do the same. Parliament was advised by no less a figure than the Prime Minister that the urgency over these 'weapons' made war inevitable. Lord Hutton is not expected to go that far back in his deliberations, but he should. He cannot get to the bottom of matters surrounding Dr Kelly's death without looking at the central issue at the heart of all this. Why were we misled into an illegal and immoral war, and who was responsible?

Unfortunately, if predictably, the report focussed on the battle between the Government and the BBC over the September 2002 dossier. The inquiry shifted attention away from the war itself, preferring to fix on Campbell's vendetta with the BBC. An opportunity for an independent view of the run up to war was lost – either deliberately or inadvertently.

Much of the Government's concern seemed to revolve around a series of reports aired on BBC radio early in May 2003, wherein the BBC's defence correspondent, Andrew Gilligan, claimed that the aforementioned dossier had been sexed up from the original bland (and unhelpful) intelligence announcement. There was little initial fuss made about Gilligan's report. The ordure really hit the fan when Campbell appeared before the Foreign Affairs Select Committee. As I wrote on 4 February 2004:

> The Hutton inquiry was a diversion born of a diversion. When Alistair Campbell went into the Select Committee on Foreign Affairs, it was considering the events that led up to the declaration of war on Iraq. In my view, he quite deliberately and

successfully set out to divert the Committee, which ended up with the sad loss of Dr Kelly and all the events that have stemmed from that.

I had already expressed disappointment with Lord Hutton's report, in *Tribune* on 30 January:

> . . . critics had hoped that Lord Hutton would be the man who transmuted Tony's evasion and legalistic explanations into the charge of liar . . . Indeed, we had the head of the Iraq Survey Group – David Kay – resigning, and saying that there had probably been no WMD in Iraq . . . For Tony Blair, however, such expert opinions had always been an irrelevance. He believed – and apparently continues to do so – that Iraq possessed WMD, and were 'a clear and present threat' to the United Kingdom. Last weekend, he shifted slightly towards an intelligence explanation – he believed what the intelligence had told him. What sophistry! Remember, as Hutton illustrated, it was the essence of the situation prior to the war that intelligence had to be 'sexed up'. In turn, that was presented in dossiers containing forgeries and plagiarised material . . . A Labour government misled Parliament and people about the reason for going to war on Iraq.

However, careful reading of the report prompted a couple of gems which could not be ignored. For example, 'Mr A', a civil servant working in counter-proliferation arms control, said:

> The perception was that the dossier had been round the houses several times in order to try to find a form of words which would strengthen certain political objectives.

To most objective observers, this justified Gilligan's assertion that the dossier had been 'sexed up'.
Even more informative were the words of Scott Ritter in a *Times* interview of 28 December 2003:

> The aim was to convince the public that Iraq was a far greater
> threat than it actually was . . . Stories ran in the media about
> secret underground facilities in Iraq and ongoing programmes
> [to produce weapons of mass destruction]. They were sourced
> to western intelligence and all of them were garbage . . . Kelly
> was a known and government approved conduit with the media
> . . . What M16 was determined to do by the selective use of
> intelligence was to give the impression that Saddam still had
> WMD or was making them and thereby legitimise sanctions
> and military action against Iraq.

There appeared to be ample scope for charging the intelligence community
with conspiring with the Government to sell a wholly fallacious account of
Saddam's alleged ownership of weapons of mass destruction. This could only
have been done to mislead the British public, and to give Prime Minister Blair
his excuse for war against Iraq.

Lord Butler

Nothing is easier than self-deceit. For what each man wishes,
that he also believes to be true.
Demosthenes (384-322 BC)

Robin Butler is the stereotypical Whitehall mandarin, a man of many accom-
plishments. He is also an amiable and an honest man, immersed in the ways
of Whitehall – he is, after all, a former permanent secretary and cabinet
secretary. There was nobody better suited to conduct the review of the intelligence leading up to the Iraq war, although, as with the Hutton Inquiry, he
had restricted terms of reference.

Nevertheless, because he was the quintessential establishment man, many feared
at the time that his appointment was the means to a whitewash of foul play in
government. After all, there was widespread cynicism about both the intelligence
services and the Blair Government. The former had a long and inglorious history
of duplicity as far as many Members of Parliament and commentators were

concerned. Their views had long been confirmed by publications like Peter Wright's *Spycatcher*, although more recent failures of intelligence had led to serious questions about the efficiency and value of our intelligence services. Thus, I could ask the Prime Minister on 4 October 2001:

> Will he tell the House what convinces him that, given the tragic
> failure of the intelligence community before the 11 September,
> its competency has improved since?

Even the Prime Minister knew in the early days post 9/11 that there was little concrete information on which we might proceed. As he told the *Observer* on 14 October 2001:

> I think what people need before we take action against anyone
> is evidence.

Naively, Francis Maude was wrongly to state the obvious in the House of Commons the very next day:

> No one suggests that one embarks upon military action against
> a country such as Iraq on suspicion: that would be absurd.

Nor had his own party's spokesman begun to understand the realpolitik facing the world:

> I do not think that any government would manufacture a bogus
> excuse to go to war with another country and another govern-
> ment.

Menzies Campbell was less gullible, asking in the House on 27 November:

> How many of those Muslim countries would continue to
> support the coalition if military action were launched against
> Iraq, as has been foreshadowed in the past twenty four hours,
> without incontrovertible evidence?

Evidence – or rather, the lack of it – was shaping up as the first hurdle for the Bush/Blair axis to overcome. This was recognised by everyone, as Hugo Young and Michael White advised us in the *Guardian* of 30 November 2001:

> 'Incontrovertible evidence' would be needed according to Blair and Chirac, of Iraqi complicity in the attacks on America before they could endorse US threats to extend the anti-terrorism war to Baghdad.

But the Joint Intelligence Committee was to admit on March 15th that:

> Intelligence of Iraq's WMD and ballistic missile programmes is sporadic and patchy. Iraq is also well practised in the art of deception, such as concealment and exaggeration. A complete picture of the various programmes is therefore difficult.

By 16 April, Jack Straw could insist to the House that:

> So far as the evidence is concerned almost all of the evidence on Iraq's development of WMD is already available and published.

This included the notorious allegations about the purchase of uranium yellowcake from Niger, based on bogus documentation. The real issue was not the 'evidence' but how it was presented. As Jonathan Powell – Blair's chief of staff – hinted in an email on 5 September to Blair's press guru, Alistair Campbell, the Government's expert on presentation:

> What did you decide on the dossiers?

As the real evidence was to show, the whole question of objective analysis of intelligence was subsumed into a presentational programme designed to fit Prime Minister Blair's political requirements. This was despite the Joint Intelligence Committee's continued judgement on 9 September 2002 that:

> Intelligence remains limited and Saddam's own unpredictability complicates judgements about Iraqi use of these weapons. Much of this paper is necessarily based on judgement and assessment.

Their assessments were, however, confused at best. As the Butler review was to show, quoting John Scarlett from 19 September 2002:

. . . Intelligence indicates that Saddam is prepared to use chemical and biological weapons if he believes his regime is under threat.

This was omitted from the final version, presumably because it went against the Government's case. The suggestion was that Saddam would use WMD in panicky self-defence. The Government picture was of a more aggressive and confident leader, likely to attack without provocation. In fact, his forces had been degraded since his 1991 defeat, and the Anglo-American aerial bombing programme. He was truly a danger to no-one outside of Iraq.

Even the title of Scarlett's draft was altered from *Iraq's Programme for WMD: the Assessment of the British Government*, to the more definitive final version title of 24 September 2002 – *Iraq's Weapons of Mass Destruction* – now given in the British Government presentation.

The much-trailed dossier was to be the basis for the case for war. It asserted Iraq's possession of WMD, and the claim that these non-existent weapons could be primed for use within 45 minutes. It was also claimed that British bases in Cyprus, for example, were within Saddam's range. None of this was true, but it frightened many people into innocent support for the Government's deeply flawed case.

I told the *Mirror*:

> There are no new killer facts in this document. The dossier is a judgement. It's full of unsubstantiated assertions and allegations. There is nothing we don't already know.

These conclusions were not rocket science. Many others immediately reached the same judgement. The dossier brought no new knowledge of Iraq to the table, and Saddam had not suddenly become a greater danger. The question in many minds was why there was a sudden urgency to tackle Saddam. As I said:

> I do not think it adds anything to the sum total of our knowledge of what a nasty regime there is in Iraq and what a nasty man Saddam Hussein is. I wonder about the timing of the document, and why it came into being at all. As I recall, it was promised in lieu of the kind of debate that we are [hoping for] . . .

My view was widely shared.
I had told BBC *Breakfast News* that morning:

> The dossier is a judgement, it is not attributed and it is unsubstantiated.

However, in his foreword to the dossier, the Prime Minister had written, astonishingly:

> The assessed intelligence has established beyond doubt . . . that Saddam has continued to produce chemical and biological weapons.

This was despite the United Nations weapons inspectors in Iraq reporting:

> No proscribed activities, or the result of such activities from the period 1998–2002 have, so far, been detected through inspections.

How could Tony Blair speak of 'beyond doubt'? Assessed intelligence can never be beyond doubt; and the intelligence from the United Nations inspectors gave no support to Blair's charge.
The foreword to the dossier also claimed:

> The assessed intelligence has established beyond doubt that . . . he [Saddam Hussein] continues in his efforts to develop nuclear weapons.

273

As IAEA Director-General Mohammed El Baradei was to confirm to the United Nations Security Council, on 7 March 2003:

> After three months of intrusive inspections, we have to date found no evidence or plausible indication of the revival of a nuclear weapons programme in Iraq.

The Prime Minister – or his 'intelligence' – was utterly wrong again.
By the beginning of January 2003, there was no diminution in the scepticism, and, indeed, hostility, towards the Government's evidence. Tony Lloyd asked the Defence Secretary on 7 January:

> Where is the evidence that a national consensus in favour of war exists? What evidence will he [Hoon] bring to the House to show that it exists before we go to war? Does my Right Honourable Friend accept that the prevailing mood in the country remains very sceptical and that a huge number of people believe that Britain is not acting on its own interests or in the interests of Middle East peace, but solely in the interests of the relationship with the United States?

Glenda Jackson was more abrasive on 22 January:

> . . . they [the British people] have not been convinced by arguments from the British Government that essentially attempt to delude and, in some instances, to deceive.

A weak leader of the opposition asked the Prime Minister on 29 January:

> Does he accept that the British people deserve to be given the fullest possible information about the scale and nature of the threat that we clearly now face?

To be answered by Tony Blair:

Of course we have to give people the fullest possible information, which is why we published the dossier a few months ago.

At the start of February, a second dossier was conjured up to bolster the
weak government case. The main architect of this was chief government
'spin doctor' Alistair Campbell. Central to it was a ten-year-old Ph.D.
thesis, plagiarised from the internet. I was to tell the *Mirror* on 8
February:

It just adds to the general impression that what we have been
treated to is a farrago of half-truths . . . I am shocked that on
such thin evidence we should be trying to convince the British
people that this is a war worth fighting.

Surprisingly, this woefully inept device did not, at the time, incur the full
measure of public contempt which it deserved. Still, the Prime Minister could
keep a straight face in the House on 3 February, when, referring to the second
dossier he said:

We issued further intelligence over the weekend about the infrastructure of concealment. It is obviously difficult when we
publish intelligence reports.

He went on:

They [the security services] are not publishing this, or giving us
this information, and making it up. It is the intelligence they are
receiving and we are passing it on to people. In the dossier that
we published last year, and again in the material that we put out
over the weekend, it is very clear that a vast amount of concealment and deception is going on.

The question, unfortunately, was: who exactly was guilty of concealment and
deception?

Two days later, Colin Powell was singing from the same hymn sheet, addressing the United Nations Security Council:

> Every statement I make today is backed up by sources, solid sources. These are not assertions. What we're giving you are facts and conclusions based on solid intelligence.

Two-and-a-half years later, his then chief of staff, Colonel Lawrence Wilkinson, revealed the truth about the information given to Powell by the White House for his United Nations address:

> It was anything but an intelligence document. It was, as some people characterised it later, sort of a Chinese menu from which you could pick and choose.

This sounds remarkably like the British Government's approach to its own 'sexed-up' dossier.

On 6 February, Paul Flynn reminded the House of Commons of what had been given to it as intelligence before:

> . . . is not it essential that we go forward with sound knowledge?
> . . . would it not be good to assess the value of the dossier placed before the House in September, as it has proved to be almost entirely untrue?

At Prime Minister's Questions on 12 February, while the Prime Minister maintained his air of sincerity, Alex Salmond closely questioned the changes made by Number 10 to alleged intelligence analysis:

> Does the Prime Minister accept that it is not just a question of plagiarism but of changing key phrases? The phrase 'Iraqi aid for opposition groups' in the original becomes 'Iraqi support for terrorist organisations' in the Government's Downing Street document. What possible motivation is there for making these changes apart from propagandising to war? If the Prime

Minister cannot be trusted on that, how can he be trusted on anything?

The following day, Jack Straw practised his doublespeak:

> . . . I tell the House . . . that the document itself [WMD dossier] was accurate in every particular – the part that claimed to be from intelligence was from intelligence.

The chairman of the Foreign Affairs Select Committee, Donald Anderson, for once (possibly unintentionally) touched on a key weakness in the Prime Minister's case:

> In the final analysis, we are dealing not with absolutes, but with judgements, based on the available facts, including intelligence facts.

It is true that intelligence analysis does not always deal in absolutes – judgements are required. Yet these judgements need to be factually based. They cannot be based on plagiarised fantasy or on sexed-up dossiers. It would certainly be most inappropriate to trust the judgements of people who knowingly analyse a situation on such a basis.

Our international colleagues were most unimpressed by the gymnastics of Bush and Blair. The Swiss Ambassador to the United Nations put it very simply on 11 March:

> Switzerland notes that UNMOVIC and the IAEA do not have, at this moment, conclusive evidence indicating that Iraq possesses or is continuing to produce weapons of mass destruction.

Harry Cohen reminded the House on 12 March:

> That this House notes that the United Kingdom told the inspectors of the United Nations that Iraq sought significant

quantities of uranium from Africa, despite having no active civil nuclear power programme that could require it; further notes that the Chief Nuclear Inspector for Iraq Mohammed El Baradei recently reported to the United Nations that the documents which formed the basis for this claim are in fact not authentic and that we have therefore concluded that these specific allegations are unfounded; and believes that this represents another failure for United Kingdom intelligence in respect of Iraq.

The next day, in an early day motion, it was Paul Flynn's turn:

That this House notes that the Prime Minister pointed out in his statement on Iraq on 3rd February that UNSCR 1441 imposed on Saddam a duty to give 'a currently accurate, full and complete declaration of all aspects of its programmes to develop chemical, biological and nuclear weapons, ballistic missiles and other delivery systems'; further notes in the same statement the Prime Minister informed Parliament that the Government had produced a dossier on Iraq making clear that 'there is a huge infrastructure of deception and concealment designed to prevent the inspectors from doing their jobs' in Iraq; further believes that the provenance of this dossier was not made clear, although it accepts that well researched academic publications are legitimate sources of information; further notes that the allegations made by United States Secretary of State Colin Powell to the United Nations Security Council on 5th February that a base of the terrorist organisation Ansar al-Islam, located in the Kurdish enclave in northern Iraq, contains a chemical and poisons factory, were proved to be wrong by subsequent visits by journalists; and calls upon all ministers to provide this House with accurate, up-to-date and relevant information on Iraq and terrorist threats, to permit honourable Members to make judgements on facts, not propaganda.

These were straightforward, factual rebuttals of what the Prime Minister and his government were saying. The mystery is why so many continued to believe in a totally false prospectus for war.

George Bush addressed his own nation on St Patrick's Day:

> Intelligence gathered by this and other governments leaves no doubt that the Iraq regime continues to possess and conceal some of the most lethal weapons ever devised.

He presumably meant nuclear weapons, like those held by Israel. Iraq has never possessed nuclear weapons. His British ally was also resolute in believing myths:

> I stand absolutely 100 per cent behind the evidence, based on intelligence, that we presented to the people.

This was 2 June 2003. A week later, Clare Short blew a large hole in the blanket around Blair's *modus operandi* on Iraq within his own Government, testifying before the Foreign Affairs Select Committee:

> . . . the Defence and Overseas Policy Committee never met. There was never a paper. There was never an analysis of options . . . They [Campbell, Powell, Morgan, Manning – 'that close entourage'] attended the daily war Cabinet . . . Decisions were made in the Prime Minister's study all informal around this small in-group of people . . . I think the decisions were being made by the Prime Minister . . . the decision making was sucked out of the Foreign Office . . . there was no kind of collective decision-making.

This committee reported its findings on 3 July and noted with regret:

> Conclusions and recommendations are far from satisfactory, as acknowledged, given the [full cooperation from the Government] was not forthcoming.

The committee should have had full access to all papers, witnesses, other personnel, intelligence, and other sources of evidence. These were denied to them.

Backbenchers plugged away. Lynne Jones put down an EDM on 7 July:

> That this House notes the comment from the Prime Minister in a letter dated 22 May to the Honourable Member for Birmingham Selly Oak, that 'we remain confident that Iraq sought to procure significant quantities of uranium from Africa'; further notes that in its report to the Security Council on 7th March the International Atomic Energy Agency concluded that this specific allegation was unfounded; also notes the question by the Honourable Member for Birmingham Selly Oak to the Foreign Secretary asking whether access to all information in his possession of Iraq's WMD was given to the chief Weapons Inspector and the Director General of the IAEA; and the answer given by the Honourable Member for North Warwickshire that the Government shared all relevant information about Iraq's WMD with the inspection teams from both UNMOVIC and the IAEA; further notes the question put by the Honourable Member for Birmingham Selly Oak to the Foreign Secretary asking when the United Kingdom Government gave the IAEA information upon which it based its assessment about attempts by Iraq to procure uranium from Africa; and the answer given by the Honourable Member for Rotherham, that the United Kingdom Government did not pass to the IAEA any information on Iraqi attempts to procure uranium, and therefore questions why the United Kingdom Government has not submitted the evidence, upon which it bases its assessment, to IAEA scrutiny, in line with its obligations under Security Council resolutions.

We are still unclear about the facts surrounding this wholly mendacious allegation.

The following day was another trial by ordeal for the Prime Minister before the Liaison Committee. He insisted:

I don't concede it at all that the intelligence at the time was wrong . . . I have absolutely no doubt at all that we will find evidence of weapons of mass destruction programmes.

The intelligence may well have been right. It was what he and his closest advisers did with it which is questionable. Remember that this was some months into the Iraq conflict, and he could still say:

I do stand by the essential case. I also stand entirely by the intelligence we put in the September dossier . . . do not believe that our intelligence will be shown to be wrong at all. I think it will be shown to be right . . . I have no doubt at all that he was trying to reconstitute WMD programmes.

He never budged an inch. I asked Foreign Secretary Jack Straw for a government apology on 14 October:

. . . does [the Foreign Secretary] not think it is now time for the Government to apologise for the dodgy dossier, which misled the House on Iraq in the first place?

That apology has yet to materialise. It is no more likely to do so than the independent public enquiry I asked for in the *Guardian* on 27 February 2004:

. . . we have come to expect the worst of our security services when they are guided by men and women of little principle. Yet when we bug our allies to undermine them at the United Nations, we are plumbing new depths . . . Let us recall the calamitous interaction between the intelligence services and the British Government in Iraq. There was Scott Ritter's account of M16's Operation Mass Appeal in the 1990s, designed to 'shake up public opinion' against Iraq, using dubious intelligence material. There was the alleged failure to tell the Prime Minister that the doubtful 45-minutes claim related only to battlefield munitions, and the subsequent failure to find the ubiquitous

WMD. Until we have a full, public and independent inquiry into the case for going to war against Iraq, there will remain a dark cloud over the Prime Minister.

Still, not yet beaten, I tried again to illuminate one corner of this ugly mess, with a written question to Jack Straw on the 8 March 2004:

> To ask the Secretary of State for Foreign and Commonwealth Affairs what steps have been taken to establish who was responsible for forging documents relating to attempts by Iraq to obtain uranium from Niger.

The reply from FCO Minister Denis MacShane did little to enlighten me:

> We have repeatedly made clear that our assessment that Iraq sought to procure uranium from Africa was not based upon the documents submitted to the International Atomic Energy Agency which subsequently were identified as forgeries. Since these documents did not have any bearing on our assessment, the Government has taken no steps to identify the forgers.

Later that year, in July, Lord Butler's report was published:

> . . . we were struck by the relative thinness of the intelligence base . . .

This was an indictment of Blair's 'beyond doubt' assurances, but the report rehashed what was, by and large, already known. Its credibility had already been damaged early on, as Harry Cohen noted in an early day motion on 1 March 2004:

> . . . notes that the Butler Inquiry into the Intelligence Services pre-war claims about Iraq's WMD no longer has bi-party support, and that confidence in it must therefore be seriously eroded . . .

The mandarin in Lord Butler regretted the style of Blair's Number 10. This was not mere pedantry on his part. He noted, for example, there were often no minutes of critical meetings and decisions. Much was done on the basis of a nod and a wink by Whitehall standards. Crucially, there was little evidence of what was decided at vital junctures in the decision-making processes. Reliance had to be on the recollections of participants.

What could not be denied was that Parliament had been misled. When I said so publicly in August 2004 I was stating what was blindingly obvious to all:

> That the Prime Minister has misled the Commons is not in doubt in most people's minds.

Harry Cohen was another backbencher who kept nagging away on the issue of faulty intelligence, as in an early day motion on 5 January 2004:

> That this House is aware of intelligence inadequacies in connection with the war in Iraq, including claims about weapons of mass destruction, their deployment within 45 minutes, weapons grade uranium from Niger, and sources of intelligence linked to the opposition groups with a vested interest to exaggerate and influence rather than inform; notes that much of the United Kingdom media, in April 2002, declared that United Kingdom military action based on intelligence, had killed Ali Hassan al-Majeed, known as 'Chemical Ali', in Basra; further notes that it has now confirmed that 'Chemical Ali' is alive and in United States custody and that his being alive represents another failure of United Kingdom intelligence and its sources in connection with Iraq; and believes that this whole episode shows the gullibility of the press and the fallibility of intelligence.

However, it was not necessarily inadequate intelligence. It may well have been doctored to fit in with the Government's agenda.

Meanwhile, the Prime Minister continued to bluff and bluster his way through increasing scrutiny, telling BBC's *Breakfast with Frost* on 11 January 2004:

What you can say is that we received that intelligence about Saddam's programmes and about his weapons that we acted on that, it's the case throughout the whole of the conflict . . . I remember having conversations with the chief of defence staff and other people were saying well, we think we might have potential WMD find here or there . . . Now these things didn't actually come to anything in the end, but I don't know the answer. And what I do know is that the group of people that are in there now, this Iraq Survey Group, they produced an interim report.

A fortnight later, he told the *Observer*:

I have absolutely no doubt in my mind that the intelligence was genuine . . . It is absurd to say in respect of any intelligence that it is infallible, but if you ask me what I believe, I believe the intelligence was correct, and I think in the end we will have an explanation.

The explanation may well lie in the refusal of the politicians to accept the truth of the intelligence, because it did not fit the Bush–Blair political agenda. A crack appeared when Blair appeared before the House of Commons Liaison Committee on 3 February:

What is true about . . . David Kay's evidence, and this is something I have to accept, and is one of the reasons why I think we now need a new enquiry – it is true David Kay is saying we have not found large stockpiles of actual weapons.

The very next day, Llew Smith tabled yet another early day motion:

That this House notes that the outgoing Head of the Iraq Survey group, Dr David Kay, told the New York Times in an interview published on 26 January that his team had uncovered no evidence that Niger had tried to sell uranium to Iraq for its nuclear weapons programme and that the original reports on Niger have been found to be based on forged documents, and that the Bush administration has since backed away from its initial assertions; contracts this with the reply by the Prime Minister to the Honourable Member for Blaenau Gwent on 28 October 2003 in which he said that the United Kingdom ensured that the International Atomic Energy Agency was made aware of the contents of non United Kingdom owned intelligence on apparent Iraqi attempts to procure uranium from Niger, and shared all relevant United Kingdom owned material with the IAEA and United Nations Monitoring Verification and Inspection Commission on these alleged uranium procurement activities; and calls upon the Government to explain, and publish, the exact source of its beliefs that Iraq tried to obtain uranium from Niger for its nuclear weapons programme.

He had summed up this facet of the case – the Prime Minister using flawed 'intelligence' – but held out no hope of satisfaction. On that same day, however, a ray of light broke through on Number 10's approach from an unlikely 'source' – Brian Jones, a former leading Ministry of Defence expert on WMD. Speaking to the *Independent* he ventured:

> In my view the expert intelligence analysts were overruled in the preparation of the dossier in September 2002, resulting in a preparation that was misleading about Iraq's capabilities.

Other voices were being raised about the methods employed to gain intelligence – in one instance, about friendly countries at the United Nations Security Council, who did not share Anglo-American enthusiasm for war. Lynne Jones highlighted the case of Katherine Gun in a motion tabled on 25 February 2004:

> That this House applauds the courage and patriotism of GCHQ translator Katherine Gunn who made public information about a memo from the United States Government

National Security Agency requesting United Kingdom assistance with a covert surveillance campaign of the United Nations Security Council members such as Mexico and Chile prior to voting on a resolution which would have endorsed the proposed invasion of Iraq in March 2003; welcomes the decision to drop the charges against her for breaching the Officials Secrets Act; considers that the actions of Ms Gunn qualify her as a whistleblower – an employee who, on the basis of principle, exposes a malpractice or miscarriage of justice that deserves public attention; calls on the Government to reform the Official Secrets Act so that whistleblowers are able to have a public interest defence so that if a jury can be persuaded that a breach of the Official Secrets Act is in the public interest this should be an absolute defence; and calls on the Government to make a statement on the information made public by Ms Gunn.

Barrister and politician Bob Marshall-Andrews lent his support on 1 March:

That this House expresses its grave concerns at the institution and discontinuance of criminal proceedings against Katherine Gunn; notes that the prosecution was pending for three months from the date of charge during which time legal advice must have been given at the highest level to the effect that a clear prima facie case existed against Miss Gunn; further notes that the discontinuance was coincident with requests by the defence for government documents relating to the war against Iraq; considers that the statements purporting to provide reasons for the discontinuance are presently inadequate and wanting in particularity; calls upon the Government forthwith to make public and place in the Libraries of both Houses of Parliament (a) Counsel's opinions relating to the institution, continuance and discontinuance of the case against Miss Gunn and (b) all advices on the legality of the war on Iraq provided to government by the Attorney General or Counsel retained on his behalf; and further calls for the appointment of independent senior counsel to review the proceedings against Miss Gunn and to report to Parliament on the circumstances in which they were begun and brought to an end.

His concern was plain. Disproportionate pressure was being exercised against Ms Gunn, in order to ensure that no further leaks on 'intelligence' – or lack of it – would occur.

Other probes into what was really known continued. On 26 April 2004, I put down a written question to the Prime Minister:

To ask the Prime Minister when the director of the CIA first advised the British Government not to use the allegation that Iraq could ready weapons of mass destruction in forty-five minutes.

Llew Smith was far more inventive, with a motion tabled on the 26 May 2004:

That this House notes the apology to their readers by the editors of the New York Times newspaper in its issue of 26 May because of the paper's misreporting on several occasions, in prominently placed articles, that Iraq had possession of WMD; recognises that, with hindsight, the newspaper concedes it was over reliant on so-called 'intelligence' information; notes that it concedes that 'in some cases, information that was controversial then, and seems questionable now, was insufficiently qualified or allowed to stand unchallenged' and that the 'problematic articles . . . depended at least in part on information from a circle of Iraqi informants, defectors and exiles bent on regime change in Iraq, people whose credibility has come under increasing public debate in recent weeks; agrees with the newspaper editors that it is 'past time' to turn the light on themselves; and recommends to Ministers, including the Prime Minister that they adopt this same policy of self-examination over their assertions that Iraq had WMD in the period from the publication of the Government dossier on Iraq's alleged WMD in September 2002 to the present.

Once again, unfortunately, he was whistling in the wind. So was Gordon Prentice, who picked up smartly on Lord Butler's Report:

> That this House notes with unease Lord Butler's observations on page 147 of his report concerning the nature of Cabinet discussions on Iraq; is dismayed that while a small number of key Ministers met frequently, no papers were circulated to the full Cabinet or to a Cabinet committee despite the fact that 'excellent quality papers' were written by officials and that information given to Cabinet ministers outside the inner circle and in the Cabinet forum was solely by way of oral briefings by the Prime Minister, Foreign Secretary and Defence Secretary; further notes that Lord Butler's conclusion that this practice 'reduced Cabinet Ministers' ability to prepare properly for such discussions' and this reduced 'the scope for informed collective political judgement'; deplores the way in which vital decisions on war and peace were taken on the full authority of the Cabinet but without the active participation and engagement of all its members; and calls on the Head of the Home Civil Service and the Prime Minister to give an undertaking to Parliament that the concerns expressed by Lord Butler on the machinery of government will be fully addressed.

In the United States, a far more critical report on US intelligence by the Senate Intelligence Committee put our institutional weakness into perspective. On 9 July they wrote that there was:

> . . . mischaracterisation of intelligence . . . most of the major key judgements . . . [were] either overstated, or were not supported by, the underlying intelligence report . . . [no] established formal relationship [between Al Qaeda and Saddam] . . . In the end, what the President and the Congress used to send the country to

war was information that was provided by the intelligence community, and that information was flawed.

Their frankness should be of no surprise. The American system is, after all, far more open than our secretive privilege–heavy approach to government. Lynne Jones kept up her campaign on intelligence with a detailed motion on 12 July 2004:

> That this House notes with concern the refusal of the Secretary of State for Foreign Affairs to answer Parliamentary Question 182618 of 8 July put by the Honourable Member for Birmingham Selly Oak on whether signals intelligence picked up by GCHQ concerning a visit by an Iraqi official to Niger was passed on to the International Atomic Energy Agency, instead stating that 'it would not be appropriate to comment publicly on the detail of this intelligence reporting'; notes that no detail was being requested in this question; is perplexed because previous Parliamentary questions asking what information has been passed to the IAEA by the United Kingdom Government have been answered by Foreign Office ministers; calls upon the Foreign Secretary to make it known to the House whether the GCHQ intelligence in question was passed to the IAEA, further notes that since 6th May in response to other Parliamentary questions regarding the claim in the Government's September 2002 Dossier, 'Iraq's Weapons of Mass Destruction' that Iraq had attempted to procure significant quantities of uranium from Africa; Parliamentary Questions 270513, 171178, 173387, 175493 and 175494, the Foreign Secretary has refused to answer, referring to the fact that Lord Butler of Brockwell is conducting the review; believes that by referring to the Butler Review instead of answering Parliamentary questions, the Government is replacing Parliamentary accountability with a secret inquiry on these matters; and suggests to the Foreign Secretary that by his unco-operative actions, he is undermining the House's rightful role of scrutinising the policies and actions of ministers.

She was absolutely right to demand accountability, but powerless to ensure it. Two days later, the Prime Minister again performed a verbal contortion, without any apparent immediate political damage:

> We expected – I expected – to find actual usable, chemical or biological weapons after we entered Iraq . . . .But I have to accept as the months have passed, it seems increasingly clear that at the time of invasion, Saddam did not have stockpiles of chemical or biological weapons ready to deploy.

Still there was no admission that he had been wrong all of the time. No one took responsibility, as Elfyn Llwyd noted in the debate:

> The Butler report refers to strains, mistakes, misinformation and the resultant carnage. Somehow, no one is to blame for all that.

The Prime Minister could still claim that:

> No-one lied. No-one made up the intelligence. No-one inserted things into the dossier against the advice of the intelligence services . . . There was no conspiracy. There was no impropriety . . . We all acknowledged Saddam was evil and his regime depraved.

Also on that fateful day, the *Flood Report* was released in Australia. It found that:

> [WMD evidence was] thin, ambiguous and incomplete.

Three major Anglo-Saxon nations were forced to admit in their different ways that their intelligence – or the way in which it was interpreted – was badly flawed. No one was held politically accountable in any of the three. Remember, too, that the intelligence communities of these three countries are conjoined in the massive 'Echelon' project to monitor global electronic traffic. What other monumental errors do they share?

The Butler Report advised:

> . . . we were struck by the relative thinness of the intelligence base supporting the greater firmness of the Joint Intelligence Committee's judgements on Iraqi production and possession of chemical and biological weapons.

It was, nevertheless, a curate's egg of a report, as I told the House:

> Curiously, when Lord Butler wrote about the background to the weapons of mass destruction, he did not mention where they actually came from . . . he did not mention the countries, including the United Kingdom and the United States, that provided the very weapons of mass destruction that would later become politically problematic.

Six months later, Lynne Jones was still fighting her own attritional war on governmental deceit:

> That this House notes that in response to concerns raised by Honourable Members about the validity of the case made for war, the Prime Minister referred the House to the findings of the Iraq Survey Group, for example stating on 21 January that it was the job for the ISG to find out what has happened, which it will do; notes that the ISG makes it clear that it found no evidence that Iraq sought uranium abroad after the first Gulf War in 1991, stating that it has uncovered no information to support allegations of Iraq pursuit of uranium from abroad in the post-Operation Desert Storm era; further notes that the ISG report goes on to state it had found only one offer of uranium to Baghdad since 1991, an approach which Iraq appeared to have turned down; further notes that the Government has provided no evidence to rebut this finding but is now relying on the conclusion of the Government appointed Butler Committee: but not that Lord Butler's conclusions on the

uranium claim only refer to the credibility of United Kingdom and United States assertions made prior to 7 March 2003, the date the International Atomic Energy Agency revealed forged intelligence documents; and therefore calls on the Government to provide new evidence to counter the ISG findings or withdraw their isolated claim that Iraq sought to procure uranium from Africa.

Robin Cook belatedly gave *Panorama* his take on how the Prime Minister squared his improbable circle:

He [Tony Blair] knew perfectly well what he was doing. I think there was a lack of candour . . . The reality is he believed in the evidence because he needed to believe in the evidence.

Cook believed Blair to be wilfully delusional.

Eleven days later, Bush's own panel of experts described American assessment of Saddam's weapons capabilities as 'dead wrong'. The intelligence agencies had exaggerated evidence and relied on shaky sources. Predictably, no blame was attached to the politicians.

Lynne Jones was still digging in an EDM tabled in May 2005:

That this House notes the accusations, in the Observer on 15 May, by Dr Rod Barton, an Australian intelligence officer, formerly a member of the CIA-led Iraq Survey Group, that Secret Intelligence Service [M16] Director-General, John Scarlett, whilst still chairman of the Joint Intelligence Committee, tried to influence the content of the independent verification research evaluation of Iraq's alleged WMD programme by e-mailing the head of the ISG in March 2004 proposing the insertion into the report of nine 'nuggets' of WMD-related information based on British intelligence information rather than information or discoveries originating from the ISG's investigations; believes such a report can only carry credibility if it retains its independence, and thus any such attempted 'sexing-up' of the report would be damaging to the entire Iraq inspection process; and calls upon the Prime Minister and Secretary of State for Foreign and Commonwealth Affairs to make a public statement on any involvement by John Scarlett in the drafting of the ISG report.

She, like others, will not cease, until the truth is told.

Aftermath

Of all tyrannies, a tyranny exercised for the good of its victims may be the most oppressive. It may be better to live under robber barons than under omnipotent moral busybodies. The robber baron's cruelty may sometimes sleep, his cupidity may at some point be satiated, but those who torment us for our own good will torment us without end, for they do so with the approval of their own conscience.

C.S. Lewis (1898–1963)

On 26 August 2002, it had seemed that Dick Cheney had found his own futurologist to predict the outcome of his intended war on Iraq. Speaking to veterans, he had declared:

> The Middle East expert Professor Fouad Ajami predicts that after liberation, the streets of Basra and Baghdad are 'sure to erupt in joy'. Extremists in the region would have to rethink their strategy of jihad. Moderates throughout the region would take heart.

After the war, questions to ministers and appeals for caution, turned to more accusatory statements from critics as the truth of the situation on the ground became apparent. Thus, I was quoted in the *Guardian* on 29 May 2003:

> This is absolutely dangerous for Tony Blair . . . The potential charge is that the House of Commons has been misled.

This remains a major charge against Prime Minister Blair – that, either deliberately or inadvertently, he misled Parliament. I was quoted the following day in the same paper, regarding the Security and Intelligence Committee Inquiry:

> This is going to run and run. This shows how flimsy the whole basis
> for going to war was. Either the Government misled the House for
> political reasons or they were misled by the security services.

If the intelligence had been sound, then it was a failure of political judgement which took us to war on a false prospectus. The question remains whether this failure of judgement resulted from ineptitude or duplicity.
Even at the Labour Party Conference later that year, Blair appeared wholly unmoved:

> I can only go one way. I have no reverse gear.

His Conference speech was one thing; an open debate was another. The Prime Minister's fixers ensured that there was no debate at the Conference. Disappointed, I warned in the *Mirror*:

> This is a major, major mistake. People will not understand why
> the biggest issues of the moment are not being debated.

Tony Blair had denied what were seen as traditional British strengths on the global stage. Thus, he had told ambassadors back in January 2003:

> This is not the time for British caution or even British reserve.

Despite having insisted in a speech at the George Bush Senior Presidential Library the previous year:

> As for Iraq . . . we will proceed, as we did after 11 September, in
> a calm, measured, sensible but firm way.

He had also implied a cautious and an incremental approach to Iraq to the Liaison Committee of 21 January 2003:

The two most important (factors) are . . . is it the right thing to do and can it be done? When I say is it right and is it do-able, is it do-able militarily but also is the aftermath something that you can handle as well, because I think that is important too.

His reference to thinking through 'the aftermath' did not wash with Glenda Jackson, who told the House the next day:

I do not believe that having won the war we, the United Kingdom and the United States, will be prepared to commit the money, people, material and time to create a new democratic society in Iraq.

She was right. A more serious contempt was displayed in a *Mirror* article by John Pilger, 'Blair is a Coward' in February 2003:

In 1946 the judges at Nuremberg . . . left no doubt about what they regarded as the gravest crimes against humanity. The most serious was unprovoked invasion of a sovereign state that offered no threat to one's homeland. There was the murder of civilians for which responsibility rested with the 'highest authority'. Blair is about to commit both these crimes, for which he is being denied even the flimsiest UN cover now that the weapons inspectors have found, as one put it, 'zilch'. To call Blair a mere 'poodle' is to allow him distance from the killing of innocent Iraqi men, women and children for which he will share responsibility. He is the embodiment of the most dangerous appeasement humanity has known since the 1930s.

Meanwhile, at the Scottish Labour Party Conference, Blair was testing the waters on issues of a 'moral case for removing Saddam' and 'conviction' in relation to Iraq. However, as commentator Malcolm Harrison spelt out, it was too easy to think of a war against Iraq in a simplistic way:

The obvious line, that we should bomb Saddam and get it over with because he is an evil despot who murders his own people, is to reduce the argument to a very superficial level. I wish it were only that simple. Are we ready to accept responsibility for the mayhem that might follow and a significant deepening of simmering hatreds? Is this the kind of peace we want? The maxim 'live by the sword and die by the sword' was never more appropriate.

Glen Rangwala was certainly not buying into Blair's moral case for war. As he wrote in an article entitled 'Blair's Crumbling Case for War' for *Labour Left Briefing*:

The appearance of the Prime Minister's new moral case for war from his Glasgow conference speech of 15 February, derives from the failure of his prior justification.

It was certainly not just an armchair debate either, as I reminded the House on 26 February 2003:

I . . . have noticed the Foreign Secretary's inconsistency and the various attempts to shift the goalposts . . . If we have not already signalled a firm intention to attack Iraq, I do not know what we have done . . . Like him [the Member for Rushcliffe, Kenneth Clarke] I anticipate that the overwhelming force in place to deal with Iraq is of such a nature that a campaign would, hopefully, be relatively short and sharp. What we cannot guarantee, however, is the amount of collateral damage that would ensue – apart from the wholly undesirable political outcomes, of course.

There was also the contentious issue of Iraq's oil. Tony Blair told MTV on 7 March 2003:

We don't touch it and the United States doesn't touch it.

He repeated this on 18 March in the Commons:

> The oil revenues, which people falsely claim that we want to
> seize, should be put in a trust fund for the Iraqi people admin-
> istered through the United Nations . . . The United Kingdom
> should seek a new Security Council resolution that would
> affirm the use of all oil revenues for the benefit of the Iraqi
> people.

By May of that year, a United Nations resolution tabled by the United
Kingdom and the United States gave them (especially the United States), total
control of Iraq's oil revenues. However, Resolution 1483, putting this promise
into effect, set up no UN-administered trust fund. In fact, deductions are
being made from Iraq's oil revenues as compensation for the invasion of
Kuwait twelve years ago.

While still in the Cabinet, Clare Short was telling BBC's *The Westminster
Hour* of her own concerns – echoing the arguments of Anatole Lieven and
Senator Robert Byrd – on 9 March 2003:

> The whole atmosphere of the current situation is deeply
> reckless – reckless for the world, reckless for the undermining of
> the United Nations in this orderly world, reckless with our own
> government, reckless with his [Blair's] own future, position and
> place in history.

In the eyes of many, Blair *was* behaving recklessly, endangering the lives of
Britons and Iraqis. Of course, Bush was bent on doing the same, although
cloaking the reality in pious promises, as on 17 March 2003:

> In a free Iraq, there will be no more wars of aggression against
> your neighbours, no more poison factories, no more execu-
> tions of dissidents, no more torture chambers and rape rooms.
> The tyrant will soon be gone. The day of your liberation is
> near.

In the House of Commons the following day, Blair was certainly correct to say:

> The outcome of this issue . . . will determine the way in which Britain and the world confront the central security threat of the twenty-first century, the development of the relationship between Europe and the US, the relations within the EU and the way in which the US engages with the rest of the world.

The problem was that his prognosis was dramatically opposite to that of his opponents. As Charles Kennedy put it:

> . . . we do not believe that a case for war has been established under these procedures in the absence of a second United Nations Security Council resolution . . . I believe that the impact of war in these circumstances is bound to weaken the international coalition against terrorism, itself, and not least in the Muslim world. The big fear that many of us have is that the action will simply breed further generations of suicide bombers.

There were essentially two sides to the debate – those who trusted the Prime Minister and those who did not. Speaking for the former among the Tories, Nicholas Winterton declared:

> I say to my constituents, 'On this issue, put your trust in the Prime Minister. I fervently believe, as your Member of Parliament, that he is right'. We will get it right, we will bring peace to the Middle East and we will restore the credibility of the United Nations.

He was joined on the Labour side by Barry Gardner:

> The people of this country know that our Prime Minister has behaved with absolute integrity on this issue. The people of this country therefore trust the Prime Minister on Iraq.

In the other camp, Peter Ainsworth spoke for Opposition members who had a dimmer view of the Prime Minister:

> . . . the people do not trust the Prime Minister. They do not trust him on health, education or crime. Why, therefore, should they trust him on Iraq?

He was in the same camp as Labour's Brian Sedgemore:

> It is sad that the Prime Minister should have forsaken the ideal of a tolerant and liberal internationalism in favour of the frightening concept that might is right . . . We are supposed to admire the Prime Minister because he is a man without doubts and one shorn of scepticism – two of the greatest qualities that the British people have. He just knows that he is right and is therefore prepared to ignore the advice of virtually all the leaders of the great religions in the world . . . I find that approach rather frightening. Worse than all that, the Prime Minister shows himself to be oblivious of, and careless towards, the shrewd moral judgement of the majority of British people . . . in modern democracy we need something stronger to hold on to than the slogan 'My Prime Minister, right or wrong'. He [the Prime Minister] should know . . . that when arrogance turns to hubris, comeuppance is never far behind.

There were some who looked for a higher consideration from his Parliamentary colleagues, innately decent people like Malcolm Savidge:

> There is only one issue that we must consider today; whether we should go to war at this time and set what is, to me, a terrible precedent of starting a pre-emptive war on a dubious legal basis without the support of the United Nations...It should transcend our careers, because in this context we should regard ourselves as 'here today, gone tomorrow' politicians.

Interestingly, no seat was found for Savidge by the Labour Party in Scotland after a boundary review; Sedgemore left Parliament and the Labour Party; and Gardiner was given a junior ministerial post.

Tony Blair had claimed in that great debate:

> The country and the Parliament reflect each other.

Not if John Pilger was to be believed. In March 2003 he wrote:

> . . . as a journalist, I have never known official lying to be more persuasive than today. We may laugh at the vacuities in Tony Blair's 'Iraq dossier' and Jack Straw's inept lie that Iraq has developed a nuclear bomb (which his minions rushed to 'explain'). But the more insidious the lies, justifying an unprovoked attack on Iraq and linking it to would-be terrorists who are said to lurk in every tube station, are routinely channelled as news. They are not news; they are black propaganda.

There was to be no respite for the Prime Minister and his pro-war faction. Writing on my website, I reminded ministers that:

> . . . what was illegal, immoral and illogical on Tuesday has, by today, not become legal, moral and logical. The damage already done by this war to the United Nations, the European Union, NATO, and, not least, Britain's standing in the world, is incalculable . . . Terrorism has been made more likely as hostility towards us flares and instability is reinforced throughout the Middle East. I fear it will take a lot more effort and many, many years, to repair the tattered international reputations of both the United States and the United Kingdom.

Tariq Aziz, the Iraqi Foreign Minister, warned CNN:

> American soldiers will be received with bullets, not flowers.

The propaganda war was in full flow, and encouraged Liberal Democrat Paul Marsden to table an early day motion on 26th March:

> That this House mourns the death of British journalists including the late Terry Lloyd and salutes those brave reporters trying to send impartial and fair coverage of the war in Iraq; urges the British media to use clear language when reporting the war in Iraq; deplores some journalists using technical and military jargon that act as euphemisms to reduce the implications of war; and hopes journalists and commentators will stop using particularly the terms, take out, soften up and clear out when they mean dropping bombs, firing missiles and killing people.

Lindsay Hoyle was more concerned with the Iraqi civilian population:

> That this House notes the immediate need to ensure that supplies of humanitarian aid are channelled into Iraq in order to support the Iraqi population; recognises the importance of providing food, shelter and medical aid as soon as possible in order to prevent a major humanitarian crisis; and calls on the United States and United Kingdom governments to work closely with the United Nations, the European Union, and non governmental organisations, in providing a programme of reform in Iraq which will support the humanitarian needs of the civilian population.

Prime Minister Blair tried to reassure the Arab world in an article on 30 March:

> . . . we are doing all that is humanly possible to minimise civilian casualties and finish this campaign quickly – Military forces will withdraw from Iraq as soon as practicable.

He continued:

I believe that history will judge that we made the right choice.

Paul Marsden reminded the Prime Minister of his promises – perhaps appropriately – in an early day motion on April Fool's Day:

> That this House welcomes the Prime Minister's promise that he
> will not let down the Iraqi people in delivering humanitarian
> aid and assistance to rebuild Iraq; notes that the Prime Minister
> said on 14 November 2001 that this time he would not walk
> away from the Afghan people and that he would ensure massive
> amounts of aid would be sent to Afghanistan; is greatly
> alarmed at the report in The Sunday Times on 23 March by
> Christina Lamb that in the neonatal unit of the Kabul hospital
> premature babies can only be placed in the unit's only incubator
> for 15 minutes per three hours and only when there is electricity;
> is dismayed that hospital doctors and nurses have no masks or
> gloves or sterile solutions for washing; is concerned that
> President Karzai has been unable to pay his Ministers since last
> June; condemns the lack of assistance for refugees forced to
> sleep outside and that medical students have no classrooms; and
> urges the Prime Minister to deliver on his promises to both the
> Afghan and Iraqi people.

Marsden had obviously woken up to the realities of Iraq and the war, tabling another motion on 8 April:

> That this House congratulates the British Armed Service
> personnel distributing aid to Iraqi civilians and attempting to
> maintain calm in an extremely difficult and perilous situation
> through patience and professionalism on peacekeeping duties;
> is concerned at the apparent contrast with the way some United
> States armed service personnel are operating since the war on
> Iraq commenced; with 14 civilians killed and 30 injured in a
> bombing raid on a Baghdad shopping area, 12 civilians killed
> travelling in trucks across a bridge south of Nassiriya, ten dead

and 200 wounded civilians in one residential area in Baghdad and 60 civilians killed north of Baghdad travelling by bus, all apparently shot or bombed by United States military forces; and urges the British Government to make the strongest representations to the United States Government that actions must be increased to safeguard civilians in Iraq.

Tory Bob Spink joined him a day later, in praising our troops. Like Marsden, he failed to excoriate the Government for putting British troops in this mess:

That this House congratulates British Armed Service personnel distributing aid to Iraqi civilians and attempting to maintain calm in an extremely difficult and perilous situation through patience and professionalism on peacekeeping duties; deeply regrets civilian casualties and collateral damage; and urges the Government to now focus on restoring the rule of law and order, respect for human rights, delivering humanitarian aid, the reconstruction of Iraq and encouraging the emergence of an Iraqi based system of democratic, representative administration for this previously brutally oppressed people.

Joan Ruddock, the former Labour spokesperson on women, drew on her own particular concerns and expertise:

That this House notes that while Iraqi women have suffered enormously under Saddam Hussein's regime as victims of political rape and torture, as mothers unable to provide for their children and as wives who lost their husbands, nonetheless they did make up more than 20 percent of the Iraqi workforce holding a range of professional and technical jobs, and are not subject to any state religious laws or dress code; observes that while the Iraqi Parliament was a sham, almost 20 per cent of its members were women; further notes that in Northern Iraq, Kurdish women travel freely, hold high level economic and political positions including as judges and regional government ministers; believes that in post-conflict situations, women are particularly vulnerable to violence and rape and are frequently excluded from the political forums set up by the international community; expresses concern that there appears to be no significant involvement of women in United States plans to consult on an Iraq Interim Authority and that the United Kingdom has appointed a male cleric to oversee the running of Basra; and calls on the Government to listen to the views of Iraqi women's organisations in London who have called for a secular democracy with at least 40 per cent women and 40 per cent men to be included in the Iraqi Interim Authority, for a gender balanced team to draw up the new constitution (as was done in South Africa), and for a new legal code that would guarantee the rights of women in post Saddam Iraq.

Meanwhile, on 13 April, Richard Perle was demonstrating in the *News of the World* the stereotypical lack of judgement of the American neocons:

The predications of those who opposed this war can be discarded like spent cartridges.

Mark Field, the Tory Member representing the City of London, was on the ball for his banker and financial constituents:

That this House notes that Saddam Hussein's regime accumulated almost 400 billion dollars of debt and reparation claims; believes that these are odious since the regime was oppressive and illegitimate; welcomes the Jubilee Iraq call for cancellation of these financial obligations so that the liberated Iraqi people are not made to pay the bill for the wars and oppression they suffered after Saddam; would also encourage a reciprocal cancellation by the future democratic government of Iraq of debts owed to Iraq by other highly indebted poor countries; and urges Her Majesty's Government to use all its influence in the Coalition and with creditors to ensure that none of Saddam

Hussein's financial obligations pass on to the soon to be formed democratic government of Iraq, in line with the Prime Minister's promises to the Iraqi people of freedom and renewed prosperity.

Tony Worthington's ministerial experience and general thoughtfulness came out in his motion of 14 April:

That this House notes the grave effects of the present war in Iraq on the civilian population; believes any international involvement in establishing a transitional administration in Iraq must be driven multilaterally by the international community and have a clear UN mandate; further notes the need to establish an inclusive democracy in Iraq which guarantees the rights of all ethnic and religious communities as outlined by Minority Rights Group international; believes that the people of Iraq must decide on the structure and form of its own democracy and that the new constitution should conform to international human rights standards and establish equality before the law; calls on the international community to ensure that the interim government takes into consideration a federal structure for Iraq, taking particular account of the long standing aspirations of the Kurds for self-government and to enact special measures to counteract long standing discrimination against the Shi'a and against Kurds and other minorities, including promoting their participation in central and regional government; and calls for the deployment of human rights monitors across Iraq during any transitional phase and the implementation of a major programme to facilitate the voluntary return or resettlement of refugees and internationally displaced persons.'

The indomitable Perle was telling *USA Today* on 2 May to:

. . . relax and celebrate victory.

In her resignation speech, Clare Short pointed the finger for the undemocratic style of the British Government, at the Prime Minister.

> I do think . . . that the errors we are making over Iraq and other recent initiatives flow not from Labour's values, but from the style and organisation of our government, which is undermining trust and straining party loyalty in a way that is completely unnecessary. The problem is centralisation of power into the hands of the Prime Minister and an increasingly small number of advisers who make decisions in private without proper discussion.

If, many asked, she knew this, why had she been so slow in resigning? It was difficult at times to follow her reasoning:

> I had many criticisms of the way in which events leading up to the conflict in Iraq were handled. The reason I agreed to remain in the Government was that it was too late to put right the mistakes that had been made. However, the problem now is that the mistakes that were made in the period leading up to the conflict are being repeated in the post-conflict situation. In particular, the United Nations mandate necessary to bring into being a legitimate Iraqi Government is not being supported by the United Kingdom Government . . . Under the Geneva Convention of 1949 and the Hague regulations of 1907, the coalition is legally entitled to modify the operation of the administration as much as is necessary to fulfil [certain] obligations; but it is not entitled to make major political, economic and constitutional changes. The coalition does not have sovereign authority and it has no authority to bring into being an interim Iraqi Government with such authority, or to create a constitutional process leading to the election of a sovereign government. The only body that has the legal authority to do this is the United Nations Security Council . . . The United Kingdom Government is supporting the United States in trying

to bully the Security Council into a resolution that gives the coalition the power to establish an Iraqi Government and control the use of oil for reconstruction with only a minor role for the United Nations . . . In both the run up to war and now, I think the United Kingdom is making grave errors in providing cover for the United States mistakes; but undermining international law and the authority of the United Nations increases the risk of instability, bitterness and growing terrorism that will threaten the future for all of us . . . I am ashamed that the United Kingdom Government has agreed to the resolution tabled in New York and shocked by the secrecy and lack of consultation with departments with direct responsibility for the issues referred to in the resolution.

It was also difficult to equate the political obsessions on Iraq in London and Washington with events on the ground. As 72-year-old Saleh Hamzeh Ali Moussawi told the *Los Angeles Times*:

Our home is an empty place. We who are left are like wild animals. All we can do is cry out.

This was after eleven members of his family were killed when an American tank fired on a minivan. The body count had begun, as Paul Marsden noted in a motion on 20 May:

That this House condemns the deaths of at least 4,065 Iraqi civilians in the war in Iraq, including 372 civilians killed by cluster bombs, as independently reported by Iraq Body Count; notes the misleading claim by General Richard Meyers, chairman of the military's Joint Chiefs of Staff on Friday 25th April that only one civilian has died from United States and United Kingdom cluster bombs; expresses sympathy to all the families who lost loved ones in the years under Saddam Hussein and those who have suffered further losses from the war; and urges the Government to end the use of cluster bombs in military campaigns.

Back in London, Clare Short was becoming ever more specific about the Prime Minister. On 9 June she told the *New Statesman*:

> My conclusion is that our Prime Minister deceived us.

And the Foreign Affairs Committee inquiry:

> I presume he [Tony Blair] saw it as honourable deception.

In Iraq, the carnage continued. A 'fat, painfully shy' 15-year-old was killed during a raid on his village. The offhand comment of military spokesman Lieutenant Arthur Jiminez to the *Washington Post* was:

> That person was probably in the wrong place at the wrong time.

Adam Price and Paul Flynn put down an early day motion on the use of cluster bombs in Iraq. Huge numbers of the cluster 'droplets' were already lying on the ground in the country, ready to reap a grim harvest of innocent civilians.
Lynne Jones, meanwhile, was still plugging away for an independent inquiry into the war:

> That this House notes the comments of Rodric Braithwaite, former head of the Joint Intelligence Committee, in a letter published in the 10 July edition of the Financial Times that 'fishmongers sell fish; warmongers sell war' and although 'the Prime Minister surely acted in good faith, it does look as though he seriously oversold his wares'; further notes Mr Braithwaite's assessment that 'the incentives for terrorists to attack us have probably been increased'; and calls for an independent inquiry into the way the Government sold its case for war to Parliament and to the public and the lessons to be learned from this.

As she contemplated the futility of such Parliamentary gestures, Colonel James Alles was quoted in the *Independent* on 10 August 2003 saying:

We napalmed those bridges. Unfortunately, there were people there. It's no great way to die.

More innocents killed by barbaric weapons. The Pentagon denied using napalm. It used the formal name of the weapons – 'Mark 77' incendiary bombs – a euphemism for napalm.

As the death toll mounted, there were attempts to monitor the loss of life, although governments were not interested.

Welsh nationalist Adam Price, in an attempt to flag up the reality of 'collateral' damage, tabled an EDM:

> That this House notes with deep concern that there has been no official count of Iraqi civilian deaths following the conflict in Iraq, and that it is left to unofficial researchers, such as the Iraq Body Count, to estimate figures, cited as being more than 5,000; further notes that Iraq's military dead also remain unnumbered; further notes that incidents such as the one in the Mansur district of Baghdad on 27 July where United States forces killed at least five innocent people during a failed search for Saddam, should focus attention on the loss of civilian life in Iraq at the hands of United States forces since the conflict ended; calls on the United Kingdom Government explicitly to agree with the principle that the Mansur victims and all other Iraqi victims deserve a proper inquest to put pressure on the United States Administration to launch enquiries into all the previous incidents in which civilians have been shot in Iraq since the conflict ended, including the one at Mansur; and to ensure that it is far more concerned in future with losses it inflicts on the Iraqi people and less obsessed with keeping a tally on the triumphant total of cards turned up so far in the deck of most wanted Saddam supporters.

As autumn approached, the situation in Iraq was obviously worsening. For the Tories, it was a political nightmare, given their unfettered support for the

Government in the run up to war. Spokesman Michael Ancram tried to get some political leverage with a motion asking too little, too late:

> That this House notes the deteriorating security situation in Iraq since the end of the conflict; recognises the need for extra troops to be deployed; is concerned that the lack of security has resulted in NGOs removing staff from Iraq; further notes with concern that the lack of security has forced the United Nations now to operate from a neighbouring country; remembers that on the 24 September 2002, the shadow Foreign Secretary warned the Government that if they were to embark upon war, there must be a blueprint with plans and resources so that a democratic prosperous and renewed Iraq could quickly enter the family of nations and the global economy; regrets that the Government ignored these and other warnings from Her Majesty's Opposition; further regrets that inadequate post-conflict planning has contributed to the deterioration of security in Iraq; has every faith the British troops will do their best despite political dithering; and calls for an urgent independent judicial inquiry into the mishandling of post-conflict operations in Iraq.

The industrious Price had meanwhile shifted onto the Government's authoritarian domestic stance, mirroring its right wing foreign policy:

> That this House notes with deep concern the use of powers provided by the Terrorism Act 2000 to police anti-war protests during the recent conflict in Iraq; further notes with deep concern that the use of these powers labels legitimate peaceful protesters as terrorists; condemns the use of section 44 of the Terrorism Act 2000 against protestors at the arms fair in London on 9 September; calls for the Home Affairs Committee to investigate the use of these powers to police anti-war protesters during the recent conflict in Iraq as well as the protesters at the arms fair; and further calls on the

Government to reaffirm its commitment to basic human rights by establishing an independent human rights commission, and in future to allow anti-terror legislation to be used only against individuals who pose a genuine threat to the security of the United Kingdom and not citizens practising their right to peaceful protest against their government's actions.

The whole culture of the Government had moved to the right, heralding new anti-government fronts on civil liberties and penal policy. This was happening on both sides of the Atlantic, stirring a democratic, liberal reaction to the Bush and Blair governments.

Not that the pro-war parties were particularly bothered by this in late 2003, or even cognisant of the shift which was taking place. A disdainful Rumsfeld held a National Press Club lunch in Washington on 10 September:

I don't believe it's our job to reconstruct that country. The Iraqi people are going to have to reconstruct that country over a period of time.

A more considered voice was that of Colin Powell on the NBC on 26 October:

We did not expect it would be quite this intense this long.

Six months after the invasion of Iraq, the enormity of the mistake was becoming apparent to all. Adam Price asked:

That this House notes with deep concern the serious lack of security on the ground in Iraq, demonstrated in particular by the high numbers of both coalition military forces and Iraqi civilians killed since the end of the conflict; and calls for an urgent broader inquiry into the apparent vacuum in the Government's planning where its pre-war assessment of the challenges of post- Saddam Iraq should have been.

Remember that the Prime Minister had assured the country that post-conflict reconstruction was built into government considerations of its policy towards Iraq. There was also the obvious concern about from where the money was to come to pay for this protracted commitment. Was it, I asked the Department for International Development, being taken from other needy programmes?

> Can the minister tell me whether those are the very same programmes that are being threatened with cuts in order to pay for the mess created in Iraq?

Harry Cohen listed the enormous problems in Iraq, on 26 November:

> That this House notes the report 'Continuing collateral Damage: The Health and Environmental Costs of War on Iraq 2003' by the international health charity MEDACT, which indicates that between 21,700 and 55,000 died between 20 March and 20 October, and that limited access to clean water and sanitation as well as poverty, malnutrition and disruption of public services, including health services, continue to have a negative impact on the health of the Iraqi people; and does not share the apparent view of those responsible, who fail to record or report these matters, that those deaths are unimportant.

Michael Ancram virtually repeated his early day motion of 10 September, on 20 November. It showed how little Conservative thinking had been developed with regard to Iraq, and what a catastrophically poor opposition the Conservative front bench had been in failing to challenge this calamitous adventure of the Prime Minister in Iraq.

The American approach was fairly crude, summed up by Colonel Nathan Sassaman to the *New York Times* on 7 December:

> With a heavy dose of fear and violence, and a lot of money for projects, I think we can convince these people that we are here to help them.

Muscle and money were to win the day. Nothing could be further from the truth. Nor was privatisation to be the answer. This led to traumatic crimes like the kidnap and murder of Ken Bigley. It also led to the death of the four contractors which in turn precipitated the American attack on Fallujah. David Chaytor condemned the attack, although grossly underestimating the number of people killed:

> That this House considers that the killing of an estimated 600 people, many of them women and children and innocent civilians fleeing the conflict, by United States forces in Fallujah during the first weeks of April, to have been an atrocity and calls on the Government to request the Coalition Provisional Authority to publish a complete list of fatalities, military and civilian due to the conflict in Iraq in each of the last twelve months.

As did Elfyn Llwyd:

> That this House believes that the mandate given to the Coalition Provisional Authority under United Nations Resolution 1511 will expire on 30 June when the responsibility for governing Iraq is transferred to the Iraqi people, is concerned with recent events in Fallujah where reports suggest that more than 700 Iraqis have been killed over the last month including many women and children; notes that Britain, unlike the United States, is subject to the strictures of the International Criminal Court and could face prosecution if drawn into actions similar to those carried out by United States troops in Fallujah and Najaf; further notes that troops from Spain, Honduras and the Dominican Republic have withdrawn from Iraq and that Australian troops could also leave if the opposition party wins the next general election; calls on the Government to give honourable members of this House the opportunity to debate and to vote before any more British troops are committed to serve in Iraq or are drawn to serve in

areas not currently under British Armed Forces command; demands that a further United Nations resolution is established before handover authorising a multinational command structure answerable to the United Nations Security Council rather than an occupying force; and further demands that the British Government ensures the White House does not renege on previous commitments to transfer full sovereignty to the Iraqi people on 30 June.

Makki a-Nazzal, manager of a clinic in Fallujah, showed his contempt for the West after the attack in an interview with Rahul Mahajan, for *Empire Notes*:

I have been a fool for 47 years. I used to believe in European and American civilisation.

There should be little surprise at Iraqi hostility towards the coalition forces. A Florida National Guardsman, Sergeant Mejia, told the *Guardian*:

The way we treated these men was hard even for the soldiers, especially after realising that many of these 'combatants' were no more than shepherds.

According to a poll of Iraqis for the Coalition Provisional Authority in June 2004, the United States soldiers were seen as peacekeepers by three per cent of the population; liberators by two per cent and occupiers by a massive 92 per cent. According to an anonymous senior United States diplomat in Baghdad, quoted by *Newsweek* on 12 September 2004:

We're dealing with a population that hovers between bare tolerance and outright hostility. This idea of a functioning democracy is crazy. We thought there would be a reprieve after sovereignty, but all hell is breaking loose.

This was hardly surprising given the attitude of an unnamed United States marine commander, speaking in November that year to the BBC:

You will be held accountable for the facts not as they are in hindsight but as they appeared to you at the time. If, in your mind you fire to protect yourself or your men, you are doing the right thing. It doesn't matter if later on you find out you wiped out a family of unarmed civilians.

The Iraqis in exile, who had promoted invasion, could only throw their hands up in desperation. As Ahmed Chalabi declared:

We are heroes in error . . . what was said before is not important.

George Bush had seemed incapable of seeing reality, telling America in his 2004 State of the Union speech:

No one can doubt the word of America.

He could convince America that he had the answers, he told an Albuquerque re-election rally on 11 August 2004:

I know what I'm doing when it comes to winning this war.

Throughout 2004, opposition to war in Iraq remained intense in both Britain and America. The attacks on Tony Blair intensified. Henry Porter wrote in the *Observer* on 14 March:

The Prime Minister increasingly looks more like a deceiver than a leader. It is time we confronted him with his blatant contradictions over Iraq . . . Blair remains unembarrassed by the failure to locate stockpiles of WMD, immune from any process of accountability and inconvenienced not one jot by his own party...the man who manipulates and distorts the British agenda to accommodate his addiction to power.

Dan Plesch and Glen Rangwala wrote on 1 August in *A Case to Answer*:

This report [a report on the potential for impeaching Tony Blair] sets out compelling evidence of deliberate repeated distortion, seriously misleading statements and culpable negligence on the part of the Prime Minister . . . The Prime Minister's conduct has also destroyed the United Kingdom's reputation for honesty around the world; it has produced a war with no end in sight; it has damaged and discredited the intelligence services which are essential to the security of the state; it has undermined the constitution by weakening cabinet government to breaking point; and it has made a mockery of the authority of Parliament as representatives of the people.

Frustrated backbenchers pressed in different directions. John McDonnell wanted an inquiry:

That this House believes that there should now be convened an independent inquiry into why the United Kingdom was taken to war with Iraq.

While Glenda Jackson wanted verification of the number of casualties in Iraq:

That this House calls upon the Prime Minister, in concert with the United States administration and the Iraqi interim government, to immediately institute a dedicated body to gather, collate and publish the number of Iraqi civilians killed and injured as a result of coalition forces actions since 20 March 2003; believes that such a body should incorporate procedures employed by Iraq Bodycount and those United States and Iraqi health experts whose findings, detailing 100,000 civilian deaths, was (sic) published by the Lancet on 30 October.

Meanwhile Prime Minister Blair showed not one iota of self-doubt. Speaking to British troops in Iraq on 4 January 2004, he told them:

You know how passionately I believed in this cause and in the wisdom of the conflict as the only way to establish long time peace and stability.

By August 2004, Blair seemed to be free of political danger thanks to Tory support. As I put it in a *Guardian* article, 'The Party's Over', at the time:

> Chained to the rock of Iraq, our own latter day Prometheus was released from his torment, not by Hercules, but by Howard.

I wondered whether Blair could be impeached, telling the *Guardian*:

> The time has come to look again at whether impeachment should form part of the constitutional process . . . Impeachment should only be used as a last resort, because the convention is that ministers will behave as 'honourable gentlemen' if they have misled the Commons . . . That the Prime Minister has misled the Commons is not in doubt in most people's minds.

Such a possibility was never on the cards, given the combined Labour and Tory support he had in the Commons. Yet still peace seemed as elusive as ever, as I pointed out in the House on 17 May:

> The road to peace in Iraq seems to be a journey through a vale of tears that will go on for some time. It is one of those journeys where we know where it began but do not know where it will finish.

That is as true today as it was then.

The auguries at the beginning of 2005 were no more auspicious. As Eliot Weinberger wrote on 3 February:

> I heard that a few days before he became Prime Minister, Iyad Allawi visited a Baghdad police station where six suspected

insurgents, blindfolded and handcuffed, were lined up against a wall. I heard that, as four Americans and a dozen Iraqi policemen watched, Allawi pulled out a pistol and shot each prisoner in the head. I heard that he said that this is how we must deal with insurgents.

Haifa Zangara told the *Guardian* on 22 April 2005:

> What happened to the war on Iraq? Suddenly, Iraq seems very far away once more, and the Iraqi people long forgotten. Why? Is it because Iraq has become a bleeding wound, too painful to look at, or a mess that should be avoided at elections? Or is it true that Blair genuinely believes that he has honoured his pledge to the Iraqi people? On the second anniversary of the invasion 300,000 Iraqis demonstrated in Baghdad. Three effigies of Bush, Blair and Saddam were burned. The message was clear; Bush and Blair, like Saddam before them, are legally and morally responsible for the destruction of Iraq and the daily killing of its people.

Two years on from the start of this war, the BBC's John Ware put his finger on a lesser bleeding wound than the state of Iraq. It was the state of Tony Blair's political credibility. In *Panorama*'s 'Iraq, Tony and the Truth' he set out the Prime Minister's problem:

> There is one issue none of these inquiries [into Iraq] has focused on: the evolution of Mr Blair's Iraq policy, what he said in public, what he knew in private and whether he can reconcile the two.

His failure to heal this wound can only mean one thing, as far as many are concerned, and as I put it to the *Observer* on 3 October 2004:

> The stigma of Iraq will remain with him throughout the rest of his career.

I set out a summary in a *Tribune* article on the fate of my murdered constituent, Ken Bigley, on 21 October 2004:

> Those of us who opposed the war insisted that it was both illegal and immoral. It was immoral because it was based on an entirely false prospectus for war, presented to both Parliament and people. We were, according to Mr Blair, under a clear and imminent threat from WMD. We now know that this was never the case, nor had been for a very long time. More importantly, we know from Lord Hutton, Lord Butler and Jack Straw that the Government knew that their case was a false one. No one in government attempted to set the record straight. Indeed, they went in the opposite direction – sexing up the flimsy, uncorroborated evidence supporting their case. The legality of the war has been denied by leading experts on international law. Their view was confirmed last week by Kofi Annan, General Secretary of the United Nations. Is it any wonder, then, that Government still denies us unfettered access to the full legal opinions of their own law officers? . . . It was really, by his own account, the Prime Minister's war; but only three government ministers disagreed enough to resign. It may have been driven by an individual but the responsibility is collective . . . Iraq is now a country on the brink of civil war . . . Is this the glad, confident morning expected by Mr Bush and Mr Blair after Saddam? . . . An unpopular war which has created hugely more instability in the world.

Until the long wait for honest answers to fundamental questions is over, there will remain pressure from politicians and commentators for the Government, and the Prime Minister in particular, to come clean. There is still a core of fighters for the truth pressing the case in Parliament. There must be closure on this, but that closure demands honesty, objectivity, and integrity. Perhaps Douglas Hogg saw a way on 22 November 2005:

> That this House believes that there should be a select committee of seven honourable members, being members of Her Majesty's

Privy Council, to review the way in which the responsibilities of Government were discharged in relation to Iraq and all matters relevant thereto, in the period leading up to military action in that country in March 2003 and in its aftermath.

We can but hope.

Index

A

Ainsworth, Peter
  trust, on 301
Al Qaeda 83-95
Allen, Graham
  legality of war, on 191
Allen, Richard
  America, on 120
  British national interest, on 133
Alles, Colonel James
  napalm, on 310-311
Amnesty International
  Iraq, on 9
Ancram, Michael
  deteriorating security situation, on 312
  Iraq, on 45
  motion of 13 November 2002 59
  WMD, on 143, 155
Anderson, Donald
  intelligence, on 277
  United Nations, on 208-209
Anthrax 156
Assad, President
  legality of war, on 202
Aziz, Tariq 302

B

Baath Party 1
Babylon 1
Baer, Robert
  Pentagon, on 60
Banks, Tony
  arming of Saddam, on 5
  Europe, on 67
Barrett, John
  chemical weapons, on 15-16
Berger, Sandy
  UNSCOM, on 40
Bevin, Ernest
  war, on 4
Birmingham Post
  British-American posturing on Iraq, on 39-40
Blair, Tony
  Al Qaeda, on 87
  Al Qaeda and Saddam Hussein, on 89-90, 91-92
  America, on 120, 123, 124-125, 127, 132-133
  April 1, 2002 visit to Bush ranch 123
  British foreign policy, on 35-36

D

L

M

Z